WITHDRAWN
HARVARD LIBRARY
WITHDRAWN

CONTEMPORARY PRACTICE AND METHOD IN THE PHILOSOPHY OF RELIGION
New Essays

Edited by David Cheetham and Rolfe King

continuum

Continuum International Publishing Group
The Tower Building, 11 York Road, London SE1 7NX
80 Maiden Lane, Suite 704, New York, NY 10038

© David Cheetham and Rolfe King and Contributors 2008

All rights reserved. No part of this publication may be reproduced or transmitted in any form or by any means, electronic or mechanical, including photocopying, recording, or any information storage or retrieval system, without prior permission in writing from the publishers.

British Library Cataloguing-in-Publication Data
A catalogue record for this book is available from the British Library.

ISBN: HB: 0-8264-9588-5
      978-0-8264-9588-4

Library of Congress Cataloguing-in-Publication Data
A catalog record for this book is available from the Library of Congress.

Typeset by Aarontype Limited, Easton, Bristol
Printed and bound in Great Britain by Biddles Ltd, Kings Lynn, Norfolk

Contents

Contributors	vii
Editors' Introduction	1
Imagining the Future: How Scepticism can Renew Philosophy of Religion JOHN L. SCHELLENBERG	15
MacIntyre, Tradition-Dependent Rationality and the End of Philosophy of Religion NANCEY MURPHY	32
A Contemporary Jewish Perspective on Philosophy of Religion JOSHUA GOLDING	45
The Revival of Philosophy among Muslims SHABBIR AKHTAR	59
The Study of the Self JONARDON GANERI	74
Buddhist Approaches – Not 'What?' But 'How'? DAVID WEBSTER	87
Comparative Philosophy of Religion DAVID CHEETHAM	101
'Thinking Differently' in the Context of Sikh Religion NIKKY-GUNINDER KAUR SINGH	117
Philosophy of Religion Takes Practice: Liturgy as Source and Method in Philosophy of Religion JAMES K.A. SMITH	133
Knowledge of God, Knowledge of Place and the Practice and Method of Philosophy of Religion MARK WYNN	148

Reformed Epistemology and the Recontextualizing of Natural Theology MICHAEL SUDDUTH	160
The Role of Trust and the Practice and Method of Philosophy of Religion ROLFE KING	174
The Reasonableness of Philosophy of Religion PHILIP GOODCHILD	188
Bibliography	204
Index	217

Contributors

SHABBIR AKHTAR is Assistant Professor in the Department of Philosophy and Religious Studies at Old Dominion University. He has written a number of books including *The Light in the Enlightenment: Christianity and the Secular Heritage* (Grey Seal, 1990); *A Faith for All Seasons* (Bellew, 1990) and *The Final Imperative: An Islamic Theology of Liberation* (Bellew, 1991). His research interests include the philosophy of religion, Islam, and Christian–Muslim relations. He is also a published poet.

DAVID CHEETHAM is Senior Lecturer in Theology and Religion at the University of Birmingham. He specializes in the philosophy and theology of religions. He is the author of *John Hick* (Ashgate, 2003) and numerous articles in journals including *The Heythrop Journal, Sophia, New Blackfriars* and *Theology*. His new book entitled *Ways of Meeting and the Theology of Religions* is forthcoming (Ashgate).

JONARDON GANERI has taught at the Universities of Stirling, Nottingham and Liverpool. He has been the Spalding Fellow in Comparative Religions at Clare College, Cambridge, and a Visiting Professor at the Divinity School, University of Chicago. His work is primarily on philosophical analysis within the classical Indian traditions. His best known book is *Philosophy in Classical India: The Proper Work of Reason* (Routledge, 2001).

JOSHUA GOLDING is Associate Professor of Philosophy at Bellarmine University in Louisville, Kentucky. He is the author of *Rationality and Religious Theism* (Ashgate, 2003). He has published in *Religious Studies, Faith and Philosophy, The Modern Schoolman*, and *Tradition*. He has also contributed articles to *Encyclopedia of Philosophy, International Encyclopedia for the Social Sciences*, and the *Routledge Companion to Philosophy of Religion*. He specializes in philosophy of religion and Jewish philosophy.

PHILIP GOODCHILD is Associate Professor in the Department of Religious Studies at the University of Nottingham. He has written *Gilles Deleuze and the Question of Philosophy* (Associated University Presses, 1996) and *Deleuze and Guattari: An Introduction to the Politics of Desire* (Sage, 1996). More recently, his *Capitalism and Religion: The Price of Piety* (Routledge, 2002) was an attempt to construct a Continental philosophy of religion through the encounter between questions of truth, ethics, and piety. His current research interests are in the implications for philosophical and religious thought of the collision between ecology and economy in the contemporary world.

ROLFE KING was formerly Senior Lecturer in Theology and Philosophy of Religion at Newman College, Birmingham. He is currently an Honorary Lecturer at the University of Birmingham and a Research Associate of the Queen's Foundation for Ecumenical Theological Education, Birmingham. His research interests focus on the relationship between forms of trust and evidence in the context of philosophy of religion.

NANCEY MURPHY is Professor of Christian Philosophy at Fuller Theological Seminary, Pasadena, California. Her first book, *Theology in the Age of Scientific Reasoning* (Cornell University Press, 1990) won the American Academy of Religion award for excellence. She is the author of eight other books, including *On the Moral Nature of the Universe: Theology, Cosmology, and Ethics* (Fortress, 1996; co-authored with George Ellis), and *Did My Neurons Make Me Do It? Philosophical and Neurobiological Perspectives on Moral Responsibility and Free Will* (Oxford University Press, 2007; co-authored with Warren Brown). Her research interests focus on the role of modern and postmodern philosophy in shaping Christian theology, on relations between theology and science, and relations between neuroscience and philosophy of mind.

JOHN L. SCHELLENBERG is Professor of Philosophy at Mount Saint Vincent University in Nova Scotia, Canada. His *Divine Hiddenness and Human Reason* (Cornell University Press, 1993) stimulated what is now a lively, growing debate and has made him a much-cited representative of atheism. Schellenberg has recently been investigating more fundamental questions pertaining to the philosophy of religion. The result is a series of books: *Prolegomena to a Philosophy of Religion* (Cornell University Press, 2005), *The Wisdom to Doubt: A Justification of Religious Skepticism* (Cornell University Press, 2007), and *The Will to Imagine: A Justification of Skeptical Religion* (forthcoming).

NIKKY-GUNINDER KAUR SINGH is the Crawford Family Professor of Religion at Colby College in Maine, USA. Her interests focus on poetics and feminist issues. She has published extensively in the field of Sikhism, including *The Feminine Principle in the Sikh Vision of the Transcendent* (Cambridge University

Press, 1993), *The Name of My Beloved: Verses of the Sikh Gurus* (Harper, 1995), *Metaphysics and Physics of the Guru Granth Sahib* (Sterling, 1995). She has lectured widely in North America, England, France, India, and Singapore, and her views have been aired on television and radio in America, Canada, and India.

JAMES K.A. SMITH is Associate Professor of Philosophy at Calvin College in Grand Rapids, Michigan. Working at the intersection of philosophical theology and Continental philosophy, he is the author of several books, including *The Fall of Interpretation: Philosophical Foundations for a Creational Hermeneutic* (InterVarsity Press, 2000), *Speech and Theology: Language and the Logic of Incarnation* (Routledge, 2002), *Introducing Radical Orthodoxy: Mapping a Post-Secular Theology* (Baker Academic/Paternoster, 2004), *Jacques Derrida: Live Theory* (Continuum, 2005), and *Who's Afraid of Postmodernism? Taking Derrida, Lyotard, and Foucault to Church* (Baker Academic, 2006). He is coeditor of *The Hermeneutics of Charity: Interpretation, Selfhood, and Postmodern Faith* (Brazos, 2004), *Radical Orthodoxy and the Reformed Tradition* (Baker Academic, 2005), and *Hermeneutics at the Crossroads* (Indiana University Press, 2006).

MICHAEL SUDDUTH is a philosophy lecturer at San Francisco State University and California State University, East Bay. He was formerly Associate Professor of Philosophy at Saint Michael's College in Colchester, Vermont. He has published numerous articles in philosophy of religion, including articles in *Faith and Philosophy*, the *International Journal for Philosophy of Religion*, and *Religious Studies*. His first book *The Reformed Objection to Natural Theology* is forthcoming. His work has focused on the concept of God, religious epistemology, and natural theology.

DAVID WEBSTER is Senior Lecturer in Religion, Philosophy and Ethics the University of Gloucestershire. His first book was *The Philosophy of Desire in the Buddhist Pali Canon* (Routledge, 2005). His current main research interests are in early Buddhism, and relating this to Western philosophy and everyday life.

MARK WYNN is Senior Lecturer in the Philosophy of Religion in the Department of Theology at the University of Exeter. His previous publications include *God and Goodness: A Natural Theological Perspective* (Routledge, 1999) and *Emotional Experience and Religious Understanding: Integrating Perception, Conception and Feeling* (Cambridge University Press, 2005). His current focus of research is the philosophy and theology of place.

Editors' Introduction

What is the philosophy of religion? What is the nature of its discourse? Is there any agreement concerning practice or any *normative* methodology that can be discerned? Moreover, what might be the priorities that will (or should) occupy its attention as we move further into the twenty-first century? As interest in, and awareness of, different religions increases, will philosophy of religion change? Is philosophy of religion tradition-specific or can the same philosophical methods be applied to different religions?

The above questions form the background to the present collection. The result is far from definitive, and this is not simply because the volume lacks the space, but because the editors have deliberately sought to avoid the temptation to obtain some sort of imposed comprehensiveness that would have necessitated being prescriptive about the titles of the chapters (e.g. Analytic, Continental, Reformed, Hindu, Islamic, Jewish, etc.). Instead, conscious of the fact that authors are sometimes loathe to wear particular labels or situate themselves in historic traditions, the contributors were invited to suggest their own titles. Thus, whilst the different authors in this volume represent the kinds of method and practice that were anticipated, it was intended that they should also write about their *own* understanding of the practice, method and future focus of the subject. Of course, the questions outlined at the beginning probably beg the eventual need for further collections in order to give voice to the varieties of philosophical activities and practices that occur *within* different schools of thinking and faith traditions. While recognizing this, the present book's modest aims are only offered to provoke further debate that may be expanded by other works.

The first two chapters in the book represent contrasting perspectives concerning the scope and limitation of the philosophy of religion. These contrasts introduce some of the broad strokes in the debate and set the scene for the book's subsequent chapters. Thus, whereas the first author, John Schellenberg, characterizes philosophy as a discourse which properly operates apart from traditional interests or confessional constraints, Nancey Murphy maintains that we can only engage in a tradition-dependent rationality that spells the end of the 'philosophy of religion'.

Schellenberg's chapter offers a distinctive approach to the questions we asked our contributors to address. He writes as a sceptic about religious claims, but also aims to broaden the understanding of scepticism and link the sceptical attitude to the kind of disposition that he argues philosophers in general ought to have as they pursue questions about ultimate matters. It is a scepticism that is hesitant about any firm answers being given to philosophical questions that seem deeply complex and elude resolution. Schellenberg points out that philosophy of religion is a species of philosophy, and so it must share the form of inquiry that philosophy exhibits: in particular, using pure thought to 'get to the very bottom of things'. What matters is love of the *deepest* understanding possible of the nature of ultimate reality. Schellenberg objects to the specific focus many philosophers of religion have on their own religious tradition; indeed he argues that, given the possible range of religious beliefs, to restrict oneself to focusing on the claims of a particular tradition and to seek to defend one's tradition is not to merit the title of philosopher of religion at all. For religion is so much wider than one tradition. He argues for an approach that is 'true to both philosophy and to religion' and suggests the term *ultimism* as the primary topic of philosophy of religion where differing religions have different perspectives on the nature of ultimate reality (and the link with that reality and the ultimate good). His advocacy of scepticism is not a policy of 'unbelief' pure and simple, but is based on the limited time human beings have had to reason about ultimism: we may, he suggests, be very early on in the possible development of religious ideas, so people are not justified in having the certainty that an overall answer to ultimist questions has been arrived at. In short, all current religious claims (and atheistic claims) should, at best, be advanced as hypotheses and the right attitude to them is a critical but open scepticism. Such openness may lead to new insights about both religious and philosophical possibilities. Thus, he opposes both cynicism about religious dogma and what he calls 'conservative conformism'.

Schellenberg's chapter is located within a realist tradition and raises a particular challenge to those who focus on one tradition. Nevertheless, his chapter draws attention to an issue concerning the extent of the possible range of 'ultimist' options: for Schellenberg the options appear to be many; by contrast, King's chaper in this volume suggests that if there is a God then God's options to give 'revelation' to us are very limited because we as the potential recipients of such revelation are limited. Nevertheless, such issues are important for philosophy of religion as it engages with different religious traditions: philosophers of religion need to reflect on whether the range of such options is a rather limited matrix or not: for example, how many structurally distinct varieties of theism might there be, or of non-theist religious perspectives? On the question of ultimism, some will object by saying that the philosophical preoccupation with such matters constitutes an unrealistic project; instead, we should focus on developing tradition-specific contexts of meaning and not seek to 'go the whole way down'. However, regardless of whether ultimates in knowledge are actually attainable, Schellenberg is really seeking to epitomize what he sees as an authentic philosophical attitude: a striving for truth and understanding at its most profound.

Nancey Murphy has studied how theistic epistemology in particular may compare to the underlying epistemologies that philosophers of science have argued actually operate in justifying scientific knowledge. In this volume, she considers two topics: the shift from modern to postmodern in the Anglo-American tradition and the relationship between Christian theology and the natural sciences. Her chapter aims to show that Alasdair MacIntyre's 'tradition-dependent rationality' spells the end of the philosophy of religion. (This is quite a contrast to Schellenberg's idea that the philosophy of religion has only just begun!) So Murphy has a very different vision from Schellenberg's notion of philosophy as an activity that is seemingly independent of tradition. Following MacIntyre, she argues that the Enlightenment notion of tradition-independent thought is itself historically conditioned and that modern theories about rationality have been 'too crude'. Philosophical analysis cannot begin from an 'objective' or detached point of view, instead it is important to consider particularities: '*which* community's concepts, and *when*?' Consequently, a committed 'philosophical theology' should replace the pretence of philosophers of religion being 'uncommitted to their point of view'. Moreover, she does not think that indubitable foundations can be found for Christian theism (nor presumably for any tradition of thought), and suggests that Imre Lakatos' notion of research programmes in science – establishing a core thesis and then evaluating various peripheral theses – can be adopted by Christian theology. In this way theological rationality could be put on a par with scientific rationality.

In her critique of atheism, in particular that associated with scientific naturalism, Murphy compares theism and naturalism as competing traditions. She highlights crises, as she sees them, within the tradition of scientific naturalism, especially this tradition's inability to ground moral claims. The important point is that it is necessary, under the procedure advocated by MacIntyre, 'to explore the crises and potential problems within each tradition and show that a Christian tradition is in better shape, on its own terms, than naturalism'.

One of the features of contemporary approaches to the philosophy of religion is the recognition of the expanding nature of its discourse. Moreover, an increased *cross-cultural* awareness that has been accelerated by globalization means that philosophy of religion as a mostly Christian preoccupation is being challenged. Of course, this is not meant to imply that philosophizing about religion has not already been a longstanding reality in most religions, but indicates that non-Christian traditions have not featured very prominently in the Anglo-American tradition of philosophy of religion until relatively recently. Nevertheless, things are changing. Many students who now take a course in the philosophy of religion in Western universities expect the curriculum to reflect these new realities. Moreover, looking at the attitude to philosophy in religions other than Christianity helps us to test ideas concerning the translatability or universality of philosophical concerns across cultures. Is the method and practice of the philosophy of religion significantly altered by different traditional contexts or does it remain roughly the same? Even if we see comparable interests, then we can also see different agendas and starting points. Thus, the place of philosophical critique may represent a potential challenge for most religious traditions, but there are also diverse notions of philosophy which view it, for example, as an activity continuous with religious searching and spiritual practice. Some of these issues are brought out in the next four chapters.

Joshua Golding, like Schellenberg, notes the point that philosophy of religion is a branch of philosophy and so he aims to move from an understanding of philosophy to considering philosophy *of religion* before reflecting on the latter from a Jewish perspective. Golding sees philosophy in a way that is, again, similar to Schellenberg, about 'rational reflection on fundamental questions'. It is a universal human activity. So too is philosophy of religion and other branches of philosophy that investigate ethics, politics or science. The content of the beliefs examined will vary over times and contexts, but for Golding the basic questions are still the same: is there a God? what is faith? what is the relation of reason to faith? and so on. New areas do emerge – such as the relationship between science and religion, or between religion and the public sphere. But the *primary* reason for engaging in philosophy of religion continues to be: 'to help us understand religion, and to help us evaluate its claims'.

Golding makes an interesting point when he highlights the potential value of philosophy of religion as a prophylactic against potential religious fanaticism: engaging in philosophical critique of religion makes one more aware of the complexity of the issues involved and thus less likely to be attracted to simplistic solutions that are imposed by force – literal or metaphorical. Golding concedes that religion is about much more than belief, but he nonetheless stresses that religions are ways of life that 'make claims about their own significance, by making assertions about reality'. So truth issues remain vital and he does not agree with the view that religions do not make claims about reality. Nor does he concur with those fideists who say that reasoning is not relevant to religious commitment. On the contrary, reason is very important and can be used to defend religious belief from a variety of criticisms and this is equally the case, he comments, when it comes to the intellectual defence of the Jewish faith. For Golding, 'Jewish philosophy' is not an idiosyncratic activity to be distinguished from 'reason' in general, but it is nevertheless distinctive in terms of a Jewish attitude to philosophical inquiry which he sees as giving reason a significant place in religious commitment and in the defence of faith. It is also distinctive in terms of doctrinal questions of particular interest to Jews. Thus, Golding is in agreement with the mediaeval Jewish philosopher Moses Maimonides concerning the warrant – scriptural and traditional – for reason to play a role in religious commitment. Moreover, he speaks of a religious duty to *know* God and that this involves philosophical activity in the sense that 'the way of God is a way of wisdom and understanding'.

Still within an Abrahamic rubric, in the next chapter Shabbir Akhtar considers the relationship of philosophy to Islamic thought. Akhtar suggests that philosophy of religion is not part of mainstream Islam, and he asks if there can be a philosophy of Islam along similar lines to what he sees as the philosophy of the Christian religion predominant within contemporary Western academic contexts. He notes the tension between reason and revelation and the alleged impiety of reason evaluating revelation. For the committed believer the concern may be that the philosophical scrutiny of religious claims arises from a mischievous intent. For, it is not for humans to judge the word of God and reason may be setting itself up as God to insist on sufficient secular reasons for faith. But Akhtar asks how, if reason is to be rejected, one could distinguish revelation from error? Some critical checks would seem necessary. However, Akhtar explains that philosophy in Islam was resisted – above all by al-Ghazali whose work 'signed the death warrant for philosophy in the Muslim Orient'. Philosophy came to be seen as raising doubts and threatening the certainties of faith. In his critical reflections, Akhtar suggests that 'religious belief is a sub-division of belief in general' and so must defend itself in terms of a wider account of rationality of belief; the sceptic's demand for evidence is justified. Philosophy of religion cannot assume the truth of a religion; that is for theologians to do. But just as philosophy can question the grounds for religious faith so it can question the grounds of secular reason. Nevertheless, Akhtar maintains that any 'encounter of reason and revelation produces an impasse. There is no common foundational ground, no higher court of appeal, no accepted epistemological referee.'

Moving beyond the Abrahamic milieu, Jonardon Ganeri considers the themes of this book in terms of Indian philosophy. He argues that the central topic of Indian philosophical thinking on religion is the true nature of the self. This topic is not just at the centre in terms of the amount of reflection it has generated, but is at the logical centre of Indian philosophy of religion. He identifies two crucial themes: truth about the self and concealment. In his view, the significance of the relationship between the literary form and the philosophical arguments of the classic Indian philosophical texts has been underestimated. Interpretation may depend on understanding the purpose of various literary devices, particularly if such devices help to prompt the desire to search for truth and provoke self-examination. In this sense, Ganeri sees both Hindu and Buddhist texts as 'protreptic narratives' – of an exhortatory nature. And it is not just desire, but the *right kind of desire* that matters: right desire brings about freedom from conceptual error and leads to moral progress. He suggests that even though people may be subject to significant deception and error there may still be interior 'epistemological resources available to them with which they might *lever* themselves out of error' and this includes the power of reason.

The literary form of the Upanishads, Ganeri suggests, aims to instil a desire to find out an exciting secret, and only then can one go on the journey to find out the secret 'that the self is deceived by its own desires, which cause it perpetually to look in the wrong place for itself; that the rediscovery of self is a reorientation of gaze'. The texts lead one out of illusion and to an acknowledgement that the senses deceive when they 'testify to a world of difference and differentiation'. For all is one.

Ganeri describes a similar technique of 'constructive deception' in the Buddha's teaching: the teaching is not to be taken at face value; it is to prompt a desire, a search, a way of preparation so that one can then have real insight. He introduces the notion of a 'cognitive story': 'the overall way we make sense of our beliefs, the epistemological story we tell ourselves about them'. The possibility of deception may not just apply to our specific beliefs about the world, but to our cognitive story as well. Ganeri suggests that Indian philosophy, within both Hindu and Buddhist traditions, has revolved around the debate as to whether our entire cognitive stories are in error, or whether it is just certain key beliefs about the world which need to be corrected. Finally, he calls for bold re-readings of texts in terms of what is important to the reader. These re-readings are a part of the method of philosophy of religion and are ways of avoiding potentially lifeless scholarly detachment.

David Webster's Buddhist perspective on the philosophy of religion echoes many of the issues that are brought out in Ganeri's chapter. He wrestles with the notion of philosophy as an intellectual exercise that operates outside of religion rather than *within* it. He begins his reflective piece by drawing attention to the Buddhist potential to 'make trouble' for the philosophy of religion. That is, Buddhism refuses to play the game of seeking answers to questions that, from a Buddhist perspective, are meant to remain unanswered. In fact, Buddhist philosophy disputes the value of purely doctrinal debates and prefers to ask questions of practice and method. The purely intellectual questions of belief and faith may have dire consequences for the spiritual path of meditation if it is subjugated to 'unchannelled or unrestricted reason or logic'. It is the practice of meditation rather than the adoption of doctrinal positions that is crucial: a kind of *engaged* philosophy. Moreover, whereas theistic philosophy of religion may begin with questions concerning the existence of God, Webster describes the starting point for Buddhism as an existential anxiety about the human predicament. Given this orientation, it is not really the rational critique of belief and doctrines that counts, instead it is a matter of the 'psycho-spiritual consequences of possessing certain types of belief'. At one level, it is important to gain a right view and to correct errors in understanding; however, at a more profound level there may be a danger in becoming 'attached' to right *views*. Thus, 'how do we believe?' becomes a crucial question: paradoxically, it may be 'better to be wrong in a skilful manner than to have accurate beliefs badly held'.

Following on naturally from these last four chapters, David Cheetham's contribution discusses the issues concerning the possibility for a comparative philosophy of religion. He presents the philosopher of religion as a 'properly comparative animal'. This is something that Cheetham argues is not just a prescriptive injunction that is compelled by new plural realities, but is already quite a natural feature of philosophical methods in argument and dialogical debate. Moreover, in a move that echoes Schellenberg, he suggests that because the priority is *philosophical* rather than religious then the project of philosophy of religion is necessarily inclusive of as much data as there is available. Thus, whatever the personal commitments of the philosopher, it is a kind of enquiry that cannot be restricted to one religion alone. This might be contrasted with religious philosophy (or philosophical theology) where *religion* or theology is more the priority and which seeks to critically develop a more tradition-specific line of thinking or to refine the articulation of a particular area of a tradition's beliefs. Cheetham reviews the potential pitfalls for comparative philosophy of religion as a discourse *about* philosophy rather than being philosophy *itself*: for, concerned only with the scholarly craft of comparison, we can risk sidelining basic philosophical inquisitiveness or vision. He comments that current interest in comparative philosophy of religion may actually represent nothing more profound than a broadening out of the data available for philosophical reflection and critique. That is, there is now just more material – from outside the Judeo-Christian matrix – and this has resulted in an increasing complexification of the field. Nevertheless, the possibility of a comparative philosophy of religion faces a challenge from the alternative prospect of culture-specific philosophizing. Cheetham recognizes this as a problem, but he nonetheless suggests that the effectiveness of this critique depends on the type of comparative philosophy being attempted. Even if the bolder pretensions of *universal* reason remain problematic, there may still be a certain 'contestability' (Clayton) or 'arguability' (Clooney) that is achievable. Towards the end of his contribution, Cheetham briefly considers the possible practice of a constructive comparative philosophy of religion. Thus, whilst preferring realism as a basic outlook, he proposes a kind of anti-realist strategy that may be useful in facilitating an experimental sense of *imagination*.

Elaborating on the question of the imagination and its stimuli, the next three chapters offer discussions, in different ways, about the role of symbolism, liturgy and 'place' in philosophical discourse and practice. Here we find more of an emphasis on what might be called pre-theoretic, pre-discursive elements in the philosophy of religion. That is, in the view of these writers, it is not so much a dispassionate analysis that should (or can) be the focus: rationality is not just about arguments concerning what exists or not but about how human beings *orient* themselves religiously or philosophically.

Nikky-Guninder Kaur Singh, working within the framework of Sikh religion and feminist thought, alerts us to the prejudices that may lie at the root of our reasonings. She notes that even the most critically aware or analytical authors may not be able to see clearly when it comes to self-criticism of their own prejudices. Given the dominance of male scholars in Sikh thought, her view is that such scholarship has been patriarchal and one-sided and needs to be balanced by a feminist perspective. She identifies, firstly, Sikh metaphysics; secondly, understanding Sikh scripture; and thirdly, reflection on the five symbols worn by Sikh men and women, as key areas where feminist thought can bring important corrective insights. Singh's goal is to 'bring about a change in the androcentric structure of Sikh society and culture'. This is quite distinct from the more analytic and reflective approach to philosophy: it is philosophy as *praxis*, aiming to change society and its structures. As Singh says: 'I do not want us to think differently just for the sake of mental gymnastics.' The link between ideas and changing reality is, for Singh, the transforming of the imagination so that desires and goals are changed, which leads to real action.

Reconsidering the ontological fabric of philosophy of religion, Singh rejects the emphasis on images of fatherhood for the ultimate metaphysical reality. She appeals to Sikh scriptural texts and reflections on birth, as well as to the work of object-relations psychoanalysts, as grounds for an emphasis on maternal power and the maternal as universal, contrasting mother-birth notions with a male-influenced obsession with death which she affirms has influenced how the Absolute has been apprehended. Seeing the metaphysical divine through a maternal affective lens enables a transformative release of inner life. She then argues that the Guru Granth Sahib, the Sikh Scripture, is to be understood not as the soul of the Gurus, but the *body*. The tenth Guru, Guru Gobind Singh invested the Granth with Guruship so there could be no more Gurus after the ten Gurus. Thus, Sikhs treat the Granth 'as though it were the body par excellence of the Gurus' in such actions as *sukhasan*: putting it to bed at night. But Singh discerns a deep inconsistency between this embodied treatment of the Granth and the hostile denial she has encountered from Sikh men that the book is not corporeal. She detects a hidden rejection, perhaps even a quasi-dualistic hatred, of the flesh, and suggest that this as something that has infected Sikhism in its attitudes to the human body generally.

Finally, Singh reflects on the classic symbolism of the 'five Ks'. Arguing against the dominant masculine interpretation of these, she points out that each can have a female identity. What matters is the link between these and the 'passionate experience of the divine in daily life'. She highlights uses from the Scriptures which emphasize feminine imagery in connection with the five Ks. Sikh philosophy is about a deeper truth than a truth 'out there': it is about a 'subjective and existential engagement with the ultimate reality that pours out organically into our self-understanding, and our relationships with family and society'. Sikh philosophical reflection is reflection on symbols that image the relationship to the divine, and since symbols and imagery have power to bind or liberate, feminist Sikh philosophy must find for women a liberating way to reclaim the symbols and imagery central to the Sikh tradition.

Although representing a different religious tradition, James K.A. Smith's chapter reveals a similar concern with the priority of religious 'forms of life' and liturgical practices for philosophizing. He begins by referring to what has been called the 'renaissance' in the philosophy of religion in the decades towards the end of the twentieth century. Smith acknowledges the work done by various philosophers of religion which contributed to this renaissance but highlights what he sees as a gap: the lack of focus on the practice of religious communities. His chapter draws attention to the importance of liturgy. Believers focus on 'what we *do*'; philosophers on 'what we *believe*'.

He asks whether believers even appear in philosophy of religion, which is so focused on *belief*. Moreover, he perceives a lingering Cartesian rationalism in this: construing human beings as thinking things. Religion, which is a rich form of life, becomes an attenuated list of beliefs. To remedy this, Smith argues for more attention to be given to religion as a form of life and to the complex of practices involved. This would highlight what he envisages as a much more realistic philosophical anthropology: an affective and non-rationalist one. Close attention to religious forms of life reveal that human beings are 'oriented more fundamentally by desire than thinking'. Showing similar influences to Murphy, Smith draws upon the critique of secular reason set out by Alasdair MacIntyre and John Milbank because 'they recognize the central place of practices and liturgy in the formation of human identity, and thus the role of both in the very shaping of rationality'. He also draws on Charles Taylor's work on 'the social imaginary' showing how social practices exhibit implicit understandings that precede more theoretical reflections and suggests that liturgy contains just such implicit understandings that philosophy of religion needs to attend to. However, this is still looking to liturgy for *ideas*, and Smith wants a further stage – calling for liturgical participation as itself crucial to forming the philosophical imagination and as a way to learn how to form judgements religiously. Such participation, Smith argues, may lead to a new philosophical orientation.

Mark Wynn comments on two recent analogies employed, he thinks very fruitfully, in philosophy of religion: the comparison of religious belief and scientific beliefs, and the comparison between perceptual belief and religious belief. He cites the work of Swinburne in connection with the former and that of Alston with the latter. He sees some key agreements between these analogies (as well as alluding to differences), in particular the notion of God as an individual whose reality could in principle be accepted 'independently of any deep-seated commitment'. Both these models for knowledge of God, Wynn notes, 'imply that ethical, aesthetic and otherwise engaged response to the world is not directly relevant to our knowledge of God'.

Wynn suggests another analogy, which he argues gives a greater role to how we engage with the material world. This is the analogy he sees between the concept of God and the concept of place. One parallel that he sees is between 'the relationship of God to creatures and that of a place to its parts'. He moves from there to the notion of the genius of a place, or the *genius loci* – a notion of what gives unity to a place – and suggests that this is the best way to highlight this analogy with God. For Wynn, this improves on the scientific and perceptual analogies in the sense that God is not another individual entity but is more akin to the frame of reference which makes sense of individual elements within that frame. It also allows for more personal attributes to be retained when compared to other concepts of God that emphasize that God is not an individual. The knowledge of places is also often mediated to us via narratives. Narratives about a place can make sense of particular behaviours in that place. This indicates that places can exercise a type of agency in forming part of the goal of some of our activities, eliciting certain types of behaviour.

Wynn also notes the link with pilgrimage to places of religious significance. He suggests that there may be aspects of 'pre-discursive insight into the world and the kind of ethical and other claims it makes on us' in the connections between place and notions of the body, which pilgrimages to places where relics are kept may tap into.

Turning to the questions of epistemology, Michael Sudduth notes the continued concern of Anglo-American philosophy of religion with the epistemology of religious belief and comments on the relationship between evidential and non-evidential approaches to religious epistemology. His chapter explores the question of how philosophical reflection on religious belief should be carried out from within the perspective of a particular faith. He notes that 'There there has been a strong temptation to interpret the claims of Reformed epistemology as a critique and rejection of natural theology'. Sudduth claims that there is nothing intrinsic to Reformed epistemology that entails the rejection of the project of natural theology. What Reformed epistemology denies is 'that either natural theology or the evidences it develops are necessary for the positive epistemic status of belief in God'. He distinguishes between dogmatic and pre-dogmatic conceptions of natural theology, with the former using reason from a faith perspective primarily to explore the doctrine of God as revealed in Scripture and also to defend the faith against counter-arguments. The latter, which arose in the wake of Descartes, aimed to offer arguments for God's existence prior to considerations of a dogmatic nature. Reformed epistemology rejects the need for this kind of pre-dogmatic natural theology and maintains that 'it is not possible for natural theology to constitute a foundation for dogmatic theology'. However, this is not to say that there is no value in natural theology, only that it cannot constitute a foundation for belief in God. Sudduth thus sees Reformed epistemology as rejecting the pre-dogmatic conception of natural theology, but leaves open for future research the question of whether Reformed epistemology 'entails an endorsement of the dogmatic view of natural theology'.

Following on from Sudduth's concerns about the proper epistemological or 'foundational' starting points for discourse about God, Rolfe King's chapter draws attention to the subject of *trust*. This is something that he portrays as a neglected area in contemporary philosophy of religion compared to the amount of work done examining the grounds for belief. He explores the notion of a journey-epistemology, relating religious discipleship and trust. Crucially, King maintains that what matters is grounds for trust that it is rational to go on the journey. In particular, he highlights the notion of a journey towards God and suggests that the question as to whether it is a simple matter for God to win our trust seems insufficiently examined.

King argues that a journey-epistemology involves a different kind of foundationalism compared to the foundationalism much examined by philosophers. In order to commence the journey, one has to first trust the teachings of a 'Teacher' and accept them in some way as foundational for one's life. Since the religious journey moves to an end point that is not self-evident from the start this is quite different to the usual foundationalism based on self-evident truths. Indeed, it depends on trusting the 'Teacher' that his or her self-testimony about the end point is truthful. Belief in the existence of the end point may not arise without trust in the testimony of the Teacher. If God is to get us to embark on a journey towards him then he has to win our trust so that we start the journey. The problem is that there is no independent evidence for the end point, God, since God must testify that *this* is him (whatever 'this' is, that is claimed to be evidence for God, or claimed to be God).

King argues that God only has limited options to win our trust because we are limited. Some form of divine speech and acts of power seem necessary. If so, these are part of the 'necessary structure of revelation'. To work out what would be the best plan within that structure for God to win our trust is automatically to work out what good evidence for God would be. Evidence for God cannot be separated from trust, including trust in divine self-testimony. God cannot therefore reveal himself unless we trust him. Human beings will have different 'trust policies', so there are subjective and objective elements involved. What matters is evidence for each person that is sufficient for them to go on the journey. That will partly depend on their desires and the things they value. This kind of evidence cannot therefore be separated from desires and ethical (and perhaps aesthetic) values.

King sketches scenarios that show obstacles to God revealing himself, but notes that we can make progress in understanding how God might overcome those obstacles, and thus the kind of evidence to look for. The structure of a journey-epistemology applies to many religions; deciding between different religions is akin to a situation where there are different guides all offering to take us to an attractive destination we cannot obtain full evidence for. Trust is therefore crucial, and what matters is evidence or grounds that enable us to know that we are rational to trust that we know that there really is an end point.

Within Western philosophy the distinction between the analytic tradition and the Continental tradition of philosophy is popularly represented in terms of different *approaches* to philosophy. Thus, the analytic tradition is often portrayed as being concerned, above all, with clarity of thought whereas the Continental is associated with more literary, hermeneutical styles of discourse. In truth, such elements are exhibited in *both* traditions: there can be some very lucid Continental writers and some rather abstruse analytic ones! However, the issue is perhaps less a matter of distinguishing actual methods one from another and more one of identifying the purpose of philosophical arguments and their ability to act as effective 'forms' of persuasion. In the final chapter of this book, Philip Goodchild manages to combine elements of the concern for 'reasonableness' in the analytic tradition with the hermeneutical strategies resonant with a Continental approach that seeks a 'wise understanding'. He finds the analytic approach problematic, with its concentration on rigorous arguments which seem to 'rarely achieve persuasive conclusions'. Goodchild is concerned with the formation of thought itself. He concentrates on Anselm's idea of 'faith seeking understanding'. Faith is oriented toward the future; it is a matter of hope and desire as well as beliefs, but it is not a matter of certainty. Thought is formed by orienting oneself and there is a rationality of judgement involved in this process that can be explored. That is, the dimensions of reason actually present in this type of thought can be disclosed and developed. Anselm is located in the Augustinian tradition of the 'illuminated idea', this can be contrasted with the 'clear and distinct' ideas of the Cartesian tradition that still so influence the analytic tradition in seeking clarity and propositional truth. The illuminated idea of 'God' is something that is beyond our understanding. So, Goodchild questions whether evidence and argument is the appropriate form of reasoning here. The notion of correspondence to ideas that is used in evidential reasoning breaks down when it comes to considering metaphysics and religion, for neither reality nor God can be readily considered as individuated facts or things. Metaphysical and religious thought cannot be about ideas as representations. For Goodchild the evidential approach therefore contains an implicit metaphysic and is not neutral: 'it imposes its own metaphysics as the only valid one for rational argument'.

Goodchild argues that Anselm's approach of faith seeking understanding, including even his ontological argument, is very different. The concept of 'that than which nothing greater can be conceived' is not intended as a proof per se but is for contemplation, and contemplation itself may lead to disclosure. True attention leads to insight and wisdom. Goodchild indicates that Anselm would consider the analytic, evidential model of philosophy of religion to be lacking in wisdom, and thus foolish. Wise reflection on concepts and the cultivation of a contemplative approach can lead to creative insights into reality.

Finally, all the chapters of this book help us to gain a perspective on the current state of debate in the philosophy of religion and the various trajectories that might constitute its future. Of course, it is unlikely that any one of the 'methods' that have been presented in this book will gain overall dominance in the future practice of the subject, however it seems that some issues have a certain perennial quality. The concern about the relationship between philosophical critique and religious faith and the question of whether the philosophy of religion is something that emerges from *within* faith traditions or is properly external to them. The question of the *universal* applicability of the philosophy of religion – does the future involve all religious traditions in a sort of trans-cultural philosophical discussion, or is a more viable project(s) one of tradition-specific philosophies that acknowledge their 'confessional' allegiances? Moreover, underlying many of the chapters in this book is a sense that the philosopher herself is also a legitimate focus of attention. So, what are the prejudices or dreams that direct the course of human rationality or even frame the questions that seem important? Perhaps the task of the philosopher of religion is one that seeks not just conceptual clarity or interpretative creativity but a grasp of what is a *wise* method practice and method?

Imagining the Future: How Scepticism can Renew Philosophy of Religion

John L. Schellenberg

There is a familiar sort of doubting attitude or scepticism, expressed as agnosticism about traditional theism, that operates quite comfortably within the parameters of contemporary philosophy of religion. It makes few waves. Nothing of the current emphasis on God and Christianity is disturbed by it (the agnostic is in doubt about the traditional God but not about his centrality to matters religious). And the thrust of its critique is not easily translated into a positive message for our field of study or a new vision of how it might be developed.

The scepticism of my title is very different. It *challenges* much that can be found in contemporary philosophy of religion, including agnosticism about theism. Furthermore, it suggests *alternatives*. These challenges and suggested alternatives are born of a sense that even the twenty-first century may well represent but an *early stage* in a long process of human development (this developmental and temporally qualified stance is indeed the most distinctive feature of the scepticism I have in mind). The imperative of fuller maturation and the future's bearing on the present are its constant themes.

The nature of this scepticism, as well as the renewal it may promote in philosophy of religion, will be more fully discussed shortly. But to ensure that the stage is properly set for this discussion, I first need to say something about some broader issues.

1. The Nature of Philosophy

Whatever else philosophy of religion may be, it is a species of *philosophy*. This is rather forcibly indicated whenever we utter its name. And anything we say about the proper purposes and priorities of philosophy of religion must be compatible with that fact. So let me address, as my opening question, what philosophy should be taken to be. This is a big question, but I shall have to be brief. Despite my brevity I will be drawing on all the resources available to me, including (implicitly) all the main figures in philosophy's history. The upshot is philosophy as I have known it; quite a bit of knowledge by acquaintance will be involved. In other words, this section will, to a considerable extent, be me as a philosopher reflecting on who I *am* as a philosopher. (If you think that what I describe is not a philosopher, then you should try to figure out why not – and then you should also get in touch with the editors of this book, who, so you must suppose, have misidentified one of their contributors!) If what I have to say about this matter is right (and if what I say later about scepticism is near the mark), I should remain very much open to criticism concerning my conception of philosophy, and I do. But then, there is nothing in this chapter that purports to be, at bottom, anything other than a proposal to be discussed.

Whatever else philosophy may be, it is a form of inquiry. So what form? Let me make three suggestions, which will subsequently be defended. (1) First, philosophy is a form of inquiry whose *subject matter* is absolutely unrestricted: that is, anything and everything and even nothing comes under its gaze. (2) Second, philosophy is a form of inquiry whose *aim* in respect of its subject matter is simply understanding, but – and this cannot be too strongly stressed – understanding of the most fundamental kind; philosophy's passion is to get to the very bottom of things and nothings and ultimately to see how everything hangs together. (3) Third, philosophy is a form of inquiry whose *method* for prosecuting its aim, thus passionately embraced, is sheer thought and the criticism of thought (here we see reason in its purest and most relentless form; philosophy runs on the imaginative intellect alone and is supremely self-critical, hoping by this means to further its aim: argument is its life-blood).

By thus identifying the distinctive subject matter, aim, and method of philosophy we can hope to distinguish it from other forms of inquiry. But some will be dissatisfied. My first point especially may seem implausible or unhelpful. In saying that philosophy's subject matter is *unrestricted*, have I not I been rather less than straightforward and definite? And how, in any case, can we suppose that just any question is a philosophical question? (Surely there are clear counterexamples to this, for instance *this* question: 'How many words are there in the next sentence?')

But it does not follow from my claim that philosophy's subject matter is unrestricted that just any question is a philosophical question. Non-philosophical questions arise from approaching realities also open to philosophical investigation with non-philosophical aims. (The question mentioned above is indeed non-philosophical, but the facts represented by the sentence it refers to and by its own words are packed with material – for example, concepts of space and inference, number and reference – that is ripe for philosophical exploration.) And I would suggest that it is precisely in its unrestricted subject matter that we see quite a *definite* way of distinguishing philosophy from other sorts of inquiry, which are focused on this or that aspect of what is open to examination, but never the whole. (For a quick insight into what we are discussing here, consider how 'What is science?' is not a scientific question and 'What is theology?' not a theological question, whereas each of these questions and also the question 'What is philosophy?' fall within the purview of philosophy.)

It may be insisted, however, that philosophy's subject matter surely does not include that of *science*. Scientific inquiry is focused on obtaining a fine-grained understanding of the physical world (and let us include social worlds within this); philosophy on certain general and fundamental questions about matters beyond the reach of science, like moral right and wrong or free will. So we should say that philosophy directs itself only to those *non-scientific* concerns.

In reply, I would want to point out that in thinking about substances and properties and relations and the nature of space and time philosophers are thinking precisely about the fundamental nature of *physical things*, and so physical things are included in philosophy's subject matter. Now of course, there are still aspects of modern science that are absent from philosophy. However this difference is not to be understood on the level of subject matter, but rather, again, by reference to the very basic nature of the understanding sought in philosophy (feature 2), and in light of the fact that it relies on pure thought (feature 3).

It should also be noticed here that (a) the fact about an intellectual division of labour between philosophy and science the critic has introduced is but a *contingent* fact, and moreover one obtaining only in the modern era; and that (b) even here, as in any possible world, individuals who try to figure out, purely through critical reason and without recourse to specialized scientific techniques, how physical things are constituted and the deepest and widest patterns of their interaction, are doing philosophy – however *bad* the philosophy may be. Imagine a philosopher who, due to some cataclysmic event, finds herself socially isolated and bereft of the knowledge previously acquired by her in science and philosophy, but who, because of an indomitable spirit and intellectual curiosity, starts exploring the world again, as it were from scratch. Might we not find her wondering what the world is made of, considering the merits of theories concerning this spun from the intellectual threads left to her; and would we not want to call what she is doing philosophy?

A similar tack may be taken in response to the suggestion that if philosophy's subject matter were unrestricted, philosophers would not devote so much of their attention to *us* – to human beings. Here we also have a contingent fact. The preoccupation in question arises from the fact that, concerned with achieving fundamental understanding, with getting to the very bottom of things, philosophers have naturally found it an important task to understand what understanding *is*, and how it may best be achieved. This requires them to investigate the categories of human thought and language in which things are apprehended by us – the ways in which things are represented to us and the problems and possibilities associated with *reliable* representation. Hence thought is directed not just outward at the external world but, as is often said, back at itself, and more intensely – one might say obsessively – so that if it were directed at itself *simply* on account of the fact that our thought is part of the 'anything and everything' open to philosophical exploration: understanding how our thought works, as all would agree, may also be a means to better understanding *other* things, and its importance in philosophy is thereby increased.

But let me once again underline the contingency of all this. If these problems of epistemology and the philosophy of mind had already been solved, human beings might represent a much smaller concern for philosophers. Broadening this point a bit, we may note that, contrary to what some would find congenial, philosophy's subject matter is not to be understood as *consisting* in what we discuss in our Introduction to Philosophy classes, namely God, free will, mind and body, knowledge, goodness, and so on, and thus as restricted in this way. For example, not in every possible world do philosophers worry about the mind/body problem or about whether a theory of right action must be subsidiary to a theory of virtue! In some possible worlds, presumably, these problems have been solved, and other questions arising from the desire to achieve understanding of the most fundamental kind are rationally addressed. More could be said about this, but I think that what has been said will help us to see how my claim as to the unrestrictedness of philosophy's subject matter may be defended.

What about feature 2? Is it really fundamental understanding that philosophers seek? To some extent this has already been addressed. Here I would add: that philosophers have the aim I have attributed to them explains why we see individual philosophers constantly seeking to arrive at new and broader and ever deeper ways of looking at things in their areas of concentration – which, incidentally, inevitably brings their areas of concentration into conversation with others. It also explains why there is such an emphasis on exposing as many mistaken forms of thought and misunderstandings as possible. Fundamentally, however, what one wants to say to any critic on this point is the following: can you really imagine a philosopher resting content with what he knows is some understanding that *has not* yet got to the bottom of things?

This may make the philosopher sound rather audacious and even unrealistic. Do we not all know nowadays that every human practice, including the practice of philosophy, reflects the 'location' of the practitioner in some way and is thus limiting? Yes, we do know this. But knowing it should only increase our humility and our urge to collaborate (and something like it may *itself* find a place in philosophy, as we will see later on when we come to scepticism). If instead one thinks on this basis that understanding of the world is impossible and ceases to seek it, one ceases also to be a philosopher. Or if one becomes *complacent* about one's location and ceases to criticize it, then also one has passed out of philosophy. What a genuine philosopher wants to see from her location is still, deeply, some aspect of the world. The philosopher will take from her location every insight it permits, and she will not hesitate to trade it for a broader, deeper perspective if such becomes available.

So philosophers seek understanding. But is understanding the *only* thing that philosophers seek? *Qua* philosophers, yes. And given the difficulty involved in finding it, perhaps we can understand why! Notice that even the subject area of applied philosophy, which seems focused on practical problems and the realization of instrumental benefits, can be subsumed here. A philosopher engaged in applied philosophy will want to *understand how* philosophy is properly applied to this or that practical problem; all of the applications involved are *intellectual* applications. Independently, she may act on this practically useful understanding, but this is applied philosophy in quite another sense, which presupposes a distinction between the activity of philosophy and the application thereof. (Here 'applied philosophy' does not name a region *within* philosophy.)

What about method (feature 3)? I suppose it might here be objected that the restriction to reason and thought is somehow overly narrow. To this I am inclined to reply that while various emotional or moral dispositions, say, might be conducive to thinking well, it is still *thinking well* that philosophers are concentrating on, in pursuit of an understanding *embraced* in thought. But why say *sheer* thought, as though special techniques and technologies are ruled out? Well, it is perhaps not inconceivable that there should emerge from philosophical thought more exact intellectual procedures than have so far been devised that can decisively be brought to bear even on the most fundamental matters, where so little can be assumed; and I would not wish to understand philosophy's method in such a way as to exclude them. But should the procedures that emerge take us too far from the operations of the intellect – if, say, they required dependence on the word of a divine being discovered to exist – I would be inclined to say that philosophy had been transmuted into something else. This, I suspect, is because philosophers want to figure things out for themselves, and also because, while such procedures might generate a form of knowledge, they would not yield *understanding*, a unified conception of things, with connections laid bare, and it is precisely understanding that philosophers seek. In any case, even here and even now, without decisive procedures of any kind but powered by imagination, philosophy's method of relying on thought alone can be applied in an infinite number of ways, and can endlessly open up new windows on the world.

Perhaps we could put the essential point here this way: philosophy may utilize, but it cannot altogether rely on, the results of empirical observation and experiment. It must appeal to all the reaches of reason and seek continually to extend its scope and power (and in this its *lack* of narrowness is shown). In philosophy it is all about critical reflection – processes of reasoning, conceptual analysis, theory construction and appraisal, which, because of the uncompromising and thoroughgoing nature of the quest, are continually subjected to criticism and refinement by the very same reason that is their source.

Suppose that, on the basis of such arguments as I have briefly given, my three features are determined to survive scrutiny. Summarizing, and also finding the connections among them, we might then say that philosophy represents and expresses a kind of *unbounded intellectual curiosity and drive to understand* – curiosity that is unbounded in respect of what may provoke its interest, how deeply it will want to understand it and its relations to other things, and what intellectual means it will utilize in seeking to do so. Philosophy is at bottom sheer thought and criticism of thought enlisted by a love of the most fundamental understanding of the world. (If I am right about this, then the previous sentence and the arguments I have used to support its claim themselves constitute a piece of philosophy.)

We can draw a moral from this story. For it immediately follows from my depiction of philosophy – and this is a matter of no small importance – that Canadian or American 'philosophers', who dismiss so-called Continental or feminist thinkers out of hand; and French 'philosophers', who caricature and scorn analytical techniques; and postmodernist or feminist 'philosophers', whose fundamental starting point is some adversarial political stance; and 'philosophers' of religion, whose most basic orienting ideas are religious and who have determined (as a matter of religious commitment perhaps) that they will not be budged therefrom, if any such there should be, and while in the grip of such dispositions, are not really doing philosophy. In all such cases, one finds the love of understanding essential to true philosophizing and the collaborative spirit it should foster either absent or subordinated to other loves and allegiances, and this, if I am right about its nature, is quite incompatible with philosophy.

2. Application to Philosophy of Religion

If the conception of philosophy I have just outlined is correct, then we must be approaching a correct conception of philosophy of religion when we think of it as a form of inquiry that runs on sheer thought and criticism of thought enlisted by a love of the most fundamental understanding *about religion*. Then we should find, wherever philosophy *of religion* truly exists, an intellectual curiosity about religion that is *unbounded* in respect of how deeply it will want to understand religion and its relations to other things, and what intellectual means it will utilize in seeking to do so (with certain expectable consequences such as the porousness of boundaries between philosophy of religion and other philosophical sub-disciplines and the absence of partial allegiances deeper than allegiance to the pursuit of understanding). What this implies, we can immediately see, is that at least the following questions will be regarded as important by a philosopher of religion. (1) What *is* this form of life – or these forms of life – we call religious? (What, if anything, is distinctive about religious attitudes and dispositions?) (2) What attitudes should we take to the conceptions and claims at the heart of religious forms of life? (3) How are the latter related to conceptions and claims in other aspects of our experience – for example, in art and science? (4) Can they contribute anything useful to achieving fundamental understanding in other parts of philosophy – that is, parts of philosophy not specially directed to religion? (Can they show, for example, that from religion emerges a good way to live? The best? Do they in any way help us understand the most basic structure of reality?)

Just by reflecting on these questions we can already see the *narrowness* of much that passes for philosophy of religion in contemporary culture. For example, rather little attention has been given to question (1). Many 'philosophers of religion' simply take their *own* form of religion as a point of departure, rarely thinking about what religion *is* or about what is included in forms of religion other than their own. Indeed, often they use their standing in the field primarily as a vehicle for *defending* their own form of religion and resisting others. Thus philosophy of religion is transmuted into apologetics.

Think here of Alvin Plantinga's recent *Warranted Christian Belief* (2000) which, while it displays its author's considerable analytical and rhetorical skills and also exposes his impressive achievements in other areas of philosophy, can hardly be said to rise to the standard of philosophy in much of what it says about religion. Plantinga's curiosity does not really extend to religion (for he has hardly begun to explore it), but rather to how the justifiability of adhering to his particular brand of religion – orthodox Christianity – can be defended. The love expressed in his work is for *God*, as God has always been understood and experienced by him, not for an ever deeper understanding of religious matters, which would take him into non-defensive conversation with religious ideas and religious thinkers from far and wide. Thus while Plantinga is widely regarded as one of the most important living philosophers of religion, most of his relevant work does not seem to amount to *philosophy* of religion at all.[1]

Similar points must be made in respect of question 2. It is usually quite uncritically assumed by philosophers of religion that the possible attitudes one might take to the conceptions and claims central to religious forms of life are these three: belief, disbelief, and scepticism (often the latter reduces to the agnosticism mentioned at the beginning of this paper, since the focus is on theism). And a religious form of life is usually uncritically assumed to entail belief. A fuller discussion of the attitudinal possibilities here that frees itself from a restriction to the most familiar (usually Western) forms of response is only now beginning (see Schellenberg 2005: ch. 6, as well as the works of authors discussed therein). Most 'philosophers of religion', moreover, have a rather limited set of religious conceptions and claims to work with, often, again, restricting themselves to Christian or at any rate theistic ideas. Interestingly enough, this point appears to apply not only to well-known analytical philosophers like Plantinga and Richard Swinburne, but also to such vociferous critics of theirs from within contemporary 'philosophy of religion' as the Wittgensteinian, D.Z. Phillips, and the postmodernist feminist, Grace Jantzen. Both of the latter thinkers, now sadly gone, contributed much to many discussions, but in their discussions of religion they too restricted themselves, in most cases, to Western religious forms of life and avenues of critique.[2] Here John Hick (1989) provides a better example of what is needed, but it must be said that not many are following his lead.

The limitations of purportedly philosophical treatments of religion already mentioned must also – by implication and in obvious ways – limit the usefulness of what has so far been accomplished by philosophy of religion in respect of questions 3 and 4. The reader should check this for herself). In short, it does not take much to see that the attempted approximations to philosophy of religion we have at present – and this despite the widely proclaimed resurgence of interest in this field of study – must be awarded a somewhat less than satisfactory grade when judged by reference to certain essential concerns and the standard of philosophy raised in the previous sections.

3. A Way Forward

So how can we do better? How can we develop an approach to philosophy of religion that is true both to philosophy and to religion, shirking neither the complex and challenging tasks associated with the search for fundamental understanding nor the complex and challenging forms that religion can take? (This will turn out to be a sceptical approach when all is said and done, but here we are still working our way toward that realization.) Clearly a *broad* picture of religion is needed, one that takes us beyond the parochial concerns that, as we have seen, threaten to derail the contemporary pursuit of fundamental understanding about religion. (Whatever exactly it may be, religion is clearly much broader than Christianity or theism.) Thinking about this requirement in connection with the nature of philosophy suggests the following starting point: philosophers should, when analysing 'religion', focus quite generally on a concern with *ultimate* things. That is, from the bewildering plethora of religious possibilities they should choose ultimistic religion as their own first concern – this is because of their interest, as philosophers, in the deepest truths about the nature of reality and the deepest truths about value, which ultimistic religion can be seen as in its own way addressing, and because a focus on ultimistic religion can accommodate religious phenomena of various kinds from around the world and down the centuries. Somewhat more fully: this approach would involve thinking of religion as instantiated by those persons whose most fundamental or ultimate disposition is to conform their lives to the truth of a certain proposition about ultimates – the proposition that there is a metaphysically and axiologically ultimate reality in relation to which an ultimate good can be attained (for short, an ultimate and salvific reality). I call this basic religious proposition *ultimism*, and the various ways of filling it out are *elaborated forms* of ultimism.[3]

Quite probably, not everything that is religious or that might with some plausibility be called religious can naturally be fitted under the ultimistic definition (though a great deal clearly can). But that is no matter if we see that what we have here is really a *technical* definition crafted to meet various desiderata, having to do with respecting the nature of philosophy and the broadening of philosophy of religion from its present often parochial concerns, and also the focusing of its endeavours by means of a clear idea that all can rally around. Filling this out a little: my suggested definition of 'religion' provides a useful and quite natural development of what is at present the focus of much inquiry on the part of philosophers concerned with religion – namely, the claim of traditional theism and various more specific claims entailing it – and also, thereby, a proper home for continuing inquiry into such matters. By selecting the foregoing definition to guide their activities, philosophers will prompt themselves to remember that their concern ought to be not only with theistic religion but with the central type of which it is an *instance*. Traditional theistic religion ultimizes, but so do many other important forms of religious life. The traditional idea of God shared by most Jews, Christians and Muslims is indeed a conception of something ultimate, relationship with whom constitutes our deepest good and our most urgent calling. But both monistic and dualistic Hindus say something similar about Brahman, emphasizing the overriding importance of commitment to the religious path in one of its many possible forms as a way of finally securing release from *samsara*. And for Buddhists, the idea of the Buddha-nature or of Nirvana, the emphasis on enlightenment, and the wholehearted pursuit of the Noble Eightfold Path, function in a similar fashion. Philosophers of religion, with their concern for no-holds-barred exploration of the deepest issues, must surely be interested in all such forms of life. This concern appears most adequately reflected by the definition of religion I have put forward, which puts investigation into matters theistic in its proper context (clearly sanctioning such investigation while at the same time balancing it with other aspects of the broader concern of which it should be seen as a part).

So a fair-minded and open-minded (i.e., truly intellectually oriented) focus on ultimism and ultimistic religion is my first recommendation. Exploring this recommendation further will, I suggest, yield at least a satisfying *first* answer to our question 1 from before (perhaps one to be revised or built upon by subsequent generations of philosophers, depending on what investigation on its basis yields) and at the same time a satisfyingly broad yet clear point of departure for tackling questions 3 and 4.

How about question 2? I suggest that a great deal more investigation into alternative religious and non-religious and anti-religious attitudes is called for as we think about how to respond to this question. As mentioned earlier, it is usually assumed that belief, disbelief and a doubting scepticism are the only options here, with a seriously disproportionate amount of attention going to questions about the rational justifiability of *religious belief* (where the object of belief, as might be expected, is usually quite narrowly assumed to be some theistic proposition). But there is good reason to suppose that the spectrum of possible and significant attitudes is considerably wider than that, requiring investigation also into such things as the nature of religious hope and of a non-believing form of faith, and, further, into the standards by which such attitudes should be evaluated. (Recent investigation already confirms that an attitude and approach to living grounded in it can be quite substantially and authentically religious even without the satisfaction of the believing impulse, and that quite non-evidential standards may be applicable to the evaluation of such things taking us well outside the emphasis on evidence virtually omnipresent in contemporary philosophizing about religion. (See Schellenberg 2005: ch. 6 for more on this.)

Having identified the relevant range of attitudes, it would be possible to organize much of the work that needs to be done in philosophy of religion around it, together with the ultimistic focus previously described. If we bring ultimism (or each of various elaborated ultimisms) and a suitably broad and representative set of attitudes together, then we can engage in the comparative discussion involved in asking which of the latter is most appropriate to the former – ideally, which represents the *best* response. And this could be quite fruitful, in relation to the questions earlier mentioned. For example, suppose that from such investigation it emerged that *belief* in the truth of some *elaborated* ultimism was strongly epistemically justified for all of us (grounding the best response anyone could make, not just a response one might hope intellectually to get away with), and that the view in question had clear and detailed ethical and metaphysical implications. In that case many theoretical questions about how to live and about the basic structure of the world would be answered (after all, we have *epistemic* justification here). Furthermore, the attitudes appropriate to other religious and non-religious claims would also be discernible. And other results, involving some other proposition and perhaps some other attitude or form of justification, might be expected to be similarly fruitful. So just by taking on board my recommendations about ultimism and open-minded examination of *various* elaborations thereof as well as openness to a wider range of religious and non-religious attitudes, we can start making some real progress in the philosophical quest for understanding that is instantiated by philosophy of religion.

4. Sceptical Interlude

However now we come to a dip in the road that will have decisive consequences for how the rest of the present story about philosophy of religion is told. This section may depress some readers with its commentary on our place in time, but ultimately it is only from within the dark valley of scepticism I will be urging us to enter that we will most effectively find our way forward into a brighter future.

I noted, in an earlier section, that even *extant* forms of religious life are relatively poorly or incompletely understood by many of those who venture to pronounce on them philosophically. What must now be added to this is that what we presently see in the way of religious life may itself be only a *start* along the way to any religious insight that is available to us humans. Our present circumstances and ideas may represent but an *early stage* in a long process of development. (This thought has application to more than just religious ideas – though it need not lead to the global scepticism of the Pyrrhonians – but I will here be applying it exclusively to religion.) To suppose otherwise is to gloss over all the horrors and distortions in the history of human religion, which have kept us at an even lower level of intellectual and spiritual maturity than we might otherwise have attained to in the very short time that we have had to think about ultimate things, and also to forget its future, which may turn out to be very long indeed – vastly more extended than the few thousand years we have turned in so far.

Of course when it comes to religion, forgetfulness about the future is all too common; critics and adherents alike love to focus on what has already transpired. As a result of this orientation, we tend to behave as though what the world has so far seen in the way of religious ideas is all it will ever see. The latter is a rather curious notion (though, given our arrogance, not a surprising one). After all, as indicated, we've have only been thinking about this religion thing for a few thousand years, and according to science, intelligent life on our planet could survive for as long as *several hundreds of millions of years more*! (If you represent the potential lifespan of intelligence on our planet as a straight line extending from one end of a full-length classroom blackboard to the other, the portion already traversed will not take you to the end of the first centimetre.) What do you suppose we might be able to come up with in the way of religious ideas given another hundred million years or so? Might it be something more interesting or plausible than what has been developed so far? Who can say? It boggles the mind simply to think about it. But that is just the point. Especially due to factors uniquely operative in the present case (it has proved rather difficult to be coolly rational about religious matters in our past, and still is; and the object of study in the religious case must be as rich and sophisticated as any could be!), the only realistic conclusion from serious reflection on both past and future is that we may well be stuck somewhere *far back* in the very beginning stages of development where religious understanding is concerned. The ideas religious inquiry has turned up to this point may well be – to adapt Hume – but the first rude essays of an infant species. Many more rich layers of development and maturation, of very demanding sorts, requiring much time, might need to be laid down before any human being can hope to access such religious truths as there may be. To think otherwise might be something like expecting someone from the Middle Ages – or a Neanderthal – to be capable of understanding the propositions of string theory in contemporary physics.

What this neglected point implies is that we are completely unjustified in believing that the human species or any of its members has *already developed* to the point where either the *truth* of ultimism (whether generic or in some elaborated form) or the *falsity* of ultimism could become available to our awareness.[4] Of course we cannot say with any definiteness that the requisite development has not occurred, but we certainly cannot say it *has* either. There are simply too many glaring deficiencies in our relevant development so far and too many possible changes and intellectual enrichments in our future to make such a claim justified. The scepticism of my title is a response to *this* awareness – quite an elementary awareness, though one seldom achieved. It is an attitude of doubt directed precisely to the proposition belief of which is here proscribed – the proposition, to repeat, *that the human species (or some member thereof) has already developed to the point where either the truth or the falsity of ultimism can become available to our awareness*. But it will be clear to see that following hard on the heels of this scepticism must be another: a scepticism directed to the claim *that ultimism is true* (and by the same token to the claim that it is false). The combination of our limitations and our immaturity is fatal to justified belief of any such proposition. In other words, human belief of generic ultimism or of any elaborated ultimism must be declared *premature*. Of course the flip side of this insight is that any inference to the truth of naturalism – to the reliability of *ir*religious belief – is equally premature (naturalists tend rather optimistically to take extant forms of religious belief as the only religious competitors they need worry about). We may all be much closer to the beginning of a proper assessment of religious possibilities than we would care to admit. (Perhaps it is because we *do not* care to admit this that we so easily ignore the future and the rather large question mark staring us in the face. For a much fuller defence of the scepticisms described here, see Schellenberg 2007.)

5. The Way Forward Expanded and Extended

These facts about the justification of religious scepticism, when we allow them within range, must sponsor a radical rethinking of what we are about as philosophers of religion. We must now try to imagine, for example, how we might start the programme of religious investigation anew, with a focus not just on actual but also on *possible* elaborations of ultimism. In other words, we have turned up another question eminently appropriate for philosophy of religion. (5) What *new* religious conceptions and claims can be developed, and are any of them *superior* in various respects to extant ones? This question has not been touched at all by philosophers. But it is important that we come to grips with it, both to do our part in helping religion develop and adequately to pursue the aim of examining possible theoretical links between philosophy and religion (question 4 above). Such explorations may, for all we know, turn up theoretically useful notions, and also ones which, acted upon, generate forms of religion that deserve a positive evaluation from rational inquirers (question 2).

Of course, instead of helping to pave the road forward, one might be moved by such scepticism-inducing facts as I have mentioned to retreat into some intellectual enclave, defined by one's particular 'location' in the blooming, buzzing confusion of life – conservative Christian, radical orthodox, postmodernist, postcolonial, feminist, Buddhist, Hindu, Islamic, Jewish, liberal, aesthetic, analytic, or whatever – to which one stubbornly clings as providing one's fundamental point of orientation. But the picture of things one can carve out from within such an intellectual enclave, with one's back to the world, has little hope of resembling the *world*; it will only be a tunnel leading further into one's location. And it is the philosopher's glorious though painful duty, as we have seen, to try to understand the world. To have any chance of succeeding in this, we must not shrink from the world's apparent confusion but rather open ourselves to it even further. Fortunately, scepticism itself informs us that this quest for fundamental understanding need not be in vain. For although it tells us that we do not know enough, it also tells us that *we do not know enough to know that we will never know more*. Hope remains reasonable. And the true philosopher will always seek to follow the rays of hope into the light of day.

Suppose, then, that we will continue to do philosophy of religion, on the assumption that the understanding we seek is possible, approaching our quest from a sceptical direction. We will not settle down for good in the halfway house of scepticism, content to throw objections at passers-by, but will do what we can to approach a fuller understanding of our subject even though we are sceptics and indeed by *means* of our scepticism. What might such a positive scepticism look like? How *can* scepticism be positive and illuminating?

Well, let us not forget that without it we would probably still be contentedly hunkering down in the halfway house afforded by some extant religious view or some anti-religious naturalism, mistaking it for our final destination. The larger view we achieve by stepping back from the plausibilities of the present and noting our place in the larger scheme of things is already illuminating. Furthermore, with our sceptical insight into the lack of justification attaching to those other perspectives, we have moved a long way toward an answer to our question 2 above, for now we know that, whatever else it may involve, the proper *present* attitude toward religion (since the proper attitude to ultimism, itself entailed by every religious claim) will include *doubt*. Scepticism, in other words, is itself at least a partial answer to that question. And now another insight, signalled by the words 'partial' and 'whatever else it may involve': given scepticism, perhaps one of those earlier mentioned *non-believing* religious attitudes, which must be mixed with scepticism, will turn out to be the proper attitude toward religious claims (in particular, the claim of ultimism), all things considered. If that were so, then scepticism need not even stand in the way of a religious form of life, instead facilitating (for example) a life of faith![5]

So there are some definite trade-offs here. Scepticism certainly taketh away, but it also giveth. Seeing how very far the proper paths of inquiry about religious matters may stretch into the future need not remove all possibility of insight in this connection if that awareness *itself* is pregnant with insight. And another insight too is sponsored by scepticism: precisely when we see how our immaturity has infected many religious ideas, we can see that those ideas should properly be set aside while we investigate the strong possibility that they are *not* – as we seem so often to suppose – ideas than which none greater can be conceived. I am thinking in particular about certain traditional ideas of a personal God which imbue the deity with many of our own deformities or, alternatively, with benevolent or loving dispositions that are belied by intimate familiarity with the world. Indeed, there are powerful arguments for atheism – for a denial of the agnosticism mentioned at the outset of this paper – that even a religious sceptic of my sort can convincingly give, despite her scepticism, because of the fact that in discussing traditional theism we are 'closer to home', dealing with notions that are far from incomprehensible.[6] The basic idea of a personal God, as traditionally understood, is derived from what we know of ourselves – and from human qualities that we *do* understand even at the present stage of our development. All of the atheist's claims about how *such* a God might be expected to behave are unaffected by the awareness that many *other* conceptions of the divine remain to be explored. (Remember here that theism is but a species of ultimism, and that to deny that this species is realized is *not* to deny ultimism but rather quite compatible with complete scepticism about whether ultimism is true. Ultimism is a huge disjunction of possibilities, with traditional theism but one of the disjuncts.) And perhaps something similar applies to many other presently held religious conceptions and claims. Therefore, all things considered, we must say this: scepticism in philosophy of religion need not lead to a dead end, but rather functions as a gateway to important new insights about intellectual tasks as well as intellectual and religious possibilities.

6. Creative Criticism

Let me draw some threads together in a slightly different manner to give a closing summary of where our travels in this chaper have taken us. I suggest we construe the relevant alternatives somewhat more starkly, with the religious scepticism I have defended poised as a middle way between two extremes. These extremes, which should be familiar from earlier discussion, I call *corrosive cynicism* and *conservative conformism*. Corrosive cynicism (sponsored especially by certain popular postmodernist sensibilities) and conservative conformism (typified especially by certain strands of 'philosophy of religion' found in religious America) should equally be anathema to any philosophy of religion practised in the twenty-first century, aware both of its identity as philosophy and of its place in time, and should be replaced by *creative criticism*, deliberately and persistently and systematically applied and reapplied in a coherent pursuit of the above-mentioned complex aim (the aim represented by questions 1–5, together with any new aims that subsequent reflection supports). An emphasis on creative criticism is not only at the heart of the specific positive sceptical approach I have sought to outline. It unites us with every true sceptic and indeed returns us to scepticism in the best and fullest sense of the word, which emphasizes the unsettled and curious stance appropriate to one in the midst of difficult inquiry about important things (*skeptikos* – persistent inquirer), a stance that includes a willingness always to clear the table and see things afresh. All these scepticisms, so I claim, are needed in philosophy of religion. Only appropriate doubt about what we have achieved thus far will take us to a future understanding worthy of the imagination.

Notes

1. As support for the argument here, see especially Plantinga 2000: chs 12 and 13. See also Plantinga 1993.
2. See, for example, Phillips 1999 and Jantzen 1999.
3. For more on these matters, see Schellenberg 2005: ch.1. Note here that by saying that the reality in question is *ultimate* (both metaphysically and axiologically) and *salvific*, we 'posit' certain positive properties. We certainly have nothing as lacking in content as John Hick's 'Real', which, influenced by Kant, he describes as in itself completely unknowable and indescribable (see Hick 1989). Hick has been much criticized for this feature of his 'religious hypothesis', which is otherwise admirable in many ways, but it is important to recognize that – although Hick sometimes uses such labels as 'the Ultimate' in place of 'the Real' – my notion of generic ultimism does not share this feature.
4. Notice that this is compatible with the falsity of some *elaborated* ultimism becoming known to us (more on this later). This would not entail the falsity of ultimism in the same way that the *truth* of an elaborated ultimism would entail the *truth* of ultimism.
5. This possibility is explored and defended in J. Schellenberg *The Will to Imagine* (forthcoming).
6. For a fuller defence of this claim, see Schellenberg 2007: pt 3.

MacIntyre, Tradition-Dependent Rationality and the End of Philosophy of Religion

Nancey Murphy

1. From Where I Stand

Philosophy of religion from the perspective of assorted traditions – until recently this could only have meant assorted *religious* traditions, yet philosophers contributing to this volume are willing to place themselves in traditions as well. So here I am, a Christian of an Anabaptist, or Radical-Reformation, sort, educated in the Anglo-American philosophical tradition. I have devoted a great deal of attention to two topics relevant to this assignment. One is to argue that there has been a shift from modern to postmodern categories in Anglo-American thought, marked by the rejection of foundationalism in epistemology, of referentialism in philosophy of language, and of reductionism in metaphysics (N. Murphy 1998). I have also written extensively on positive relations between Christian theology and the natural sciences (e.g., Murphy and Ellis 1996).

The results of these two projects have brought me to see Alasdair MacIntyre's writings on rationality as by far the best available. I shall describe his account of 'tradition-dependent rationality', including its application to theistic traditions, and argue that it requires a significant shift in understanding the relation of philosophy to religion, in fact, making philosophy of religion obsolete. Then I shall turn to the question of the relation between Christianity and science, and suggest that while science itself is no enemy of religion, there has developed alongside of the Western religions what I shall call the modern scientific-naturalist tradition, which is in serious intellectual competition with theistic worldviews. I end with a sketch of how the arguments would have to go if one were to show the rational superiority of a theistic position, and in the process illustrate a MacIntyrean approach to philosophical reflection on religion.

2. Why MacIntyre?

One of MacIntyre's own epistemological theses is that justification needs to take narrative form: a theory is justified by showing how it overcomes the problems that its predecessors could not overcome. I can only hint at the problems MacIntyre's writings have taken in stride. Two streams of thought involve the historicization of reason in its empiricist and rationalist forms, respectively. One well-known name in philosophy of science evokes the first narrative. Thomas Kuhn (1970) described science not as progression toward universal truth but as a history of competing paradigms, dependent for their development on historical accidents and metaphysical commitments, incorporating their own standards of scientific practice and reasoning, and (no less than theology) embracing commitments to classical texts.

The other series of developments began with W.V.O. Quine's (1951) criticism of the analytic–synthetic distinction, which doomed analytic philosophers' quest for timeless and universal 'conceptual knowledge'. Instead, philosophy must be, in Jeffrey Stout's (1981) terms, 'conceptual archaeology': analysis of central philosophical concepts such as *truth, knowledge, justification, meaning* will have to begin with the particularities of history: *which* community's concepts, and *when*?

For many, the only possible result of the historicization of both science and epistemology itself is relativism. If standards of justification are paradigm-dependent, if the very concepts of justification, truth, and rationality are historically conditioned, then there is no objective place to stand from which competing claims to knowledge can be adjudicated.

The relativist conclusions in the philosophy of science of the 1970s was one of the contexts to which MacIntyre responded. The other was philosophical ethics. In *After Virtue* (MacIntyre 1984) he argued that moral positions could not be evaluated apart from traditions of moral enquiry. Yet, without a means of showing one tradition to be rationally superior to its competitors, moral relativism would follow. In two succeeding books (MacIntyre 1988; 1990) he has elaborated his concept of a tradition and shown by example the possibilities for such comparative judgements.

Traditions generally originate with an authority of some sort, usually a text or set of texts. The tradition develops by means of successive attempts to interpret and apply the texts in new contexts. Application is essential: traditions are socially embodied in the life stories of the individuals and communities who share them, in institutions, and in social practices. Some traditions are explicitly theistic, but at least by default every large-scale tradition incorporates an account of ultimate reality and resources for understanding the purpose of human life.

MacIntyre's contribution is to show that it is sometimes possible to compare rival traditions and judge one to be rationally superior to another. A first step is to construct a narrative account of each tradition: of the crises it has encountered (incoherence, new experience that cannot be explained, etc.). Has it been possible to reformulate the tradition in such a way that it overcomes its crises without losing its identity? Comparison of these narratives may show that one tradition is clearly superior to another: one tradition may be making progress while its rival has become sterile – has failed on its own terms. Notice how this conflicts with the relativist assumption that any tradition will seem to be perfectly in order in the eyes of its adherents.

To further explain MacIntyre's account it is useful to relate his work to the philosophy of science. Kuhn's *Structure of Scientific Revolutions* (1970) was seen by many as an irrationalist account of science. Imre Lakatos responded with what he thought was a more rationalist account. He argued that one could choose between competing research programmes on the basis of one being more 'progressive' than its rival. Loosely, a progressive programme is one that anticipates empirical discoveries, while a degenerative programme only explains new discoveries after the fact (Lakatos 1970). Paul Feyerabend (1970) countered that this criterion is inapplicable because sometimes degenerating programmes suddenly become progressive again, so one never knows when it is rational to give one up. Lakatos never gave a satisfactory answer to this challenge. The account I have given so far of MacIntyre's position on competing traditions would be open to the same Feyerabendian challenge. MacIntyre's insight is that there may be an *asymmetry* between the rivals. From the point of view of one programme it may be possible to explain *why* the other programme failed, and failed *at just the point it did*. One example is the competition between the Copernican and Ptolemaic programmes. The crisis to which Galileo responded involved inconsistencies of Ptolemaic astronomy with both Platonic astronomical ideals and Aristotelian physics, and the latter was inconsistent with empirical findings on terrestrial motions. Galileo resolved the crisis by reconceiving astronomy and mechanics. At last, the history of late mediaeval science could be cast into a coherent narrative. MacIntyre says:

> The criterion of a successful theory is that it enables us to understand its predecessors in a newly intelligible way. It, at one and the same time, enables us to understand precisely why its predecessors have to be rejected or modified and also why, without and before its illumination, past theory could have remained credible. It introduces new standards for evaluating

the past. It recasts the narrative which constitutes the continuous reconstruction of the scientific tradition. (MacIntyre 1989: 146)

'What the scientific genius, such as Galileo, achieves in this transition, then, is not only a new way of understanding nature, but also and inseparably a new way of understanding the old science's way of understanding nature' (MacIntyre 1989: 152). Thus, scientific reason turns out to be subordinate to, and intelligible only in terms of, historical reason.

A similar point can be made regarding competing traditions. When a tradition falls into crisis, it is sometimes impossible for protagonists to understand the exact nature of their disagreement with a rival's point of view. This limitation can only be overcome if there are participants within the traditions with enough empathy and imagination to understand the rival tradition's point of view in its own terms. If this is the case:

> Protagonists of each tradition, having considered in what ways their own tradition has by its own standards of achievement in enquiry found it difficult to develop its enquiries beyond a certain point, or has produced in some area insoluble antinomies, ask whether the alternative and rival tradition may not be able to provide resources to characterize and to explain the failings and defects of their own tradition more adequately than they, using the resources of that tradition, have been able to do. (MacIntyre 1988: 166-67)

MacIntyre's epistemological prescriptions would sound unrealistic were they not worked out in conjunction with detailed historical and constructive arguments that they serve to describe. His goal in *Whose Justice? Which Rationality?* (1988) was to show the superiority of his rejuvenated form of the Aristotelian–Thomist tradition to one of its most significant rivals, the Enlightenment tradition. To do this he needed to show three things: (1) that the Enlightenment tradition of 'traditionless reason' is incapable of solving its own most pressing intellectual problems – in particular, the problem of the tradition-ladenness of standards of rationality; (2) that his own version of the Aristotelian–Thomist tradition has a good chance of solving the problem; and (3) why we could have been so misled by the tradition that claimed to reject all tradition. He makes his argument by assuming the standpoint of tradition-constituted reason and then by using that perspective to diagnose the mistakes of his predecessors: the Enlightenment tradition cannot tell its own story intelligibly because its own standards of rationality require such standards to be universal and not historically conditioned. His own account is vindicated by the extent to which it sheds new light on this aspect of intellectual history.

An interesting feature of MacIntyre's historical account, for present purposes, is his claim that Christian sub-traditions have reformulated epistemology in line with their accounts of God and human nature. For example, the Augustinian tradition began with a Platonic epistemology, but adapted it to its theology. Augustine transformed Plato's *Ideas* into exemplars of created things in the mind of God. It is God present to the mind, as light is to the eye, that enables humans to apprehend truth. Augustine's conception of the fallen will impacted upon his epistemology. MacIntyre says:

> The intellect and the desires do not naturally move towards that good which is at once the foundation for knowledge and that from which lesser goods flow. The will which directs them is initially perverse and needs a kind of redirection which will enable it to trust obediently in a teacher who will guide the mind towards the discovery both of its own resources and of what lies outside the mind, both in nature and in God. Hence faith in authority has to precede rational understanding. And hence the acquisition of that virtue which the will requires to be so guided, humility, is the necessary first step in education or in self-education. (MacIntyre 1990: 84)

MacIntyre's account of tradition-constituted rationality completely overturns the assumptions of modern epistemology, according to which rationality needed to be universal and timeless. Modern epistemology was taken to provide the standard by which any account of reality (theological or otherwise) and any account of morality was to be judged. Epistemology was thus logically prior to theology, ethics, and every other discipline. Yet MacIntyre provides historical evidence that theology is, in some instances at least, logically prior to both ethics and epistemology, and that moral formation is temporally prior to the pursuit of knowledge.

3. The Beginning and the End of Philosophy of Religion

Richard Rorty (1979: 131) says: 'The notion that there is an autonomous discipline called "philosophy", distinct from and sitting in judgment upon both religion and science, is of quite recent origin' (1979: 131). It was after Immanuel Kant, in the nineteenth century, that our modern distinction between science and philosophy took hold. Philosophy *of* religion came into existence when philosophers took their job to be the examination of the foundations of assorted bodies of (putative) knowledge. Rorty argues that with the end of foundationalism there is no longer a place for philosophy as cultural magistrate. If so, then there is no longer a place for philosophy of religion.

If MacIntyre is right about the tradition-dependence of reason – of all reason – and we interpret the intellectual world as a tangle of traditions, then the relations among philosophy, religion, and the rest of scholarship will be seen to shift. We see a variety of traditions and sub-traditions, some theistic and some not. We find philosophers within each tradition at work on its own particular problems. These problems bear more or less similarity to the standard list of topics that the Enlightenment *tradition* has labelled 'philosophy of religion'.

For Christians the place of philosophy of religion is taken over in large part by what has been designated philosophical theology. Philosophical theologians address nearly all of the same problems that philosophers of religion have, but without the pretence of being uncommitted to their point of view.

One important difference between philosophical theologians and philosophers of religion is that the former do not engage in arguments for the existence of God. From a location within the Christian tradition such arguments are unnecessary. In modern philosophy of religion, excerpts were collected from Anselm and Aquinas, Descartes and Paley, and placed side by side as more or less successful attempts to achieve the same goal. From the perspective of both Rorty and MacIntyre, such collections are anachronistic. For example, Rorty says of Descartes that he would not have perceived himself as contributing to philosophy but rather to research in mathematics and mechanics, and to the liberation of intellectual life from ecclesiastical institutions. Also there have been a number of sensitive reinterpretations of the works of Anselm and Aquinas. One particularly germane to my purposes is Seungoh Chung's. Chung locates Thomas's famous five 'proofs for the existence of God' within his project of synthesizing the Augustinian and Aristotelian traditions. Thomas had no need to argue for the existence of God because that was a given. What he did need was to settle the question of the nature of rational enquiry and to justify his account of theology in that light. The point was to show that an Aristotelian mode of enquiry can arrive at the existence of God. Then, because Aristotelian enquiry is conducted in pursuit of a *telos*, a single unified explanation of the subject matter, the role of God in fulfilling the various aspects of an Aristotelian explanation in turn validates the form of enquiry (Chung 2007).

In place of such arguments, philosophical theologians have worked on the topic of theological method; this includes attempts to answer the question of whether and how theological systems can be rationally justified. This has been a preoccupation throughout the modern period because modern epistemology presented particular problems for theology. A shift from ancient and mediaeval to modern theories of knowledge created one of the most severe 'epistemological crises' for the Christian tradition. Jeffrey Stout (1981) argues that the most significant epistemological change at the dawn of modernity involved a change in the meaning of the word 'probable'. Mediaeval thinkers distinguished between *scientia* and *opinio*. *Scientia* was a concept of knowledge modelled on geometry; *opinio* was a lesser but still respectable category of knowledge, not certain but probable. But for them 'probable' meant subject to approbation, theses approved by authorities. Theological knowledge would obviously fare well in this system, being that which is approved by the highest authority of all, namely God.

However, the multiplication of authorities that occurred with the Reformation made resort to authority a useless criterion for settling disputes. The transition to our modern sense of probable knowledge depended on recognition that the *probity* of an authority could be judged on the basis of *frequency* of past reliability. Here we see one of our modern senses of 'probability' intertwined with the mediaeval sense. Furthermore, if nature itself has testimony to give, then the testimony of a witness may be compared with the testimony nature has given in the past. Thus, one may distinguish between internal and external facts pertaining to a witness's testimony to the occurrence of an event: external facts have to do with the witness's personal characteristics; internal facts have to do with the character of the event itself, that is, with the frequency of events of that sort. Given the problem of too many authorities, the task increasingly became one of deciding which authorities could be believed, and the new sense of probability – of resorting to internal evidence – gradually came to predominate.

Stout traces the fate of theism after this epistemological shift. The argument from design was reformulated so that the order of the universe supplies only empirical evidence for God's existence, not proof. In an early stage of development it became necessary to provide evidence for the truth (that is, revealed status) of Scripture as a whole. If such evidence could be found, then the content of Scripture could be asserted as true. In a later stage it was asked why the new canons of probable reasoning should not be applied to the contents of Scripture themselves. Claude Welch (1972: 59) writes that by the beginning of the nineteenth century the question was not merely *how* theology is possible, but whether theology is possible *at all*. Stout's prognosis is grim: theologians must either seek some vindication for religion and theology outside of the cognitive domain or else pay the price of becoming intellectually isolated from and irrelevant to the host culture.

My own view is much less pessimistic. I have argued that theology's failure in the past to meet modern standards of justification is due not to the irrationality of theology but to the fact that modern *theories* of rationality have been too crude to do justice to theological reasoning – and not only to theology, but to scientific reasoning as well. To support this latter claim, consider reactions to Kuhn's *Structure of Scientific Revolutions*. Kuhn showed that scientific practice at its best not only did not measure up to, but actually violated, the methodological norms of then-current theories in the philosophy of science. There were two conclusions one could draw: either science is irrational or else the positivists' theories of rationality were inadequate. Philosophers of science have largely taken the second view. Only now do we have theories of reasoning that are (in Feyerabend's terms) 'sly and sophisticated enough' to do justice to the complexity of scientific reasoning. I would say all the more so regarding theological reasoning.

Modern philosophical theologians have pursued Descartes's quest for indubitable foundations. I have argued (N. Murphy 1996) that there turned out to be only two options: one was the attempt to 'undergird' a scriptural foundation, and the other was the turn to a sort of religious awareness that was universal and self-authenticating. The forced choice between these strategies, I argue, is largely responsible for the sharp separation between (modern) liberal and conservative Protestants. The conservatives kept the scriptural approach, while liberals, following the lead of Friedrich Schleiermacher, took the second.

One of my projects has been to attempt to show that theology can, in fact, measure up to current standards of probable reasoning. I have argued that theological schools come very close to fitting Lakatos's description of scientific research programmes. They are organized around a core thesis, generally about the nature of God. They have auxiliary hypotheses that are subject to change (doctrines), and draw upon their own sorts of evidence, some scriptural and some empirical. The empirical data include religious experience and historical events. Comparable to Lakatos's and Kuhn's 'theories of instrumentation' in science (theories that warrant the use of the kinds of data being employed) theologians have a theory of revelation or inspiration to warrant the use of biblical texts, and a theory of discernment to judge whether putative religious experiences are genuine and thus provide legitimate data for theology (N. Murphy 1990).

Another successor discipline to philosophy of religion, one with a long history, is apologetics. If philosophical theology is scholarly work done within the tradition to overcome its internal crises, then apologetics is a closely related discipline that compares the Christian tradition to its competitors in the hope of showing one's own tradition to be rationally superior.

MacIntyre, being interested in traditions of moral enquiry, divides the contemporary intellectual territory among three rivals: his own Aristotelian–Thomist tradition, the Enlightenment tradition, and the 'genealogical tradition' – contemporary followers of Friedrich Nietzsche. Theological interests lead one to cut up the territory differently; for example, Thomas Aquinas would be situated in the Christian tradition rather than described as a successor to Aristotle. Many of Christianity's rival traditions are the other religions.[1] However, I shall concentrate on what I call the modern, scientific, naturalist tradition.

4. Naturalism as a 'Theological' Tradition

Historian James Turner (1985) argues that unbelief was not a live possibility in the West until late in the modern period. I claim that atheism must be seen not merely as the excision of God from an otherwise intact worldview. It is rather the development of a competing worldview; in fact, naturalism has grown to incorporate all (or nearly all) of the characteristics MacIntyre attributes to a large-scale tradition. The sense in which naturalism fails to fit MacIntyre's account is as follows. He says that a tradition is characterized by ongoing arguments about how best to interpret and apply the tradition's formative texts. For naturalists there is nothing comparable to the texts that inform the Aristotelian and Augustinian traditions (the Homeric epics and the Bible, respectively). The naturalist tradition can be traced in part to David Hume's corpus, but Hume's writings do not provide an all-encompassing worldview. Another early text was Baron d'Holbach's *System of Nature* (1770), which did present a systematic treatment of the world as a whole, humanity's place in it, immortality and, the structure of society, yet this text plays no continuing role in shaping the tradition.

Merold Westphal distinguishes two sorts of atheism. One is evidential atheism, represented by Bertrand Russell's account of what he would say if he were to meet God and God asked why he had not been a believer: 'not enough evidence God!' Given the difficulties already noted in adapting theological reasoning to modern canons of rationality, this response is readily understandable.

But if religious claims are false then one needs an *explanation* of why they are so widely believed; just as, if there are no witches, we want to know what caused people to believe there were. Hume and d'Holbach began the attempt to explain the origin of religion naturalistically. They argued that religion is a response to fear of the unknown, coupled with superstitious attempts to control or propitiate unseen powers. Such attempts continue today.

But why does religion persist in the modern world, now that we understand natural causes? Explanations here come from Westphal's second variety of atheists, the masters of suspicion. Karl Marx, Friedrich Nietzsche, and Sigmund Freud practise the hermeneutics of suspicion, the 'attempt to expose the self-deceptions involved in hiding our actual operative motives from ourselves, individually or collectively, in order not to notice... how much our beliefs are shaped by values we profess to disown' (Westphal 1993: 13). These three develop their suspicion with primary emphasis, respectively, on political economics, bourgeois morality, and psychosexual development, and each subjects the religion of Christendom to devastating critique.

Two further steps were needed to make atheism a viable position. It would be possible to say that religion may be an illusion, but a harmless or even beneficial illusion in that it shores up morality. So two sorts of arguments were needed. One was to show that religion did not serve to reveal anything about the moral order that we could not get by the use of human reason. Most of the work in philosophical ethics during the modern period had this as its aim. The other was to adduce historical evidence that religion has, in fact, promoted the worst evils in history – or at least more evil than good. So within the space of two and a half centuries, roughly from 1650 to 1890, unbelief has become a live possibility.

Recall that a tradition incorporates an account of ultimate reality and an account of what is most important in human life. The latter is essential as a foundation for ethics. It involves an epistemology, and is embodied in social practices and institutions.

The naturalist account of ultimate reality is the universe itself. Some naturalists give this thesis a religious tone and salvific trappings. For example, Carl Sagan offers a mix of science and what one might call 'naturalistic religion'. He begins with biology and cosmology, but then uses concepts drawn from science to fill what are essentially religious categories – categories that fall into a pattern surprisingly isomorphic with the Christian conceptual scheme. He has a concept of ultimate reality: 'The Universe is all that is or ever was or ever will be.' His account of ultimate origins is Evolution with a capital E. Sin originates in the primitive reptilian structure in the brain, which is responsible for territoriality, sex drive, and aggression. His account of salvation is gnostic in character – it assumes that salvation comes from knowledge. The knowledge in question is scientific knowledge, perhaps advanced by contact with extra-terrestrial life forms who are more advanced than we. He bases ethics on the worry that the human race will destroy itself. So the *telos* of human life is simply survival. Morality consists in overcoming our tendencies to see others as outsiders; knowledge of our intrinsic relatedness as natural beings (we are all made of the same star dust) can overcome our reptilian characteristics (see Ross 1985).

Richard Dawkins offers a naturalistic account of the meaning of life: he believes in a universe indifferent to human preoccupations, one in which the good life involves pursuing 'all sorts of closer, warmer, human ambitions and perceptions', including especially 'the feeling and awed wonder that science can give us'. This is 'one of the highest experiences of which the human psyche is capable. It is a deep aesthetic passion to rank with the finest that music and poetry can deliver. It is truly one of the things that makes life worth living and it does so, if anything, more effectively if it convinces us that the time we have for living is finite' (Dawkins 1998: x). Mary Midgley's book, *Science as Salvation* (1992) provides an extended argument and set of examples to show that naturalism is more than a philosophical position allied with the sciences themselves, but is rather a worldview and a way of life.

The most important practices and institutions embodying the naturalist worldview are found in science. One might not think of the discipline of history as a naturalist practice, but one of Hume's main philosophical and historical goals was to supplant the traditional Christian story line of creation, fall, and redemption by a new unity of action based along secular and humanistic lines. His six-volume *History of England* was written from a purely secular point of view in order to show that history can be understood perfectly well without the 'prophetic–providential' mode of interpretation that was common in his day (Livingstone 1984). Now, even Christian historians practise their craft on the basis of naturalist assumptions.

5. Theism and Naturalism as Competing Traditions

To proceed in MacIntyrean fashion to pursue the sort of apologetics I have described above would involve raising the question of the major crises faced by Christians and naturalists, and seeing whether each tradition is able to overcome its own. This is easier to do for the Christian tradition because Christian scholars are so well aware of their own intellectual challenges. I mention only three for lack of space.

One I have already described. This is the challenge of justifying theological claims according to the canons of modern empiricist epistemology. I consider this crisis to be well along the way to resolution. I and a number of others have shown that theology does (or at least can) measure up to current standards of scientific reasoning. The present chapter intends to take another step by describing how, according to MacIntyre's theories, the whole of the Christian tradition could be justified over against its rivals.

A second crisis is brought to light by the naturalists' claims that Christianity promotes more evil than good. Resolution requires frank acknowledgement of the extent to which evil has been done in the name of Christianity, and an explanation of why there has been such inconsistency between preaching and practice. My Anabaptist sub-tradition has an answer. The major evils (crusades, inquisitions, burning of 'heretics') are not intrinsic to Christianity but are the result of 'Constantinianism'. This term refers to Constantine's adoption of Christianity as the religion of the empire, but it is used broadly to refer to all sorts of weddings between the church and worldly powers. Solution of the crisis is not merely verbal; it requires deep changes in the social embodiment of Christianity, one of which is the separation of church and state.

A third crisis has been Christianity's relation to science. The appearance of conflict with science has made Christianity appear irrational, and this is heightened by the fact that the naturalist tradition has such a close relation with science. Fortunately, recent historians have made it clear that Christianity and science are not generally in opposition – the conflicts have been greatly overblown (See Lindberg and Numbers 1986). In addition, there is now a significant body of literature in which scientific and theological positions have been shown to be compatible and mutually supportive.

To my knowledge the contemporary proponents of scientific naturalism are unaware of intellectual crises facing their own tradition; the subtradition of Marxism is a notable exception. I suggest three places to look for trouble. The first is the persistence of religion, now that we are supposed to know of its primitive origins and the disguised motives that have kept us in its thrall. Like the Marxists' state, religion was supposed to wither away.

The second difficulty is to provide an account of the 'moral bindingness' of morality. The Enlightenment involved an experiment to see whether traditional morality could be justified on the basis of human reason alone, and MacIntyre (1984) is not alone in arguing that the experiment has failed. Current attempts to account for morality scientifically, such as in the works of sociobiologists, *might* succeed in explaining why humans are moral, but the greater their success in showing biological *causes* of moral behaviour, the less reason there is to take those behaviours to be obligatory. Midgley claims that the prevalent moral stance of naturalism is valorization of the life of the scientist, but science cannot provide any rational *justification* for this point of view.

The inability of science per se to provide grounds for moral claims is but one instance of what I see to be the most significant of naturalism's problems. The claims made by so many naturalists to the effect that science is the only way to genuine knowledge are self-referentially incoherent. Scientific research cannot support this claim itself or any of the philosophical and quasi-religious ideology that constitutes the naturalist tradition.

So the apologetic task would be to explore the crises and potential problems within each tradition and show that a Christian tradition is in better shape, on its own terms, than naturalism. This would be the first step. The final step would be to show that a Christian point of view can explain the failures of its rival.

6. Overview and Evaluation

This short chapter really needed to be an entire book. I have made many claims that I have not been able to justify. The most significant is my advocacy of MacIntyre's understanding of rationality as the best available. I have not been able to argue my case and would not be able to do so without including, as he himself has done, historical exemplifications of his theses.

I have drawn conclusions from MacIntyre's work regarding the best way, now, to understand the relations between philosophy and religion. Religion is no longer to be seen as a topic to be studied *within* the field of philosophy; rather, philosophy should be seen as located within various traditions, some religious and some not. I have claimed that unbelief in the contemporary West should not be thought of as mere disbelief in God. Rather there has grown up *around* the sciences a new, affirmative worldview, and for many there are associated quasi-religious trappings. Finally, I have projected a pessimistic view of the possibilities for a coherent naturalistic position, so long as it is committed to science as the only source of knowledge, and especially as it claims to be able to answer questions of morality and the meaning of life. My prognosis for an Anabaptist-Christian tradition is much more positive. Much more needs to be said on all of these points.

So this is a sketchy essay, but the purpose of this book is to point philosophers with religious interests in new directions, and I hope I have succeeded in this task.

Note

1. MacIntyre, in personal conversation, said that he does not consider his work to be a valuable model for approaching religious pluralism because he does not see the religions to be in competition. So I am suggesting a use that he would not sanction.

A Contemporary Jewish Perspective on Philosophy of Religion

Joshua Golding

1. Introduction

From my own perspective as a contemporary Jewish philosopher, I shall attempt in this chapter to address the following questions. What is philosophy of religion? Why is philosophy of religion important? What role does philosophy of religion play in religious life? In particular, what is Jewish philosophy? Is there a distinctively Jewish approach to philosophy of religion? Or, is philosophy of religion essentially a universal discourse that is not particular to any tradition? What is the relation between philosophy of religion and Judaism as a religion? Is philosophy of religion an integral part of Judaism, or is it, so to speak, a meta-discourse that stands outside Judaism? Finally, what are the key emerging issues in philosophy of religion and particularly Jewish philosophy? What are the priorities that will (or should) occupy its attention as we move further into the twenty-first century?

2. What is Philosophy?

One starting point for this discussion is the notion that *philosophy of religion is a branch of philosophy*. Ideally, before tackling the questions above regarding philosophy of religion, we must first address similar questions about philosophy itself. What is philosophy? Is philosophy a universal inquiry or is it specific to particular cultures or traditions? Why is philosophy important, and why should we engage in it? Needless to say, these are broad questions, and it is impossible here to give them full treatment. Instead, I shall simply sketch a certain conception of philosophy, without an elaborate defence. In light of this conception, I shall then proceed to the questions above regarding philosophy of religion and Jewish philosophy.

What, then, is philosophy? Etymologically, philosophy is the *love of wisdom*. But what does that mean? My conception is that philosophy is *the passionate pursuit of the understanding of fundamental truths*, that is, *the activity of asking fundamental questions, and attempting to answer those questions with rational support*. Of course, what counts as '*understanding*', what counts as a '*fundamental truth*' or a '*fundamental question*', and what counts as '*rational support*' may be a matter of debate. To enter such questions is to engage in philosophy, that is, to ask what it means to pursue fundamental truths with reason. The nature of reason and its limits is itself a philosophical topic; philosophy is fundamentally self-reflective. Still, the notion that reason is at least one guide (if not the only guide) to truth seems to be a central operating tenet of philosophical activity. It may not be a simple matter to defend that tenet. For the present purpose, we may say that philosophy is the *attempt* to pursue fundamental truths with reason; whether it succeeds, or even, whether it is doomed to fail, is another matter.

Based on a certain premise which shall be articulated in the next paragraph, it follows that on this conception, philosophy is essentially a *universal human activity*.

To be sure, the *content* of philosophy, that is, the particular claims, issues, and arguments, are different in different times and climes. The content of philosophy evolves, as new theories are invented, old theories are discarded, and still others once discarded are rehabilitated or resuscitated. Furthermore, the content of philosophy changes as it takes into account new developments in other areas, such as, for example, science, art, politics, and current events. It is also true that different philosophers working within different cultures or traditions are concerned with somewhat different questions, and their answers to those questions are shaped and moulded, and, in some cases, bound or limited, by their particular culture or tradition. But, at its core, the activity of philosophy itself is essentially the same: rational reflection on fundamental questions.

The argument in the previous paragraph is based on the premise that the activity of rational reflection, much like the capacity for throwing an object, or tilling the soil, is essentially unchanged and universal since the origin of humanity. While of course one may develop new purposes and even new ways of throwing an object, such as in baseball or basketball, it is still the case that the action of throwing an object is unchanged. And, while one may develop new techniques for tilling the soil, by using new instruments and new technologies, the essential act of tilling the soil is still the same. Similarly, while one may develop new techniques of reasoning and argument, such as, for example, Socratic dialectic, or symbolic logic, or even 'deconstructionism', the fundamental activity of reasoning is unchanged. I realize that this view of reason may be controversial, but I shall not here attempt to support this view any further. It is on this basis that I regard philosophy as a universal human activity.

It is worth pointing out that the present conception of philosophy differs from another possible use of the term 'philosophy' that is found in some mediaeval literature, and also in some secondary discussions of mediaeval literature. This is where the term 'philosophy' is used to designate a certain specific body of notions, doctrines, and arguments put forth by a certain specific set of authors, primarily Aristotle and his followers. It is in this vein, for example, that Thomas Aquinas refers to Aristotle as 'The Philosopher', indicating that Aristotle was the philosopher *par excellence* (e.g., see Aquinas 1981: p. 11 ; s. I.2.2). It is also in this sense that Blaise Pascal contrasted the 'God of Abraham, Isaac, and Jacob' with 'the God of the philosophers'.[1] Similarly, for example, it has been claimed (Davidson 1974) that certain mediaeval Jewish thinkers argued that there is an obligation to study 'philosophy' in this sense. By this it is meant that there is an obligation to study certain specific works, to wit, those following in the Aristotelian tradition. This is also the same use that certain Jewish figures such as Meir Ibn Gabbai (1480–1540) or Judah Loew of Prague (1525–1609) employ when they attack 'philosophy'. What they often mean to criticize is the philosophy *produced by Aristotle and his followers.* Depending on the context, they may or may not also mean to criticize the activity of pursuing the understanding of fundamental truths with reason. (For discussion and references, see Golding 1997.)

I believe there is also a current use of the term 'philosophy' which is similar to the one just mentioned. On this use, to study 'philosophy' is to study certain works which are produced by people known as 'philosophers', including, in this case, a much broader list than just Aristotle and his followers. Again, this use is different from the conception offered here. On my perspective, philosophy is the pursuit of understanding fundamental truths with reason. Thus, to be interested in philosophy is first and foremost to be interested in pursuing fundamental truth with reason; it is only secondarily to be interested in the works of any particular individual author or school of thought.

Given the present conception of philosophy, what is its purpose? *Why* should one engage in philosophy? For those who believe that reason is a guide, or at least one guide, to fundamental truth, the question then becomes, why pursue fundamental truth? This question seems so basic that perhaps one might despair of answering it well. Perhaps the best we can do is as follows. If one does not *already* care about the pursuit of truth, nothing one can say will be satisfactory to answer the question as to *why* one should pursue fundamental truth. But if one cares about truth at all, it follows that one should engage in philosophy, since philosophy pursues the most important or profound truths. It seems that for anyone who is thoughtful enough to pose the question, *why engage in philosophy?* there will be a satisfactory answer. For, anyone thoughtful enough to pose this question is likely to think that reason plays at least some role in the pursuit of truth, and that there is some value in seeking truth. Those who do *not* think that reason is a guide to fundamental truth will have no motive to engage in philosophy, except perhaps as a pastime. For the present purpose, this tentative answer will have to suffice. But we shall return to this issue later in this chapter.

3. What is Philosophy of Religion?

Given the present conception of philosophy, what is *philosophy of religion*? Where *x* is some specific subject matter, such as ethics, politics, science, or art, the 'philosophy of *x*' is *the passionate pursuit of the understanding of fundamental truths regarding x*. Thus to philosophize about religion is to pose fundamental questions about religion, and to attempt to answer those questions with rational support. The philosopher of religion asks questions such as, what claims does religion make about fundamental truths, and can those claims be substantiated with rational support? Is religion, or, is some particular religion, true, valid, and worthy of adherence? What reasons if any can be given for supporting the claims of religion, or of some specific religion? Unlike the theologian or catechist, the philosopher of religion is interested not merely in *describing* the claims of religion, but also in the *evaluative* question of whether the claims of religion are reasonable and true. Of course, this does not prevent a person from being both a theologian and a philosopher.

Furthermore, philosophy of religion investigates how religion relates to other important spheres of life, such as, ethics, politics, science, and art. Again, unlike the sociologist or historian of religion, who is also interested in this subject, the philosopher is interested especially in the normative question as to whether religion or religious claims are subordinate, or superordinate, to these other areas. Thus, for example, philosophy of religion asks whether science is in any sense superior to religion, or vice versa; whether ethical claims can in any sense trump religious claims; whether aesthetic value can in any sense be more supreme than religious values, and so on. Again, this does not prevent the same person from being a sociologist and historian of religion, as well as a philosopher of religion.

As indicated, such questions may be raised about religion in general, or about a particular religion. Moreover, such questions may be raised by religious as well as non-religious philosophers; they may be raised by members of a certain religion about the claims of their own religion, or about the claims of another religion. Thus philosophy of religion is carried out in a wide variety of contexts.

It follows from what we have said that, like philosophy, philosophy of religion is essentially a universal human activity. But, once again, it is surely the case that the *content* of philosophy of religion, that is, the particular claims, issues, and arguments, will differ from time to time and place to place. This is especially true insofar as philosophy of religion responds to new developments in science, art, politics, and current events. Furthermore, insofar as different religions teach different doctrines, it is a natural occurrence that what concerns one philosopher working within one tradition will differ from that which concerns another philosopher working in a different religion. Thus, a Christian philosopher might be concerned with a philosophical treatment of the doctrine of the Trinity; a Jewish philosopher may be concerned to explicate the doctrine of the chosen people; a Muslim philosopher may be concerned to explicate the doctrine that Mohammed is the seal of the prophets. At the same time, to the extent that different religions make the same claims or at least overlapping claims, philosophers of religion in different traditions will share some concerns. Thus for example, both Jewish, Christian, and Muslim philosophers are equally concerned with explicating the notion of God, and with the question of whether belief in God is rationally defensible. On the other hand, non-religious philosophers may be concerned with those aspects of religion which they believe to be most profoundly mistaken or wrong, or perhaps simply with those aspects of religion which they happen to find most interesting or engaging.

As we move further into the twenty-first century, what are the key emerging issues in philosophy of religion generally? Before speaking about 'emerging' issues, I submit that *the basic questions* in philosophy of religion today are still the very same perennial questions which have faced philosophers of religion for centuries. The central question of philosophy of religion is: 'Who or what is God, and, is there rational support for believing and/or having "faith" in God?' And this question brings with it many other questions, such as: 'What is belief?' 'What is faith?' 'What is reason, and how is it related to faith?' Since it is the case at least for the three main monotheistic religions that our conception of God is largely shaped by the Bible or the Koran, another very important question is: 'What is the conception of God that emerges from these texts, and is the notion of God rationally coherent?' If there are different ways of reading and interpreting the texts, which conception of God is the most plausible? Furthermore, since each of these traditions affirms some notion of revelation, another important question is: 'What is the nature of revelation and/or religious experience?' Is there some rational way of verifying or confirming those beliefs that are based on purported revelation or religious experience? Finally, once again, what is the relation between religion and other important spheres of human life, such as, science, politics, ethics, and art? To some degree these questions have been discussed and debated since the time of Philo, who may be regarded as the first philosopher of monotheistic religion. It is also the case that these questions have not be conclusively answered or 'settled'. This is why the work of figures such as Philo, Augustine, and Aquinas, as well as Hume, Nietzsche, and Wittgenstein are still very much relevant to contemporary discussions in philosophy of religion. In my opinion, these classic authors will continue to be relevant in the foreseeable future.

Having said all this, it is still true there are certain 'emerging' areas or questions where 'cutting edge' work is being done in philosophy of religion today. It seems for example that the interface between contemporary science and religion is likely to receive more treatment in the near future. As contemporary physicists continue to advance new theories (and refine old ones) regarding the nature and origin of the cosmos, philosophers of religion will continue to refine the debate regarding the implications for such theories for the belief in God as creator and/or designer of the universe. Similarly, as contemporary biologists continue to do the same regarding the origins of life and especially human life, the debate regarding the implications of such theories for the belief in God as intelligent designer will be further refined.

Furthermore, current events and political movements also affect the direction and focus of philosophy of religion. A range of issues that are very topical today concern the relation of religion and the public sphere. Such questions include the following. 'What is the proper role of religion in the public sphere?' In particular, what is the proper role of religion in the context of a liberal democracy such as the United States or Great Britain? As the phenomenon of 'globalization' continues, questions about the relation between different religious traditions have become more pressing as well. For example: 'What is the meaning of "religious pluralism"?' In what sense if any can different religions, that make apparently conflicting claims, be true? Can a religion that makes some universal claim to truth find room to 'tolerate' another religion which makes apparently different claims? What is the meaning of tolerance? All of these questions have been discussed before, but they are likely to receive further treatment for some time to come.

Finally, it seems to me another issue that probably should receive more philosophical treatment is the nature of spiritual experience and its connection with traditional religion. Many people today talk of their spiritual experience as a real phenomenon in their life. Since the 1960s in the West there seems to have been a popular interest in meditation and mysticism. What connection if any does this phenomenon have with traditional religious belief, dogma, and commitment? What is the relation of ordinary religious experience and mystical experience? Can such experiences be used to justify a belief in God or in other traditional beliefs about God? These are important questions that remain to be explored.

Now let us turn to the question, *why* should a person engage in the philosophy of religion? Depending on who the person is and to what religion (if any) he or she happens to adhere, the reasons for engaging in philosophy of religion will differ. But one thing is certain: we are all human beings. Insofar as we are human beings, we should engage in philosophy of religion for the same reason that we should engage in philosophy generally. For those of us who believe that reason is at least one guide or path to truth, we need to philosophize about religion if we are to succeed in understanding the deepest or most fundamental truths about religion. We need to engage in philosophy of religion in order to evaluate rationally the claims of religion, lest we simply believe blindly and perhaps falsely. I hasten to add that one need not think that reason *alone* is a guide to truth in order to realize and accept that philosophy of religion plays a role in our understanding of religion and its teachings. And, as stated earlier, the nature of reason, its limits, and its relation to faith or religious commitment is itself a vexed issue; it is perhaps the central issue of philosophy of religion, since its inception and to this very day. Nevertheless, insofar as we are human beings, the main reason for engaging in philosophy of religion is to help us understand religion, and to help us evaluate its claims.

It is worth noting here that, very often, a religious person who engages in philosophy of religion becomes more self-critical and circumspect about his or her religious beliefs. Through philosophy, one becomes aware of problems and questions regarding the meaning and truth of one's beliefs. Indeed, in order to engage in philosophy, it seems that one must question or call into doubt those beliefs which one holds dear. (For a discussion of doubt in the Jewish context, see Lamm 1972 and also Golding 1992.)

For a religious person this can be unsettling, to say the least. After all, it is well known that some religious people come to abandon their religious beliefs after having engaged in philosophy of religion. On the other hand, for some religious people, philosophy brings them to what they consider to be a deeper understanding and appreciation of their religious convictions.

Some of these people come to the conclusion that in their estimation, their religious beliefs are rationally defensible, or at least, that their religious beliefs do not violate any canons of reason. But almost everyone who studies philosophy of religion comes away realizing that there are complex issues involved in religious belief, and that it is foolish to think that one's own belief (or lack thereof) is so patently true that anyone who disagrees is either a blithering idiot or a wanton sinner.

One outcome of this is that philosophy of religion can serve as an antidote, or, perhaps rather, a prophylactic, against religious fanaticism. By a 'fanatic' I mean someone who believes that his religion is the correct one for all mankind, and that any means including violence and terror may be used to impose his religion on others. Of course, as indicated earlier, those who utterly reject reason as a path to truth have no use for philosophy of religion, or philosophy in general. Famously, Santayana wrote that those who do not study history are condemned to repeat its mistakes. A less familiar adage is that unfortunately, those who are most in need of the study of philosophy are least disposed to engage in it. It is not an accident that, generally speaking, religious fanatics (indeed, fanatics of any sort) tend to bear a hatred of philosophy. But while it may be impossible to disabuse a fanatic of his fanaticism, it is not impossible to steer a person away from fanaticism *before* he becomes a fanatic, through philosophy of religion. Thus, there is great social utility in studying, teaching, and spreading philosophy of religion.

So far we have discussed the reason for engaging in philosophy of religion insofar as we are humans. Insofar as we are members *of a particular religion (or sect)*, the reason or motive for engaging in philosophy of religion will differ depending on our religion (or sect). Some religions are more friendly to philosophy than others. Obviously, a religion which *rejects* reason as a guide to truth altogether will have little use for philosophy and will discourage it, not by reason (for that would be to engage in philosophy!) but by force. On the other hand, a religion which endorses or encourages reason as a guide or means to truth is bound to be more friendly to philosophy. Adherents of such religions believe that philosophy can illuminate and enrich one's religious faith. Secondarily, philosophy of religion can also be employed in the aid of apologetics, that is, in the attempt to fend off critiques of religion (or of a particular religion) from the outside. For such religions, there will be a *religious* motive for engaging in philosophy of religion. Such is the case, as I shall argue in the next section, for Judaism.

Before moving on, I wish to comment briefly on two perspectives on the relation of philosophy of religion and religious life which are different from my own. One perspective (more fashionable some time ago, in the wake of Wittgenstein's work) is based on the notion that religion does not make claims about reality; it consists in a way of life rather than a set of beliefs. Thus it is argued that philosophy is irrelevant to genuine religious life, because philosophy investigates whether certain claims are true or false, and this is not what religion is about.

In response, I can readily agree that religion is not *only* about belief, and perhaps even that it is *not mostly* about belief, but rather about practising a way of life. Still, it is certainly the case that many religions, including Judaism, Christianity, and Islam do on the face of things make numerous and quite profound assertions about reality. These religions are not only ways of life. Rather, they are ways of life that *make claims about their own significance, by making assertions about reality*. Part of the religious life involves believing, or knowing, certain truths, and living in accord with those truths. Hence, for these religions at least, philosophy is relevant to genuine religious life.

Another, perhaps more popular, perspective different from mine involves the notion that philosophy of religion is religiously out of place because religious commitment is not based on reason but faith, where faith is conceived as some sort of wholly non-rational commitment. (I say 'wholly non-rational' because if there is any portion of the commitment which is rational, this perspective would not after all be different from mine.) We may refer to this perspective as *extreme fideism*. On this perspective, it is claimed that philosophy is irrelevant, a waste of time, or perhaps an outright danger for those who are genuinely religious, since it can lead one away from religious conviction. This brings to mind what I referred to at the outset of this chapter as the central operating tenet of philosophical inquiry, namely, that reason is a guide, or at least one guide, to fundamental truth. The extreme fideist rejects this tenet, or at least, he claims that regarding the truths of religion, reason is entirely useless.

My response to this perspective is that it is impossible for the extreme fideist to support or defend his position rationally. For once the fideist engages in the effort to rationally defend his position, he thereby concedes that reason plays some role in our access to fundamental truth regarding religion, and he thereby engages in the activity of philosophy of religion. The fideist cannot defend his position; he can only assert it and then admit that he cannot defend it. This seems absurd. Now, the fideist himself may not be bothered by this absurdity. But, anyone else contemplating adopting fideism might very well be bothered by this absurdity.

In fact, historically, there have been many great religious thinkers who have attacked or disparaged 'philosophy'. These include such figures as al-Ghazzali, Pascal, and the Jewish Kabbalist Ibn Gabbai. It is interesting that all of these figures engage in arguments to try to show that the principles of their faith cannot be demonstrated with reason, or more generally, why reason is inadequate or impotent to access fundamental truths. Very often, what these thinkers were doing is not criticizing the use of philosophy in the sense employed here, but rather criticizing a certain body of literature which they designate as 'philosophy'. By doing so they are in effect *agreeing* that reason plays some role in our access to fundamental truths.

A particularly instructive case in point is Pascal. As mentioned above, Pascal distanced himself from what he called the "God of the philosophers'. He also claimed that there is no way to rationally prove or disprove God's existence. Yet in his famous argument known as 'the Wager' (1958: 65–66) he claimed that it is rational to believe in God, based on the potential value to be gained if it turns out that God exists. It is not our business here to assess the Wager. My point is that by making this argument, Pascal engaged in philosophy of religion as conceived here. Thus, despite his critique of 'philosophers', today Pascal counts as a 'philosopher of religion'.

Given the present conception, is philosophy of religion an integral part of religion, or is it, so to speak, a meta-discourse that stands outside of religion? The answer depends on the context in which philosophical activity takes place, as well as on the particular religion in question. When an atheist engages in philosophy of religion, he is not self-consciously engaging in a 'religious activity'. Instead he would seem to be engaging in a meta-discourse about religion. On the other hand, when a religious person engages in philosophy of religion, that might count as a religious activity, if his religion endorses and encourages the pursuit of fundamental truth with the aid of reason. If it does not, or if his religion discourages philosophy, then, from that perspective, he is engaging in a non-religious or irreligious activity. As I have indicated, in my view, Judaism supports the use of reason in the pursuit of fundamental truth. Thus I shall argue in what follows that for Judaism, philosophy of religion is an integral part of religion.

4. What is Jewish Philosophy?

Just as philosophy of religion is a branch of philosophy, so too Jewish philosophy may be viewed as a branch of philosophy of religion. On my conception, Jewish philosophy is philosophical investigation of Judaism, that is, rational reflection on the fundamental teachings of Judaism. It is the endeavour to articulate and understand rationally the fundamental claims or doctrines of Judaism, and the endeavour to think critically about whether it is rational to accept or believe those doctrines. Thus Jewish philosophy includes what might be called Jewish theology, namely, the endeavour to articulate the doctrines of Judaism regarding the nature of God. However, Jewish philosophy goes beyond this in that it not only articulates views, but also rationally critiques them. Included within Jewish philosophy is the question of whether (and if so, to what extent) it is appropriate, desirable, or even possible to rationally substantiate or defend the teachings of Judaism. Like philosophy itself, Jewish philosophy is self-reflective.

Is there a distinctive 'Jewish' approach to philosophy of religion? I believe that in one way, the answer is 'no', but in another two ways at least, the answer is 'yes'. The answer is negative in the sense that, as I have already claimed, reason is universal. There is no such thing as *Jewish reason* as opposed to *Christian reason* or *Muslim reason*. In this sense, there is no distinctively Jewish way of *doing* philosophy of religion.

On the other hand, there is a sense in which there is a Jewish approach to philosophy of religion, namely, insofar as Judaism favours and endorses philosophical inquiry regarding its own fundamentals. I agree with those mediaeval Jewish philosophers, most prominent among them, Moses Maimonides, who interpret the traditional sources of Judaism (i.e., the Hebrew Scriptures and the Talmud) to teach that there is a substantial role for reason to play in religious commitment. Many verses in Scripture indicate that it is a religious duty to *know* God,[2] and that the way of God is a way of wisdom and understanding.[3] In general the Talmud extols wisdom and in particular it is taught that one must *know* how to 'answer the heretic'.[4] Surely there are various ways of interpreting such passages? But the most straightforward way to interpret these passages is as an endorsement of the effort to rationally understand God and the Torah. Now it is also the case that some scriptural and Talmudic passages indicate that man's ability to understand God, and God's ways, are limited.[5] But this only raises the question of how these passages are to be interpreted, and how they are to be squared with the other passages that endorse the pursuit of the understanding of God and Torah. Indeed, many of the passages indicating that man's intellect is limited can be interpreted to mean that *regarding certain areas or issues*, man's intellect is limited. In any case, it is part and parcel of Jewish philosophy itself to sort out what aspects of Judaism are rationally available to us, and what aspects are not. In sum, although this approach may be shared by other religions as well, it is fair to say that there is a 'Jewish approach' to philosophy of religion. And that is, that Judaism endorses and encourages the activity of Jewish philosophy.

It might be objected that it is anachronistic to claim that the Hebrew Scriptures or the Talmud endorse the activity of philosophy. It will be insisted that the Hebrew prophets did not engage in philosophy, nor do the Rabbis of the Talmud. How then can it be asserted that the traditional Jewish sources endorse philosophy, if indeed the seminal characters and personalities of Judaism did not themselves engage in it?

My response is that this objection employs a conception of philosophy that differs from mine. Earlier I pointed out that my conception does not identify philosophy with a specific school of thought or method of philosophizing, such as that of the ancient Greeks. I concede that the prophets and the rabbis of the Talmud did not engage in philosophy *in the manner that the ancient Greeks did*, but I do not concede that the ancient Hebrews did not engage in philosophy in the sense articulated here. For example, the book of Job may be read as an attempt to understand or explain the question of why the righteous suffer. The book of Ecclesiastes may be read as an attempt to explore and debate the value and purpose of human existence. Some passages in Psalms may be read as the attempt to argue that there is a God based on the order of the nature. Numerous passages in the Talmud address the question of what man can and cannot understand about God's ways, and often there is sharp disagreement. To be sure, the ancient Greeks, and especially Socrates, Plato, and Aristotle, developed the exercise of reasoning to a high level of rigour and precision. The Socratic quest for definitions of terms, the Platonic theory of the Forms, and the development of Aristotelian logic changed the face of philosophy forever. No one who knew of the Greek contribution to philosophy could ever philosophize in quite the same way as before. Jewish philosophers since Philo were heavily impacted upon by Greek philosophy, and this is only natural. But it is equally true that Jewish law, custom and lore developed and evolved over the centuries, sometimes under the influence, and sometimes in response to, developments outside of Judaism. The same thing is true of Jewish philosophy. The fact that Jewish philosophy evolved since the time of the ancient Hebrews does not show that the ancient Hebrews did not engage in philosophy as conceived here.

There is yet another, more obvious, way in which Jewish philosophy is distinctive. Namely, there are some particular issues or problems which are of exclusive interest to Jewish philosophy. The same is true for any other religion. Of course, Judaism shares in common or at least overlaps to some extent with other religions in certain claims; in that regard, the content of Jewish philosophy overlaps with other religious philosophies. However there are certain claims and doctrines which are peculiar to

Judaism; thus, philosophical treatment of such subjects fall under Jewish philosophy specifically.

What are the key emerging issues in Jewish philosophy? What are the priorities that will (or should) occupy its attention as we move further into the twenty-first century? I submit that all the issues mentioned above as central to philosophy of religion are relevant to Jewish philosophy. In particular, the issue of how to resolve the modern theory of evolution with the biblical account in Genesis still deserves further attention. But there are also certain perennial issues which are deserving of new treatment. Perhaps the most basic question for Jewish philosophy is: 'What, in the first place, are the doctrines of Judaism?' More particularly, what are the strictures if any to be placed on what qualifies as a 'Jewish' view? To put it in somewhat old-fashioned terms, what counts as 'heresy' from a Jewish point of view? It seems to me that after all these years, this still remains a vexing question that has not been resolved. (For recent discussions of this issue see Kellner 2006 and Shapiro 2003.)

Other important issues include the following: 'What is the meaning and significance of the doctrine that Torah is "from heaven" or divine'? 'To what extent can the Torah be interpreted metaphorically or allegorically, and to what extent must the Torah be interpreted literally?' 'What is the relation of secular wisdom and secular culture to the wisdom and ways of the Torah?' 'What is the meaning and significance of the doctrine of chosenness, that is, the doctrine that God chose Israel from among the nations?' 'Is the doctrine reasonable to accept?' 'What does Judaism teach regarding other religions?' 'Does Judaism teach that it is the only true religion, or, can Judaism sustain some form of religious pluralism?' 'Who is the Messiah, and what role will the Messiah play in God's plan?' 'What is the nature of the messianic age?' 'What is the role of the state of Israel in modern Jewish religious life?' 'What is the significance of gender in Judaism?' 'How should Judaism respond to the modern phenomenon of feminism?' 'What is the Jewish mystical tradition or "Kabbalah" and can it be explicated and /or defended rationally?' These are some of the issues that will occupy Jewish philosophers in years to come.

Given the present conception, what is the motive for engaging in Jewish philosophy? For a committed Jew there are two reasons or motives. As argued above, insofar as we are all human, the essential motive to engage in philosophy is to pursue the truth. Again, this motive will be operative only for those who value the pursuit of fundamental truth, and who think that fundamental truth is at least partly accessible through reason. Secondly, insofar as a person is a religious Jew, he or she has a religious motive to understand rationally (as far as one can) the basic teachings of Judaism. On this conception, Jewish philosophy is an integral part of Jewish religious life.

Notes

1. The source is a document found sewn in Pascal's clothing when he died (see Milligan 1922: 172). But a similar distinction runs throughout Pascal's work (see, e.g., 1958: 115).
2. Deut. 4.39; 7.9; Hos. 2.22.
3. See Deut. 4.5–6; Isa. 33.6; Prov. 1.7; 2.6; 9.10; Pss. 111.10.
4. See Mishnah *Avot* (commonly known as Ethics of the Fathers), 2:19.
5. See Job 38; Babylonian Talmud *Hagigah*, 11b.

The Revival of Philosophy among Muslims

Shabbir Akhtar

1

An intellectual deficit in the House of Islam is the lack of a living philosophical culture which could fruitfully influence its religious outlook. Muslim society has been, internally, spared irreverent and abusive criticism, but it has also forfeited an experience of the rigours of thoughtful secular probing which can extend the range of religious integrity and invigorate the intellectual and moral health of a civilization. Historically, many intelligent believers, some of whom were men and women of genius, were siphoned off and wasted in the pursuit of mysticism and asceticism, leaving a residue of only ambitious, politically inclined, miscreants who had an easy way with the subservient masses.

There is no extant rational theo-philosophical tradition in mainstream Islam. Even the word for philosophy, *al-falsafa*, is borrowed from Greek. It does not occur in the Quran though the Scripture is self-described as 'consummate wisdom' (*hikmah balighah*; Quran 54.5). In rejecting anything that smacked of pagan pride (Q 48.26), the Quran condemned secular Arabic poetry for its moral laxity (Q 26:224–26) and rejected magic and astrological practices, especially divination (Q 5:90–91), partly for their connection to false gods. Would a 'Greek Quran', revealed in ancient Athens, have condemned secular philosophical theorizing about the examined life?

The proposed discipline of a philosophy of Islam, a part of the philosophy of religions, is partly similar to philosophy of religion as normally understood, namely, a philosophical exploration of Christian themes with analogues in Judaism and Islam. Establishing a distinctive philosophy of Islam is part of a second larger ambition: to revive among Muslims the tradition of philosophy itself. Arab or Muslim philosophy was inspired by Islam's encounter with Greek philosophy and is therefore closely related to much of Western philosophy. Islamic philosophy is not part of the theological heritage of Islam; in this regard, it differs from Eastern philosophical systems which were always integral to their associated religions.

Can a modern Muslim, as intelligent and reflective heir of his or her faithful tradition, establish, in an analytical idiom, a philosophy of Islam? Since there is no existing Muslim philosophical tradition, we must borrow terminology from the analytical philosophy of religion developed primarily to reflect Jewish and Christian concerns. While natural (philosophical) theology is an endeavour common to these three faiths, many other Judaeo-Christian intellectual interests, both in philosophy of religion and theology, find no parallel in Islamic thought. There are distinctive issues in the epistemology of Islamic doctrine, such as the Muslim interest in revelation.[1]

Philosophy of religion in Western academic departments is a philosophy of the Christian religion.[2] Some philosophers assume that the major problems of the philosophy of religion arise in every monotheism. This is, as we gauge from the sociology of philosophical debate, only partly true: Islamic thought does not attach much significance to the problem of evil (and the associated problem of the overwhelming amount of suffering it causes) in a universe created and ruled by a good and omnipotent God. Theodicy (the rational and moral justification of the ways of God), including the justification of natural and moral evil in a God-governed world, do not exist in orthodox Muslim reflection. Curiously, Muslims do not see the presence of evil (and the associated suffering) as an argument against the existence of a powerful but morally good God. By contrast, this disquiet has been the most enduring source of the rejection of a just and loving deity in many formerly Christian nations, an anxiety taking a place as prominent as reservations based on the alleged scientific refutation of religious belief in the age of reason.[3]

2

We establish a religious context for the revival of philosophy among Muslims by questioning the ancient view that Quranic exegesis is an exclusively *theological* discipline as opposed to a form of reflective philosophical inquiry. In the aftermath of authentic revelation, why should the role of human reason be drastically attenuated to being, in legal contexts, analogical, and otherwise merely exegetical? For Muslims post-revelation, why should all applied reasoning, all theology, and all philosophy collapse into hermeneutics?

The Arabic word *'aql*, translated as 'reason' or 'intellect', literally means, in its verbal form, to tie or tether something; perhaps the rational quest needs to be controlled and disciplined. The opposite of *'aql* is not faith but rather *naql*, meaning 'imitation', that is, in effect, the faithful transmission of a received tradition. The Islamic sciences are divided into *'aqliyy* and *naqliyy*, the rational and the imitative (or transmitted) sciences.[4]

Abu Yusuf Ya'qub ibn Ishaq al-Kindi (d. c. 866–73 CE), the father of Islamic philosophy and the only important ethnically Arabian philosopher,[5] saw *'aql* as intellect or even soul and often contrasted it with matter. He was impressed by Platonic views of the intellect (*nous*) as the essential or immortal aspect of the human personality. Today we can identify reason with any general critical orientation. Theoretical reason is the faculty transcending unrefined common sense and providing *a priori* principles (of logical consistency) to guide the understanding of experience. More broadly, reason is the accumulated and critically organized common sense of our species with a normative kernel of widely accepted moral values and ultimate ideals. For the secular thinker, such a reason expresses itself abstractly as the intellectual self-sufficiency of human nature with a correspondingly optimistic assessment of unaided human rational potential. No wonder then that all cogent objections to revelation, including moral ones, have been dressed up as *rational* objections to faith.

In a vignette in a Meccan revelation, the prototypical disbeliever is portrayed as thinking and determining matters, weighing the issues, apparently reflecting long and hard and then, suddenly, frowning and scowling and, in his groundless pride, turning his back on guidance (Q 74:18–23). His perversity inspires him to concoct an intellectually specious critique of the word of God. Since both specious and cogent objections to revelation equally appear as reason's bid for an independent stance in the face of an allegedly compelling revelation, one urgent philosophical task is to distinguish the two. All objections to revelation, whether genuine or spurious, are presented as rational. Yet many objections to revealed imperatives, as opposed to metaphysical dogmas, need not be even intellectually viable, let alone wholly rational. Our sinful passions and instincts are strong enough, if not altogether autonomous, to be the real motivation behind such rejection.

The Quran does not exalt reason as autonomous and disembodied – as an abstract faculty or power of the kind extolled in Cartesian rationalism where it is potent enough to discover truth by doubting all which can be doubted and then building a structure of deductive truths on a foundation of the remaining indubitable axioms. In the larger Islamic tradition, reason is intuitive and participatory, aware of its secondary role. Such reason partly overlaps with sound intuition. It can be analytical and discursive which coincides with its exegetical, legal, or analogical roles – all aimed at expounding and extracting new judgements from revered old texts. After the appearance of the revelation, the consensual reason of all competent believers guarantees infallibility in the understanding of the revelation. Collective, socially exercised, reason cannot be mistaken. This sociological theory of consensus is supported by the fairly strong prophetic tradition: 'God will not permit my community to agree on an error'.[6]

3

What is the Quran's stance on reason and its uses in the religious life? After answering that question, we address the charge of the alleged impiety of rational methods.

The Quran incessantly uses verbs of reflection and consideration. The Quranic mandate ordering the use of the intellect is a religious obligation. The signs of God (*ayat Allah*) are pointers towards an infinite reality behind the finite phenomena of nature. The Muslim Scripture condemns the disbeliever as unintelligent and irrational, a dumb animal, for failing to use his reason to ponder the divine signs. The devout believer engages in 'deep reflection' (*tadabbur*; hyperbolic form; to meditate earnestly; *yaddabbaru*; Q 38:29). The sinners in Hell regretfully confess: 'If only we had listened (to the warning of prophets) and reasoned correctly (*na'qilu*), we should not now be among the companions of the blazing fire' (Q 67:10).

The Quran has a special reason for endorsing a pre-eminent role for reason in the life of faith. Muhammad's pagan compatriots quickly noticed that Muhammad brought no miracles of the older dramatic type (Q 6:35, 37, 124; 13:7, 27; 21:5; 29:50) such as the ones given to Moses (Q 28:48) – although the Quran counters that those dramatic signs were also rejected in their time. Muhammad was distressed by these pagan taunts and desperately sought a divine sign (Q 6:35). Islam had no probative miracles, no candidly performed marvels that might compel belief. The Quran records the miracles associated with Moses, Abraham, and Jesus, John, and other prophets and adds that the Arabic scripture Muhammad brings is a sufficient miracle of reason and speech (Q 29:50–51). Muslims add that it excels the sensual miracles of earlier messengers since those miracles cannot be reproduced today.

Muhammad is asked to resurrect the pagans' forefathers (Q 44:36; 45:25), to put the Quran to better use by using it to make the dead speak (Q 13:31). The prophet does not (or cannot) resurrect the dead. The Quran, like the New Testament, complains that such dramatic signs will be dismissed by disbelievers as mere magic (Q 6:7), that only the wicked demand special signs and portents (Q 6:109–11; see also Mt. 12.38–39; Lk. 16.19–31). If the former generations, the pagan forefathers of Muhammad's contemporaries, are not to be resurrected, then there is an increased need to offer impressive reasons for the possibility of the resurrection transpiring in the envisaged after-lives of the living sceptical pagans. The objection was made continually by Muhammad's enemies. Since the challenge remained unanswered on their terms, the Quran is forced to argue its case – albeit on its own terms.

A frequent Quranic contention is the argument from analogy with the dead earth which is revived periodically by rainfall from Heaven (Q 29:63; 30:24; 41:39; 43:11; 50:11) Again, the God who can create man from nothing (Q 19:9) or 'a base fluid emitted' (Q 86:6) can surely bring him back to life. These claims are embellished with much rhetoric and effect; there are however only a few substantial responses to the pagan reservations about the Quran's claims about the resurrection (Q 36:77–83; 75:1–6, 36–40). The Quran also counters the pagan demand with a counter-demand in a *tu quoque* rejoinder. The pagans demand a resurrection of their dead forefathers while the Quran challenges the disbelievers to prevent the death of their existing tribesmen (Q 56:83–87).

4

Philosophers of religion probe the consistency, coherence, truth and plausibility of religious beliefs presented as truth-claims – but the value and function of such philosophical scrutiny of religion is not self-evident.

The religiously committed approach to the Quran may be incompatible with the rational philosophical approach. Believers suspect a mischievous sceptical intent in the proposed application of philosophical methods to religious faith. It is blasphemous for a philosopher to judge the word of God, favourably or otherwise. Is there not a concealed intellectual arrogance behind the practice of philosophizing about religion? The Protestant theologian Reinhold Niebuhr speaks on behalf of most believers when he writes: '(T)he reason which asks the question whether the God of religious faith is plausible has already implied a negative answer to the question because it has made itself God and naturally cannot tolerate another' (1949: 165–66).

Believers of all faiths would reject the extreme rationalist view that having faith depends on having good secular reasons, in the form of conclusive and compelling evidence, for believing that one's faith is true. Understandably, believers would not allow reason a decisive role in the *validation* of revealed religious beliefs since such beliefs are thought to be known to be true on revealed grounds. The argument is, as the quotation from Niebuhr implies, that if reason assesses the evidences and credentials of faith, then it is reason, not faith, that is supreme – hardly a religiously acceptable position.

The intelligent believer rejects only the final self-sufficiency of unaided human reason; he endorses the integrity of its reduced, exegetical role. Reason explains, develops, and utilizes revealed ideas; it does not originate them. What is unknowable by reason is still believable by reason, although one cannot believe what one cannot understand. Furthermore, for Muslims, reason in the aftermath of revelation is not the potentially anarchic reason of the private individual but rather the communal and consensual reason of the paradigmatic community, the community that, according to Muhammad, cannot agree on an error. This is the collective exercise of reason by the utopian society of faithful believers. In practice, it is the fallible opinion of a select constituency of jurists with political interests and human prejudices.

The believer acknowledges the importance of reasoning: it supplies a procedure, a reliable method, for ascertaining all truth, including revealed truth. If we reject reasoning in matters of faith, how are we in practice to distinguish revealed truth from impressive-sounding falsehood? Moreover, if we reject rational assessment of faith, reject the need for rationally grounded criteria for judging the truth of religious claims, we risk leaving a believer's will vulnerable to the onslaught of false but emotionally appealing views. Does anyone commend a religion of fanatically intense conviction, without resources for self-criticism? A faith deprived of independent critical checks administered by reason is liable to evoke fanaticism and sentimentality, thus falling easy prey to the secularist's charge that religious conviction is ideological in a pejorative sense. Reliance on reasoning is therefore legitimate. Only if we endorse the supremacy of reason *tout court*, allowing it to intentionally usurp the place of God and his word, are we guilty of Niebuhr's charge of idolizing our fallible intellects.

5

There is scope for detached reflection and reasoned speculation about one's religious beliefs and allegiances. In the cool hour, one should ascertain the objective validity of one's faithful convictions. In ages of religious fervour, there would be little room for such detachment but we today need perspective in our world of plural ideological offers. Life is short and our state desperate but, as the Quran admits, we have some time, a few years perhaps, to make a considered critical judgement (Q 35:37). A fair-minded God would understand our reluctance to make a capricious choice, an urgent leap of faith in the dark.

Even if it is granted that the rational scrutiny of faith is religiously permissible, is it religiously desirable? Does philosophy benefit faith? The Spanish–Arab philosopher–jurist Abu al-Walid Muhammad ibn Rushd (d. 1198 CE; known as Averroes in the Latin West) held the questionable view that the Quran demands the study of philosophical wisdom, although admittedly only by a certain class of people. According to the orthodox view, represented forcefully by the philosopher–theologian Abu Hamid Muhammad al-Ghazali (d. 1111 CE), in his spiritual autobiography 'The Deliverer from Misguidance' (*Al-munqidh min al-dalal*), God wants merely a faithful response from us.[7] Summarizing there his attack on Islamo-Hellenistic philosophy, he contends that God does not want us to indulge in philosophy and speculative metaphysics. The kind of faith that pleases him is the effortlessly child-like faith of those who said: 'We hear and we obey' (Q 2:285; 5:7; 24:51). In giving us the truth, the Quran does not intend to satisfy our idle curiosity. Rather, God shines his light directly into our hearts to liberate us from bondage to false gods so that we may attain to faith. Following al-Ghazali's lead, and fortifying an existing and already inveterate hostility to autonomous reason, orthodoxy solidified into the view that the goal of the religious life is only to please God while the concomitant purpose of revelation is solely to guide us towards heaven, claims for which there is substantial Quranic support.

Muslim thinkers from the late ninth to early twelfth Christian century produced a relatively autonomous philosophical tradition free from religious domination. The attempt to synthesize the rational Greek elements and the revealed Quranic ones begins late in Islamic history, an indication that this impulse was external, not latent. There was no Arab philosophy under the hereditary system of Sunni caliphs known as the Umayyads (661–750 CE), which deteriorated into an ethnic rather than religious dynasty. The earliest philosophical efforts were made under the more religiously open-minded and politically universal rule of the Abbasids (750–1258 CE) based in Baghdad. The work of Islam's earliest thinker, Al-Kindi (d. *c.* 866–73 CE, reaches a climax in the Arabo-Islamic philosophy of the twelfth-century thinker Ibn Rushd (Averroes), the greatest representative of Arab Aristotelianism.

Al-Ghazali was disturbed by the philosophers' eclectic and cosmopolitan approach to knowledge because, for him, every significant belief or project must find a basis in the Quran or in the mind and policy of Muhammad.

If Islam is the best religion, how is it possible for God to have overlooked anything major or seminal – such as philosophy was claimed to be? Al-Ghazali showed conservative thinkers the impiety of placing excessive confidence in the prowess of philosophical reason. He signed the death warrant for philosophy in the Muslim Orient.

The battle for philosophy which began with al-Kindi was won for religion by al-Ghazali who was distressed by the impiety of excessive confidence in the prowess of philosophical reason at the expense of revealed guidance and by the heretical conclusions that reason often implied.

Ever since his single-handed demolition of the Muslim philosophical edifice, most ordinary Muslims have concurred with al-Ghazali that philosophy fathers unnecessary doubts and hesitations, raises questions about the duties of the faith and replaces the certainties of faith with the ambiguities, confusions and conjectures of unaided reason. God had mercifully supplied mankind with the knowledge required for success in the lifestyle he has chosen for us (Q 5:3). There is neither the time nor the necessity for philosophy in a world awaiting 'the hour' and blessed with the benefit of the most comprehensive and clear Scripture given to mankind. For Al-Ghazali, the implication of the view that philosophy is needed is that the Quran is deficient in guidance. Fortunately, God has supplied truths we could not have discovered alone – and done so in a language accessible to the simple believer. Which philosopher could improve on that arrangement?

Modern Muslims think that the philosophers were unfaithful to the spirit of Islam when they sought to replace its certainties with doubt and perplexity of foreign origin. Orthodox Muslims sensed the unsettling power of the independent rational mind and wanted to curb its freedoms. The rebellious mentality plagued the labours of orthodoxy as believers worked hard to provide detailed guidance for living the God-fearing life, an ambition cultivated from the Quran (see Q 3:104; 9:122). This ancient suspicion of Greek philosophy has, after the experience of Western colonialism, broadened to all relatively modern Western intellectual designs, especially orientalism.

Theology, as a subject disciplined by the supervision of jurisprudence (*fiqh*), relied on the exegetical use of reason – to extract new opinions from sacred texts, to understand and explicate Scripture. In effect, theology was a form of hermeneutics and in that sense was practised systematically as early as Abu Hanifah (d. 767 CE) and Malik ibn Anas (d. 795 CE), two of the founders of the four mediaeval Sunni schools of law. The role of reason was modest, not ambitious or subversive. Its stimuli were internal and indigenous.

6

Three presuppositions — hypotheses placed temporarily beyond criticism — are required to establish the proposed discipline of 'philosophy of the Islamic religion'. As the minimal assumptions of an objective and detached study of Islam, these three assumptions, each controversial but defensible, also underlie any philosophy of monotheistic religion.

Firstly, religious belief is a subdivision of belief in general. As a category of conviction, it is not *sui generis*. It need not differ, epistemologically, from other beliefs such as historical, or political, or moral belief. The religious status of a belief does not endow it with any special quality called 'religious' that might make it automatically either true or false, or implausible or plausible. Nor does any psychological certainty automatically accrue to a belief solely because it is religious. A person entertains a religious belief in precisely the same way, with the same attendant risks of error, as she entertains any other belief. There is nothing special about religious belief except its object.

This is part of a larger concern. For some thinkers, notably Kierkegaard and the later Wittgenstein, the religious use of the verb 'to believe' is entirely different from its use in non-religious, scientific and commonsensical ones. This in turn implies a total opposition of religious belief and all other kinds of belief. We are here rejecting this dangerous dichotomy. Our stance has wider implications. The sceptic's demand for evidence in the ordinary sense of this word is justified and begs no question. Religious belief sets out to be rational; and it is a critic's right to convict it of irrationality if it violates a generally and sufficiently comprehensive accepted standard of rationality.

Secondly, the object of religious belief, while confessedly special to the believer, must not be assumed to be so special that it is considered the cause of the belief itself arising in the believer's mind. The existence (or non-existence) of God is irrelevant to the possibility of holding the view that there is a God or of experiencing God. If there is a God, he would probably use the psychological need for him to be a basis for a belief in him. But the mere fact that men and women believe in God does not entail that the human mind is an arena for the direct activities of God (or his angelic agents). We could believe in God even if he does not exist; this is no different, in terms of the logic of the situation, from the way we could believe in some fabulous entity of folklore.

The third assumption is partly related to the first but adds a new dimension to the notion of belief. Even if religious belief is a special gift of grace, it is at another level simultaneously a purely human conviction whose content is subject to ordinary rational appraisal and scrutiny. Religious belief is not autonomous.

A corollary of the third assumption is that even if authentic revelation is the only source of fully true religious ideas, the thinker may still reasonably assess the truth and plausibility of revealed claims once these have appeared in the human world of reason. The element of grace does not add an extra dimension to the *content* of the belief. Admittedly, the religious belief may be held with far greater psychological certainty than most beliefs, even to the point that the believer welcomes danger and death, although many secular political beliefs are actually held with equal intensity. None of this immunizes the religious belief against secular scrutiny.

These assumptions allow for the possibility that a Muslim philosopher of religion can question and assess both the rationality and the truth of the Quran; the assumptions relate solely to the most general features of any supernatural faith. The theologian, by contrast, expounds the faith and asks to have, at most, the right to assess the rationality of the faith, as part of an attempt to defend it against outsiders and heretics. Typically, he assumes its truth as a presupposition of his professional task. The philosopher, *qua* philosopher, can assume neither the rational plausibility nor the truth of the Quran's claims. The analytical philosophy of a religion, narrowly conceived, analyses the logic of the religious ideas and uses of language and elucidates the meaning of relevant concepts but reserves judgement on the truth or falsity of the beliefs entertained. I understand it more broadly as aiming at conceptual analysis and logical rigour as a means to an end, namely, as a prelude to the more substantive inquiries that arrive finally at truth.

A Muslim believer might object that, in making this trio of assumptions, I have begged the question against Islamic orthodoxy: making these assumptions privileges the sceptical position, placing the burden of proof on the Muslim's shoulders. This is a valid but answerable objection. No method or project, whether sceptical or committed, can be free of presuppositions, even prejudices. The least controversial method is the one nourished by the least number of controversial assumptions. But crucial questions are begged inevitably no matter where one starts or terminates an inquiry. In a secular age, it is easier to argue persuasively for the position outlined above. If we start with those three assumptions and no more, we are still capable of reaching conclusions favourable to religious belief. This position begs the question against one robust religious position, but it does not beg the question against all religious positions. The religious believer might be dissatisfied with this last claim. He would say that these assumptions are dictated by a secular view of revealed knowledge. We have reached a stalemate.

7

Although the Quran does not explicitly ban free inquiry, we cannot convincingly extract from it a celebration of free inquiry in the modern sense of an unending quest that need not terminate in an already acknowledged creed or conviction. The Quran does not order Muslims to undertake a critical philosophical study of revealed religious convictions; there are no specifically or exclusively Quranic grounds for this distinctively secular rational ambition. Devout believers (of all faiths) see no value in free and sustained philosophical inquiry into religious claims since they think that revelation already and uncomplicatedly contains the whole truth.

It is indirect proof of the intractability of the reason–faith dispute that we are obliged to deflect the debate onto a less philosophical plane — into a factual or sociological view of 'rationality', as opposed to reason, and as a corollary, onto a novel division of labour within the institutional pursuit of knowledge. We can secure a temporary truce between the free-thinkers and the religious jurists and theologians by partitioning religious studies into three categories. The first include descriptive (partly interpretive) academic disciplines, such as the comparative and historical study of religion. Secondly, the normative disciplines include areas such as *kalam* (theology, literally speech, but amounting to dialectic), the various branches of Islamic law and jurisprudence, *al-'aqida* (roughly corresponding to dogmatics in Christian theology). These prescriptive branches of knowledge legitimately and confessedly rely on the authority of revelation. The descriptive set of disciplines are relatively recently established; their establishment and flourishing presuppose a measure of healthy respect for the autonomy of secular reason and for a private agnosticism which dictates a student's preference among religious schemes. The normative disciplines, by contrast, grew out of the historical and current practice of the institutionalized and often empowered faith.

Thirdly, in a class of its own, is the generic discipline called philosophy of religion as such. This is a rational examination of competing religious claims, without deference to the authority of any revealed criterion for judgement. Philosophy of religion is parasitic on the existence of religion. Theology openly relies on the authority of revelation while the philosophy of revelations treats all types of religious faith, Scriptures, and experience as its domain and employs only unaided reason to guide its investigations. It does not presuppose the privileged position of any type of faith. It aims, through conceptual analysis and elucidation, at discovering what religious truths, if any, are implied by the findings of the established descriptive–interpretive disciplines of comparative religion and the psychology, anthropology, phenomenology, sociology, and the history of religion; the philosopher may also investigate the implications of the findings gathered from the relatively new fields of the psychobiography and psychopathology of religious genius and the biology of religious belief – including the study of neurological injuries that cause religious obsession and neuron-psychiatric disorders that affect the quality of religious conviction. This reductionist medicalization of the problem of religious knowledge offends believers but the implications for the religious position are not always negative: the wounded man sometimes has the best view of the human battle.

Theologies, unlike the philosophies of religions, start with the lived faiths of religious communities; theologians expound and defend their chosen faith by using reason as a tool. It is not open to a theologian to doubt the central tenets of her chosen religion. If she does question whether a particular dogma is revealed and authoritative, she can only do so as a philosopher of that religion.

If we accept the legitimacy of these distinctions and the associated divisions of intellectual labour, then the believing philosopher of religion will, in her philosophical capacity seek exemption from the normal veto on any independent assessment of the bases of her faith in relation to other faiths and secular humanism. The theologian, or, among Muslims, the *mutakallim* or *faqih* (jurist), will work inside the orbit of her faith. Institutionally, the faithful philosopher of religion may conscientiously teach the secular university syllabus, while the theologian would appropriately teach in a seminary (*madrasah*) established by the religious authorities.

Many Muslim thinkers object to this arrangement because, in Islamic history, many jurists set themselves up as arbiters of all knowledge rather than of merely legal knowledge. The Quranic word *'ulama* means the learned ones and refers to God's most learned servants (Q 35:28). The term, like the word *al-'alimun* (those who know; Q 29:43), is vague, applicable to all religiously learned individuals, used both of the rabbinate (Q 26:197) and of the Muslim intelligentsia. After al-Ghazali, and due mainly to his writings, the word came to be used in a restricted sense to mean those trained in the religious sciences. This bifurcation of knowledge led to that deleterious split between the secular and religious curriculum in Islam that exists to this day.

8

All thoughtful adults are, in some measure, philosophers; all societies have a philosophical component in their intellectual culture. While a society devoid of disciplined philosophical thinking has no practitioners who formally articulate and formulate philosophical problems, its members still entertain philosophical prejudices – since entertaining prejudice requires no training. Many fundamental opinions are absorbed from our heritage and environment. These are philosophical presuppositions and even anti-philosophical religious believers meticulously pursue their philosophical biases. Anyone capable of sustained thinking about truth, existence, knowledge, and value (moral and aesthetic), is potentially a philosopher. If we add causation and the identity of persons and objects, we have all the central motifs of ancient and modern Western philosophy.

Perhaps, there is an intrinsic connection between philosophy and civilization. Once we develop beyond the level of customary thought, we look for a reflective morality. We wonder: 'What are the place of knowledge and the role of reason in the conduct of life?' 'What is the constitution and structure of knowledge which permits reason to perform the functions assigned to it?' 'What is the constitution of the natural universe which makes possible and supports our prevalent conceptions of knowledge and of goodness?' The quest for wisdom implicit in such inquiries is sufficiently different in trajectory to distinguish it from the search for scientific knowledge. Only if a religion could give satisfactory answers to all three questions would it abort the very possibility of philosophy.

The most developed systems of faith were, ironically, reared in the bosom of philosophical rationalism. Islam's scholastic dialectical theology was developed in ages of intense faith. The believer could reasonably claim that it is reason that is dogmatic and exclusivist. Ages of faith have nurtured great systems of reasoned conviction while, by contrast, the age of secular reason, from its dawn, has arrogantly rejected revelation *a priori*. The most rigorously rationalistic systems of philosophical theology, such as mediaeval scholasticism and Thomism, have matured in the bosom of faith. Absolute faith still allows an interface of faith and reason, an exchange between the two antagonists. But absolute reason is intolerant of the very possibility of revelation. It claims tautologically that reason alone discovers truth; and truth is that which reason discovers. The believer's methodology sanctions the use of reason in the decipherment of the linguistic truth of revelation. This is legitimate and no less rational than any secular alternative. It does not, however, stretch the resources of reason to the limit since it restricts reason to an exegetical role.

A believing philosopher of religion may judge the truth of philosophy. He might argue that secularist defenders of reason are guilty of the intellectualist fallacy of reposing an unreasoning faith in the power of reason. What is the nature or ground of rational philosophical authority? The authority of our secular age is part of the contingency of history. All the tenets of modernism – including the universality of reason, the finality of scientific method and the primacy of history – are rationally assailable assumptions.

Any encounter of reason and revelation produces an impasse. There is no common foundational ground, no higher court of appeal, no accepted epistemological referee or recognized cognitive authority who could adjudicate this fundamental dispute. The conflict between faith and reason is rooted in divergent epistemologies that dictate a different scope and rationale for curiosity. For Muslims, the problem of knowledge does not arise as a secular or autonomous matter but primarily as a religious concern. Knowledge was not an end in itself, only a means of attaining success in the religious life, just as the feverish secular acquisition of knowledge today is driven by the need to maintain power. The Quran repeatedly addresses only the question: 'What must one believe and do in order to win the pleasure of God and thus enter Paradise?' A typical passage is at Q 61:10–12. This religious focus inevitably leads to a progressive limiting of individual reason and reduces legitimate scope for speculation (Q 17:36). A corollary of this restriction on speculation is a greater dependence on authority. Could this explain the demise of the nascent philosophical enterprise among Muslims? It is such restrictive religious authority, characterized by a condescending certainty, which we must question if we are ever to establish the philosophical foundations of a more rational moral and political order.

Notes

1. The Muslim account of revelation is tributary to the Muslim insistence on the linguistic inimitability (*i'jaz*) of the Arabic Quran and simultaneously fundamental to establishing its integrity of a fully infallible inspiration. For details, see Akhtar 1991.
2. Oxford University's Nolloth chair is named for this sub-branch of philosophy of religion. Martin Buber (1878–1965) was professor of the philosophy of the Jewish religion and ethics at Frankfurt University from 1924 to 1933. I have found no post or chair named for the philosophy of Islam anywhere in the world.
3. This crucial indifference to the moral character of God might explain the lack of a tradition of conscientious atheism even in modern Islam. I develop this observation in Akhtar (2007: ch. 3).
4. The first group includes the sciences of revealed branches of knowledge: the Quran, the prophetic traditions (*hadith*), and jurisprudence. Ancillaries include Arabic grammar and the biography (*sirah*) of Muhammad which supplements the *hadith* reports. Inside *hadith* studies, sub-branches include '*ilm al-rijal* (knowledge of the men) which assesses the moral character of transmitters of traditions and is a forerunner of modern biography.

5. See Klein-Franke (1995). This article offers a convincing account of al-Kindi as a pioneering Muslim, not merely Arab, philosopher.
6. This tradition is related by the traditionist Muhammad ibn 'Isa Al-Tirmidhi in his collection (*Jami‵*) with a fair (*hasan*) chain of authenticity.
7. His spiritual autobiography was translated as *The Faith and Practice of Al-Ghazali* (Al-Ghazali 1953). More recent translations of Al-Ghazali's major works are Al-Ghazali 2000a; 2000b.

The Study of the Self

Jonardon Ganeri

1. Form and Content in Texts about the Self

If one topic can be singled out as having fundamental importance in the long history of Indian philosophical thinking within religion, it must surely be the topic of the true nature of the self. That this issue is seen as central to a range of ethical understandings and soteriological aspirations is, perhaps, evident even to the most casual observer of the Indian discussion. Less obvious is the way in which inquiry into the true nature of the self serves as the organizational centre in the development of a broader range of philosophical conceptions and approaches. In metaphysics and epistemology, in the philosophy of language as well as the philosophy of mind, sustained reflection on the nature of self functions as both paradigm and principle for conceptual elaborations whose application has a significantly wider reach. In short, beginning with the most natural sense of wonder about who, why and what we are, about where we are going and where we are from, there emerges in India philosophy in its most complete and articulated form.

The investigation of the topic of self revolves around a pair of themes, the twin themes of truth and concealment. If the true nature of self were not, in some way, concealed, if it were immediately evident, then there would simply be no substantive philosophical project of self-discovery, nor would such a project have any religious significance. Neither would there be a project of inquiry and discovery of the self if nothing could be correctly described as the 'truth' about the nature of self. We are persistently told by the Indian thinkers that the truth about the self is something to be acquired only as the outcome of a lengthy procedure of conceptual examination, self-searching, 'spiritual exercise', and textual study. One must therefore consider with some care how the notion of concealment is used by Indian thinkers to ground their conception of the project and possibility of philosophy, so understood. One must consider too what ideas of truth and knowledge are brought into play when we think of the truth as something liable both to concealment and disclosure. And from the very beginning, one must be open to the possibility that the truth about the self is that there is no self, that what is being concealed is the fact that our everyday concept of self rests on and leads us into error.

Modern analyses of the classical Indian philosophical literature have tended to underestimate the importance of the relation between literary form and philosophical argument; they have preferred instead to concentrate either on the systematicity of philosophical construction in India, or else on the history of Indian philosophical ideas.[1] One of my recommendations is that we give due weight to the importance of genre, narrative, and literary form in understanding the philosophical ambitions of the works with religious significance. Studies in the dialogues of Plato and the writings of Nietzsche have begun to reveal the importance of such considerations for a proper philosophical assessment of those texts, and I believe the same to be true, perhaps to an even greater degree, for much of the philosophical literature in classical India. One reason for this is the rich use of the genres of dialogue and commentary, which bring into play all the possibilities for narrative embedding and authorial self-distancing that Indian literature in general makes so much of. Another reason has to do with specific aspects of the subject matter under discussion. The possibility, certainly, is that knowledge of the true nature of self is non-discursive, and if this is so then the author of a text that claims to lead the audience to that knowledge has to use such narrative devices as will point his audience in the right direction, encouraging them to look or think in a certain way without the outcome being explicitly formulable in words. The author has to play a game with the listener. Again, if a presupposition for the entire philosophical project is that the nature of self is concealed, then the audience needs to be persuaded both that something is concealed and that, whatever it is, it is worthy of the effort needed to discover it. The Indian authors of these philosophical texts avail themselves of an astonishing range of narrative devices by means of which they hope to persuade the reader that the philosophical quest is indeed a quest worthy of pursuit and that there is something that will count as progress. So, for us, the form of the text is informative – informative as to the nature, value and ambition of philosophy itself.

Let me now describe in more detail how these themes are explored in Indian philosophical writing. Two streams of analysis are interwoven. One stream is an inspection of what might loosely and schematically be termed Hindu philosophy of self; the other, equally schematically and imprecisely, Buddhist philosophy of no-self. An analysis of Hindu theory will begin, naturally enough, with the canonical statements of an ideal search for self as a philosophical programme. One may hope to understand these texts as carefully crafted compositions, which exploit a variety of narrative devices in order to instil in their readers a certain sense of anticipation and at the same time to embody a distinctive philosophical vision. The texts portray the Upaniṣadic sage as someone possessed of a great reluctance to disclose the truth about the self, but this reluctance has more in common with Socratic irony than mere secretiveness – it is a device to encourage the pupil or reader to attach value to a question they might not have previously been inclined to do so. The Upaniṣad, then, I suggest, is to be understood as a protreptic narrative, an exhortation to take philosophy (here understood in terms of a search for the truth about self) seriously. I suggest too that there is, in the Upaniṣads, a well-articulated conception of the self as something which is both concealed and yet discoverable. The key expression for 'concealment' is *guhya*, a term that occupies a central position of importance in many of the Indian texts, Hindu and Buddhist, and which surfaces again in the esoteric teachings of Vajrāyana tantric Buddhism.

It is well known that the Indian school of Advaita Vedānta offers a distinctive re-interpretation of the Upaniṣads, an interpretation which has for many acquired an almost canonical status, but is nevertheless open to question. I find in the work of Advaitic thinkers attention to a problem importantly related to the question we have just been considering, the question of how the Upaniṣads are meant by their authors to be read or received. The problem refers to an apparent contradiction between form and content. If the Upaniṣads really do say, as the Advaitins claim, that all difference is an illusion, then they themselves must be illusions too; but if the Upaniṣads are illusions, they can say nothing. To this allegation of performative incoherence, some Advaitins respond with a defence of what I will call the procedural use of reason. Reason, it is argued, is able to sustain the inquiry even of an inquirer who is in a position of massive error.

A third Hindu text to concern itself centrally with the twin themes of truth and concealment is the *Mahābhārata*, a great epic several times the length of the Odyssey and Iliad combined. As an outstanding masterpiece of literature, this text too raises important issues to do with the relation between narrative form and philosophical theory. The turning point of the great battle, the central axis around which the whole story revolves, is the lie Yudhiṣṭhira utters, a lie born of desperation in the face of otherwise certain defeat. One may seek to show how different characters are made to embody different ethical voices, and how the ethics of concealment is explored simultaneously on a number of different narrative levels. We learn from the *Mahābhārata* that, if deception per se is in certain rare cases morally permissible, deceiving oneself is always destructive of the soul (cf. Psalms Wis. 1.11: 'The mouth that lies shall kill the soul.').

Many of the themes just rehearsed have important parallels, resonances, and pre-figurations in Buddhist philosophical literature. The texts that we now refer to as the dialogues of the Buddha are in fact compositions dating from some considerable time after the Buddha's death. We might certainly wonder how the character that is 'the Buddha' is constructed in these texts, and how readers of the texts, or listeners to them, are meant to hear and receive them. Again, I would argue that the texts are protreptic narratives, encouraging their readers to perform a certain kind of self-oriented examination. Not infrequently, the Buddha is represented as engaging in something less than straight-talking, giving voice to a view ostensibly his own but incompatible with his true beliefs; nowhere is this more especially so than in his teachings about the true nature of self. In pretending to advocate a view that is not his own, the Buddha is represented as one whose intention is not mere deception, any more than that of the Upaniṣadic sage was mere reluctance: once again, this is an 'ironic' deception with a protreptic import. The dialogues thereby force their readers to wonder why the truth is to be valued at all. We learn that for an inquiry into the truth to be valuable, it must be entered into for the right reasons, reasons that bear upon the moral progress of the inquirer. The point again is that an inquiry into the true nature of self is not a merely academic exercise but an attempt to free oneself through philosophy from conceptual error and what follows in its train.

One Buddhist philosopher, Vasubandhu, will argue that the conceptual error in question is that of thinking there is more to self than a stream of elementary psychological constituents. His reductionist reading of the Buddha's reported utterances marks the beginning of *formal* philosophical analysis of selfhood in the classical tradition. Another Buddhist thinker, Candrakīrti, took from the Buddha's remarks an apparently very different view. For both, however, the self is a construct rather than a given, and being a construct, it is also liable to deconstruction in philosophical analysis. Philosophers belonging to yet a third Buddhist school, Yogācāra, argue that a constructed sense of self requires that the constituents of mind be reflexively self-aware, but struggle then to explain how and where the boundaries between distinct minds could be drawn. This concern was, perhaps above all else, what drove later philosophers in the Nyāya, Vaiśeṣika and Sāṃkhya traditions to insist again on the substantive reality and genuine plurality of selves. In the Indian discussion of all this, form and argument are interwoven, and it is, to repeat, one of the objectives of philosophy of religion to demonstrate that texts which have the form of literary and even poetic compositions can be understood as giving voice to coherent philosophical

2. Polestar and Compass

The notion that the truth is concealed has been called the 'primal myth' of the Indian tradition.[2] Not every guise, however, is a disguise; even a mask can tell us something about the face hidden within. The world of error within which we dwell is not a dark impenetrable fog nor an unforgiving veil of ignorance, nor yet a shadow-world of entertaining but hollow forms (like Bacon's 'idols of the cave'). There is, the Indians say, an epistemology of error, a way of understanding how our errors work, and a hope, at least, that the world of error has within itself resources that might permit us with reason to lever ourselves out into the truth. The metaphor of concealment has, therefore, a subtly different hue than the metaphors of darkness and light that have informed comparable thinking in the West. For one thing, the error of which the Indians speak is no merely passive ignorance, but an active state of deception. For another thing, the deception is one we do to ourselves – the ignorance in which we slumber is self-imposed. And third, although it is in both cases reason that affords a 'way out', the way out that reason affords is not that of a 'first philosophy' or reconstruction from scratch, but of a 'levering out', exploiting the internal structure of error, finding its fault-lines, discovering in the *shape of the garb* truth's hidden form.

The error these Indians describe, then, is no passive mistake, it is not a lapse or an oversight or a blindness. This error belongs in the category of deceit, because like deceit it is a coin with two faces, concealing the truth by condoning the false, an active collusion rather than an act of omission. Thus Maṇḍanamira:

> This error has a double aspect, concealing the bright and projecting [an error].[3]

Lies are like this too: the liars promotes a falsehood even as he hides his own beliefs, in a characteristic synthesis of concealment and dissimulation. In his essay on lying, *De Mendacio*, Augustine says:

> Whence also the heart of him who lies is said to be double; that is, there is a double thought: the one, of that thing which he either knows or thinks to be true and does not produce; the other, of that thing which he produces instead thereof, knowing or thinking it to be false. (Augustine 1952: 833)

The truth, we are told, is hidden behind a constructed falsehood, a projection for which we ourselves are responsible. We deceive ourselves into thinking that this projection is all there is; our false beliefs are more like lies than blunders. Nietzsche understood this better than most, wondering how within the mire of self-serving self-deceit a 'will to truth' could possibly have arisen:

> Deception, flattering, lying, deluding, talking behind the back, putting up a false front, living in borrowed splendour, wearing a mask, hiding behind convention, playing a role for others and for oneself – in short, a continuous fluttering around the solitary flame of vanity is so much the rule and the law among men that there is almost nothing which is less comprehensible than how an honest and pure drive for truth could have arisen among them. (Nietzsche 1979: 80)

Is there a way out, a path from self-inflicted error to truth? Must we believe that a victim of the colossal error has no hope of finding their own way out, that their only hope is to receive a 'helping hand' from without? We should not too readily despair of our interior epistemological resources, and fall back on a soteriology of revelation or grace. Let us at least leave room for what I have called the idea of a procedural epistemology, the idea that even someone who is so massively wrong has epistemological resources available to them with which they might *lever* themselves out of error. Reason provides orientation in the space of errors,[4] and an important contrast here will be the contrast between orientation by pole-star and orientation by compass. The truth-seeker believes that the truth will lead him out of error as if it is a bright light he must follow. This is the idea behind the soteriology of disclosure – each unveiling makes brighter the place in which we live, each shrouding darkens our lives. But to orient oneself by the polestar implies that one is able see the polestar and go towards it, and so also implies that someone who is inside the error can still see through it to the outside. Orientation by polestar is the way ideals, recognized as such, function in the guidance of thought. Orientation by compass does not imply that, and so is the proper metaphor for the procedural use of reason. The compass tells us only in which direction to go from where we are; following a compass is a method that, if consistently followed, will lead us out of the fog. Orientation by compass is the way executable algorithms work in the guidance of thought. We are, the Indians might have said, more like the prisoner who, in Plato's allegory of the cave, has had his chains loosened but has not yet been lead out of the cave.[5] For the Indians, it is not the bright light of the sun outside that is to be our guide, but that application of reason which enables us to see, for the first time, the shadows as shadows. The Indians will agree with Plato when he says that the soul 'is not turned around the right way or looking where it should' (*Republic* 517d4), but they will insist that this 'turning around' or reorientation of the soul cannot be the result of the soul being 'led out' by education; rather, the soul must turn itself around from within, for it is reason alone which gives orientation to the soul.

3. The Ethics of Self-Deception

We are the victims of a grand deception, and we are the perpetrators too. The deception is one we do to ourselves, a self-inflicted state of ignorance. Or at least, that is what we are told, and we are also told that there is a 'way out', a path from error to truth, a journey of self-transformation through the acquisition of knowledge and a reorientation of mind. 'Error is not blindness', said Nietzsche, 'error is cowardice', the measure of a person's worth being the amount of truth they dare to stand, truth especially about themselves (Nietzsche 1967: 3). The unconditional will to truth is the will no longer to deceive ourselves with those cosy falsehoods and comforting lies we habitually believe. But are we sure that this is the promised path to truth, and not the propaganda of a would-be zealot? Is there not a clear risk that the only deception in play is when we are told, terrifyingly, that we dwell in massive error? Sissela Bok, in her study of the ethics of concealment, argues that attributions of self-deception are dangerous, if necessary, for they imply a denial of rationality to the one who is alleged to be self-deceiving:

> Because self-deception and secrecy from self point to self-inflicted and often harmful ignorance, they invite moral concern: judgments about responsibility, efforts to weigh the degree of harm imposed by such ignorance, and questions of how to help reverse it ... To attribute self-deception to people is to regard them as less than rational concerning the danger one takes them to be in, and makes intervention, by contrast, seem more legitimate. But this is itself dangerous ... Aiding the victims of such imputed self-deception can be hard to resist for true believers and enthusiasts of every persuasion. If they come to believe that all who do not share their own views are not only wrong but actually know they are wrong in one part of their selves that keeps the other in the dark, they can assume that it is an act of altruism to help the victimized, deceived part see through the secrecy and the self-deception. What could be more legitimate than helping to bring about a change that one takes the self-deceived person's more rational self to desire? By itself, the scope for

abuse is of course no argument against a theory that postulates self-deception. But the frequent lack of criteria for attributing self-deception or its absence represents a problem for any such theory and increases the likelihood that it will be misapplied. (Bok 1982: 64–65)

What then are the criteria for attributing self-deception, and what are the criteria for judging it? When is self-deception a harm and when a benefit or even a vital necessity? Are we indeed self-deceived about the true nature of ourselves, and even so, ought we seek to find out the truth? The Upaniṣads speak of a self that is concealed, 'hidden in the cave'. Indeed, it is so well hidden that it is a secret even to itself. The 'Upaniṣad' as a literary genre aims to instil in the reader a sense of secrecy and concealment, of there being something to which they are not privy, something exciting and wonderful. Slowly, reluctantly, we are let into the secret – that the self is deceived by its own desires, which cause it perpetually to look in the wrong place for itself; that the rediscovery of self is the reorientation of gaze. But the residual question remains – is the ecstatic feeling of relief that we are no longer the outsiders to a secret not in fact only a by-product of the instilled sense of secrecy, the artefact of a genre that works to cultivate in the audience a heightened sense of exclusion and loss? Could it be that the true experience of self, described as it is as a feeling of bliss and oneness, is in fact at one with the esoteric phenomenology of concealment and disclosure? Baladeva, the eighteenth-century follower of Caitanya, speaks of this phenomenology in his commentary on *Vedānta-sūtra* 1.1.3:

> Just as a man who thought that he was a pauper and so felt miserable, gets happiness when some trustworthy person tells him that there is a great hidden treasure in his house, and as the attainment of that treasure then becomes the object of his life, and as the information 'there is treasure in your house' is not at all useless, so too is the case with the Vedānta texts. They certainly do not teach any action, but declare the highest truth, namely that there exists a being who is the supreme end of man, whose form is intelligence and inexhaustible bliss. (Vasu 1912: 18 ap.1.1.3)

The interpretation of the Upaniṣads provided in the philosophy of Advaita Vedānta, as we have seen, represents the hidden truth as consisting in a single great fact – that all is one, all is *brahman*. The senses deceive when they testify to a world of difference and differentiation, and the false world to which they testify is discovered to be false by one who hears an oral recitation of Upaniṣadic text, speaking as it does of a hidden unity behind all appearance. But how can this be, given *ex hypothesi* that the structured

Upaniṣadic texts too are just one more part of the great delusion they themselves are meant to dispel? How can we be lead out of a deception by that which is itself a part of the deceit? Apparently, we deceive ourselves into thinking that we have a good reason for believing that the senses lie, and this self-deception successfully leads us to the truth! The startling idea is that the way out of colossal error is to embed within the illusion the catalyst of its own destruction. The Upaniṣad is a 'trojan text', a false gift that will blow up in the mind of its recipient, destroying the error of which it too is a part.

The idea of constructive deception is used to good effect in the protreptic discourses of the Buddha. The Buddha never tells his audience the truth in its naked form – he tells them a dressed-up truth, a massaged message that, if believed by them, will lead them in the direction of a reorientation of mind. There is, he therefore warns, a right way and wrong way to grasp his teachings, just as there is a right and a wrong way to take hold of a snake. His teachings, he adds by way of clarification, are a raft, to be used in the 'crossing over' and then discarded. The Buddha also claimed that he always spoke openly, without any esoteric message:

> I have taught the Dhamma, Ānanda, making no [distinction between] 'inner' and 'outer': the Tathāgatha has not the closed fist of a teacher. (*Mahāparinibbāna-sūtra*, ii 102)[6]

And yet, as the Greek King Menander observed, it is quite hard to reconcile the assertion of opened with the Buddha's famous refusal, on one occasion,[7] to answer a series of questions put to him about the immortality of the soul and the eternality of the world:

> Venerable Nāgasena, it was said by the Blessed One: 'In respect of the truths, Ānanda, Tathāgata has no such thing as a closed fist of a teacher who keeps some things back;' but on the other hand he made no reply to the [unanswered] questions. This problem, Nāgasena, will be one of two ends, on one of which it must rest, for he must have refrained from answering either out of ignorance, or out of a wish to conceal something. If the first statement [that the Tathāgata did not teach with a closed fist] be true, [his silence] must have been out of ignorance. But if he knew, and still did not reply, then the first statement is false. This is a double pointed dilemma: it is now put to you, and you have to solve it! (*Milinapañha*, 4.2.2)[8]

In exercising his right to remain silent, does the Buddha not conceal the truth from us when in his judgement his teachings will not have the transformative effect intended for them? Clearly, the internal coherence of the

Buddha's stance on silence requires that it is not zealotry but compassion which motivates him; his compassion is, as it were, a presupposition for, rather than a consequence of, the consistency of the Buddha's revolutionary project. But what prior grounds do we, his audience, have for accepting this?

In the philosophy of Madhyamaka Buddhism, there is an adaptation of the problem of deception in the Buddha's teachings, an adaptation that is curiously analogous to the reconfiguration of the Upaniṣadic problem in the philosophy of Advaita Vedānta. Now it is the status of the Madhyamaka texts that is called into question by the very fact that they speak of the emptiness of all conventional concepts, including most particularly the concept of self. We are again in the midst of a grand self-deception, this time about ourselves as unitary subjects of agency and about the workings of our minds in constructing a representation of the world. But those Buddhist texts that speak of this themselves use the vehicle of representation to communicate their idea. And the hidden truth about the self is now not that it is concealed, but that we conceal from ourselves the fact that it is not there: we collude in a false conception of self. What are the mechanisms of that collusion? What are the routes to its removal? What are the prospects for a mind that is free of self-deception, transparent unto itself? Can the ecstatic experience of selflessness be equated with the intense feeling of relief that we have when we are told that there was no secret after all, that we have not after all lost something of great value, and that we are not after all outsiders to a shared truth that only others know? A different but complementary use of the esoteric phenomenology of concealment.

Although deception implies concealment, it does not follow that concealment implies deceit, any more than to remain silent is to lie, or to conceal one's body in clothes is to hide (Sanskrit terms for 'conceal' often also mean 'clothe' as well as 'hide', and are contrasted with words for falsehood and error). To clothe the world in concepts of our own making is not yet to screen the world entirely from view, in spite of what many modern writers on Buddhism have seemed to believe. For, as Bernard Williams succinctly remarks (2002: 17): 'It is trivially true that "snake" is a human concept, a cultural product. But it is a much murkier proposition that its use somehow falsifies reality – that "in itself" the world does not contain snakes, or indeed anything else you might mention.' Some will argue that the world enclothed is still the world seen rightly – it is, in itself, a legitimate way of encountering the world. We shall then speak of 'two truths', two levels of description or viewpoints on the world, one in which the world presents itself without concealment, in all its steamy glory, the other in which it comes to us dressed-up (*saṃvṛta*). Perhaps, indeed – and this is still a further move – the world dressed-up is the only world, and our self-deception consists in persuading ourselves to hope otherwise, to think that there is a more real world (or way of encountering the world) waiting to be laid bare. The 'way out' then is to give up the seductive but grandiose allure of disclosure, contenting ourselves with the world as we find it. Heidegger argues that what he calls 'deconcealment' is the essence of truth (*a-letheia*). Our 'dressed-up' truth is not the 'distortion' of which such a conception of truth is the counterpart, even if it too is 'something concealed but which is still in a certain way deconcealed'. For 'distortion' is a mode of untruth, whereas ours is categorically described as a variety of truth. Heidegger relates unconcealment to the genealogy of philosophy:

> How and why this mode of untruth [viz. distortion] alone came into view, and to a certain extent was made into a problem, is no trivial matter, but is the ground of an innermost distress which the existence of man has had to bear ever since. This is what essentially determines the course and direction of the history of the Western spirit and its peoples ... History is nothing in itself, but exists precisely and only where something is manifest; its limit and definiteness is precisely the hidden. (Heidegger 2002: 105)

He might be right that 'distortion' as the solitary mode of untruth is the peculiar characteristic of Western intellectual history; in India the varieties of concealment and modalities of untruth have a subtly different hue.

4. Cognitive Stories and Bold Readings

Let me introduce a new idea, the idea of a 'cognitive story'. This is the overall way we make sense of our beliefs, the epistemological story we tell ourselves about them. Here is one such story, from the *Bṛhadāraṇyaka Upaniṣad*:

> As a mass of salt has no distinctive core and surface; the whole thing is a single mass of flavour – so indeed, my dear, this self has no distinctive core and surface; the whole thing is a compact mass (*ghana*) of cognition. (4.5.13)[9]

This tells us to think in a certain way about the shape of our inner lives: it is a story about the structure of our cognitive architecture. Observe now that error potentially infects both ground-level belief and cognitive story. The truth that is concealed might then be a truth about our understanding of the how, when and why of believing itself, rather than a truth about the world as revealed in the content of those beliefs. Consider again the Madhyamaka doctrine of the 'two truths'. The higher concealed truth is a truth about our beliefs, that they are empty of representational content – the only mistake we make is to attribute to our beliefs a role and function they do not have, namely representing and referring to the world. That points in the direction of a change in story and attitude, but not of outlook, as it would if we came to think that our ground-level beliefs were false. Contrast this with the Vedāntin who says that the higher and hidden truth is a substantive knowledge of an absolute unity. It is not easy to see how one could revise one's attitude towards one's beliefs to accommodate that discovery, all the while leaving the beliefs themselves intact (unless it be through quiescence in *māyā*). This all leads in the direction of an account of the attitude one has towards the goings-on of one's own mind: ironic distance, revisionary intervention, suspension, reflective modification. And that is why the problematic resolves itself into 'conceptions of the self', ways of understanding what makes me a unified and integrated focal point of belief. For how we think of ourselves as organized coagulations of belief will depend on how we think of our beliefs, and how we value them.

Let me call the conception of an inquiry into truth that sees it as operative at the ground-level, as a weeding out of false belief, 'revisionary', and the conception of an inquiry into truth that understands it as involving a fundamental shift in cognitive story 'revolutionary'. The history of Indian philosophy might be written up in terms of a great debate between the conservative epistemology of the revisionary and the radical transformation of the epistemological revolutionary, a debate that raged on a shifting sands, in which what is often at issue is, precisely who is the revisionary and who the revolutionary. Is Kṛṣṇa the moral pragmatist or the inventor of value? Is the Buddha seeking revolution in the minds of his followers, or is he simply helping to restore them to a natural condition, free from the insidious propaganda of the Upaniṣadic metaphysics of soul? Who is the revolutionary, who the conservative? Which carries the greater intellectual prestige? Which is it better to be? (Perhaps indeed all want to be 'revisionaries', if that can imply both a new vision and a revision of the old.)

I will conclude this chapter with a final remark about method. I believe that in the philosophy of religion we should seek what I will call 'bold readings' of the texts. The ambition of a bold reading is to draw out from the text – from both its content and its form – an idea that engages with the reader's sense of the important. A bold reading gives new importance to a text, suggests new insights not only into the text itself but into the things that matter to the reader. A bold reading re-situates a text in the intellectual life of the reader, often by breaking with the standard interpretation of a text that has become stale and clichéd, and it also affects the public reception of the text. A bold reading of a text is itself an event in intellectual life, signalling a retransmission, a new focus, a reorientation.[10] Bold readings, I believe, are intrinsic to the vitality of commentarial traditions, Candrakīrti's reading of Nāgārjuna being in this sense as bold as Aquinas' reading of Aristotle. If, in the interests of an exaggerated scholarly detachment, we deny ourselves the possibility of the bold reading, we will eventually drain our authors and their texts of life, vitality and, in the end, relevance. We owe it to them to be receptive, open and creative in our understanding; although we know they were not speaking to us, we are, nevertheless, being addressed. A bold reading does not extend the conversational implicature of the text beyond the speaker's intentions, to an audience unimagined by the speaker – it does not read 'meaning' into the text. What it does is to look hard at the conversation between author and intended audience, and wonder 'what is the significance of that conversation for us?' The bold reading is a contrapuntal exercise, a way to cultivate a broader intellectual sensitivity and, above all, a greater openness to the truth of another human being or culture. It is also a means to revisit the canon, to generate new readings of the old texts, and to reassert the possibility and reach of philosophical analysis.

Notes

1. The work of Radhakrishnan is representative of the first, and Frauwallner the second.
2. Mehta (1990: 282–83): 'Indra is the invincible power of breaking through, shattering obstacles, overcoming concealment. With him is associated the primal myth of the Indian tradition, the killing of the dragon Vritra, which names literally the force that covers and hides, blocks and thwarts.' He continues: 'The central image in all these myths is that of light encapsulated within a rock, which Indra liberates with his power of shattering the impenetrable, the thunderbolt, which in turn is often a symbol for poetic speech.'
3. *Brahma-siddhi* 149.16: *dviprakāreyam avidyā, prakāśācchādikā vikṣepikā ca*.
4. On reason and orientation, see Kant 1996.
5. See Plato *Republic* 514–17.
6. Text in Walshe 1995: 245.
7. See *Poṭṭhapāda-sūtra* 25 in Walshe 1995: 164.
8. Text in Horner 1963–64: 201–202.
9. Text in Olivelle 1998: 129.
10. Compare Mehta 1990: 278: 'For we in India still stand within that *Wirkundsgeschichte* and what we make of that text and how we understand it today will itself be a happening within that history.'

Buddhist Approaches – Not 'What?' But 'How?'

David Webster

In thinking about the philosophy of religion, a number of conceptual entanglements seem to hover around the very notion itself. What is it to talk about the *philosophy of religion* anyway? Is it to establish a set of philosophical approaches to the study of religion? Or perhaps to extract from the mix of sociology, ethnography, history, psychology, ethical assertion, architectural principles and the other myriad aspects of what goes to make up a 'religion' those aspects which are uniquely or distinctively philosophical?

The term itself, in both its shape and usage, seems to suggest that the philosophy of religion is not the same practice as that expressed by the term 'Study of Religious Philosophy'. It is the *philosophy* of religion, and this seems to be suggestive of a means of using or applying philosophical techniques in such a way as to clarify, identify and possibly evaluate propositions asserted by religious traditions. In this sense, it seems closer to the former of the two approaches mentioned above. In looking at actual usage, we can see something of both approaches in the thematic method applied by writers and teachers. This is to initially examine themes such as the existence of God, the origin of the universe, those aspects of religious doctrine that make claims seemingly amenable to philosophical interrogation. Then it moves to an attempt to enumerate and assess a range of responses from a range of religious traditions. In coming to consider the manner in which the study of Buddhism is pertinent here, there are a number of possible avenues one might explore. However, before I tread these routes – a comment on 'Buddhism'. There are many varieties of Buddhism, and while I will make allusions to other schools, and while much of what of what I say will also apply to them, my most conscious engagement here is with the Buddhist tradition as represented by the texts of the Pali canon and the tradition of Theravada Buddhism. It is also worth noting that some might argue that Buddhism has much more to say to psychologists than it does to philosophers of religion, and that it is barely a 'religion' at all.[1] While I am not minded to enter this debate in detail in this context, Buddhism's early phase and its inheritors (and certainly in many distinctive later forms) do seem to engage in philosophical activity.[2]

One of the clearest contributions of Buddhist ideas to philosophy of religion, as it has often been practised, is to make trouble – to be the grit in the smooth running of the machine. If we consider the themes I mentioned a moment ago – of the nature of God, the nature and significance of creation, and the like – through to topics such as the ultimate purpose and direction of the universe – it seems Buddhism, in a sense, refuses to play the game. Buddhism does not neatly line up to give a set of answers to these questions – for it seems to be concerned primarily with other matters. That is not to say that Buddhism cannot, or does not, have a view on the existence of non-worldly supernatural beings – it just disputes (in the nicest possible sense) the value of debates on such topics. If we take seriously the claim, and I think there are reasons perhaps why we should, that Buddhism has, at its doctrinal best, a tight pragmatic focus then we can see how it might wish to disregard or sideline debates that fail to pertain to its prime concerns. In the *Alagaddūpama Sutta*, the Buddha offers a summary of his teaching:

> Both now and in the past *bhikkhus*, what I set forth is *dukkha* and the cessation of *dukkha*. (M .1.140)[3]

This is often treated, alongside the Buddha's claim that there are many things which he knows but does not teach[4] (as they do not pertain to the goal), as setting out Buddhism's sphere of interest. Just to clarify its interest itself, we can turn to *Ariyapariyesanā Sutta* (the Discourse on the Noble Quest):

> Suppose that, being myself subject to ageing, sickness, death, sorrow, and defilement, having understood the danger in what is subject to ageing, sickness, death, sorrow, and defilement, I seek the unageing, unailing, deathless, sorrowless, and undefiled supreme security from bondage, Nibbāna. (M. 1.163)

Given this, we can better understand why Buddhism is often unable or unwilling to answer the questions that have been the staple of much philosophy of religion in recent decades. This may take us down a line of thinking which concerns whether or not we consider Buddhism to be a religion or not – as its concerns seem distinctive, it lacks theistic or deistic preoccupations (most of the time) and is frequently presented as a method or practice. We might wish to consider the possibility that Buddhism cannot have a philosophy of religion – as it is a philosophy in itself, and not a religion that has a philosophy. Of course, this raises much broader concerns as to whether philosophy of religion is something that occurs *within* religious traditions – or *to* them. It is worth noting here, as scholars of Buddhism from a more anthropological and sociological perspective have done, that Buddhism as practised in many cultures and the abstract, philosophical account of it we might reconstruct from its texts, or as practised in monastic contexts, are not the same. At a certain, what we might call 'folk', level, and in certain times and places, Buddhism seems very much a religion indeed – and far removed from the contemplative and analytical endeavours we are urged to undertake by the *suttas* and by monastics. While it is of limited interest here, it is a diversity we ignore at our peril.

To clarify the relation of religious philosophy to philosophy of religion, we might ask – is the Christian practice of systematic theology equivalent to Christian philosophy of religion? An answer to this would surely be 'no'. Systematic theology is a self-presentation of the tradition(s) of Christianity – a quest of faith for its self-understanding. Systematic theology looks at the consequences and details of belief through the eyes of faith, perhaps, more than analytic philosophy. Philosophy of religion by contrast, certainly as practised in the West, seems to be the development of a category of natural theology – a type of apologetics which, in seeking a rational basis for certain 'shaped' religious beliefs, is the attempt to defend the reasonableness of theism.

If we accept that philosophy of religion is something different to the self-understanding of a tradition, and is an activity more concerned with applying *to* religious traditions a certain kind of philosophy (an analytical, logical set of epistemological enquiries mostly, testing the coherence and feasibility of propositions derived from religious doctrine), then the picture is somewhat clearer. Nonetheless, Buddhism seems to persist in being awkward in respect of such an activity. Within much Buddhist thought (perhaps reaching its zenith in some forms of Zen), there is a concern over the consequences of a subjection to unchannelled or unrestricted reason or logic. This is not purely a feature of later schools and innovations (although certainly some of the later schools do respond to excessive scholasticism in such a manner), but is found in the Pali texts also. In the famous *Kalama Sutta*, the villagers are confused as to which teacher to follow – they all come along with their various ideas, claims to authority, and the like – and the villagers ask the Buddha what criteria they ought to apply in order to evaluate these claims. The Buddha's famous reply is:

> Not by reports, by lineage, (oral) tradition, collected scriptures, logical reasoning, inferential reasoning, by the result of reflection, by the appearance of a view, by what seems possible, by the importance of a teacher. (A. 1.189)

I will leave aside the claims as to whether this leads early Buddhism towards a purely or exclusively experiential epistemology, and merely note the fifth factor that is insufficient for acting as the guarantor of a theory's merit (or efficacy, for as I shall discuss, Buddhism believes ideas of value to be ones that can be applied, or practised): logical reasoning. David Kalupahana proposes that this indicates a suspicion regarding the (over-) use of reason:

> Moreover, as is evident from texts like the *Kālāma-sutta*, people had already begun to suspect the validity of reasoning (*takka*) and logic (*naya*) as means of arriving at a knowledge of truth and reality. (1976: 16)

While this is not the place to fully explicate the attitude within Buddhist thought to 'reason', it is useful to reflect on this concern about its unaccompanied use. The concern may well be seen best as a worry that logic independent of the input of certain types of experience is dangerously unbalanced. For Buddhism, this empirical balance is provided, to a degree, through the results of meditation: a kind of spiritual sense.[5] I have a feeling that some Christian theologians may have similar worries about the contemporary practice of Christian philosophy of religion, but shall leave them to speak for themselves.

These thoughts should prompt us to realize that perhaps Buddhism is not 'just' a philosophy after all – or not one at all, even if it is not a 'religion' in quite the same manner as theistic traditions are. What is central to Buddhism is not necessarily the adoption of doctrinal positions (although Buddhism has no shortage of these), but the practice of meditation. Practice needs wisdom and insight, indeed – but for a reason – to inform the practice. It is not too strong, I think to suggest that many Buddhists would be happy to defend the view that Buddhism is not about knowing the truth, but practising it. While the traditions of Buddhism certainly have become involved in philosophical analysis, and the positions posited by them are certainly open to being subjected to rigorous philosophical analysis, many would argue that this is of peripheral interest to practitioners. I will return to this notion of the role of beliefs shortly, but want to consider how this also applies beyond Buddhism.

It might also be worth considering the extent to which practising Christians are interested in the material philosophy of religion produces – are they not just practitioners like the Buddhists alluded to here? Is there not enough to do living a virtuous life, following the injunctions of faith? Why, it makes sense to ask, is there the apparent interest amongst Christian traditions in this new apologetics? It does seem to be the case that there is an increased Christian lay/non-academic interest in some aspects of philosophy of religion – what might be driving this? These factors may well be, in part, external to the tradition itself. Christianity specifically, and theism more generally, have recently, in popular culture and beyond, seen sustained assaults on their coherency and feasibility (from Dawkins, Dennett, etc.). Opponents of theism have sought to portray it not only as dangerous, as socio-ethical poison almost, but also as an irrational affectation – a mis-thinking. These critiques often suggest that if only people would think rationally, use their own reason, the fog of faith-based belief would be dispelled, freeing the individual from their prison of primitive, superstitious irrationality – this tone and line of thinking is not uncommon in the contemporary discourse concerning theistic belief. Philosophy of religion here comes into its own as the alleged provider of a rational basis for theistic belief. If philosophy of religion can demonstrate the reasonableness of theistic positions, a major aspect of this perceived attack on religious belief is fatally undermined. Furthermore, believers can be reassured that they have an answer to their critics in society, and trust that their position has good grounds. Buddhism has come under no such attack (certainly not with the force and in the sustained way that theism has), and as such has no need of such a defence or apology. It is worth noting that this has not always been the case. The *Questions of King Milinda*[6] is a statement of doctrinal positions that seems to consist primarily of the alleged rebuttal of allegations of logical inconsistency. Nonetheless, the current climate in philosophy of religion is one in which the coherency of Buddhist positions do not seem as under siege or embattled as those of contemporary theism – which is a major influence on the direction of philosophy of religion.

Having set this context, perhaps we should not ask what a Buddhist philosophy of religion would look like, but rather we should consider how Buddhist thought can add to our understanding of philosophy of religion itself. Arguably the most important contribution that Buddhism can make is the attitude it takes (or claims one ought to take) towards itself. Buddhism is (I think) unique in foretelling its own inevitable demise and disappearance from the world (rather than ultimate triumph).[7] The teaching and the practice are seen not primarily as maps of ultimate reality (as pluralists might suggest all religions map the same territory with differing means of projection), but as tools. The most powerful, and well-known, image of this in Buddhism is in the simile of the raft. This image occurs in a number of places, including the *Alagaddūpama Sutta*. Here the Buddha explains that, as with a raft, the *Dhamma* – in the sense of the teaching – is not to be held onto, or grasped at:

> In this way monks, I have shown you that the *Dhamma* is like a raft, for the purpose of crossing over, not for the purpose of grasping. (M. 1.135)

This striking image shows us limit of the teaching's use, but also (and this is less often remarked upon) just how much we need to rely upon it during the traversing of the river.[8] I will return to the Buddhist interest with the very nature and function of religious beliefs themselves shortly, but want to recall first that Buddhist thought does answer philosophical questions (or at least makes assertions about the nature of reality) and seeks to test these. We find schools of thought, and differences between them, even a tendency for excessive scholasticism – and its critique. However, what is the upshot of all of this for the practising, not of meditation, but of the philosophy of religion? What lessons might a philosophy of religion take from this?

Some are relatively clear – that we should not expect to be able to take a set of generic questions and ask them of all religions or compare the answers in a straightforward way (the differences being in the answers). As is clear from the outset of this piece – there are matters that Buddhism seems to disregard as inappropriate or unhelpful to the spiritual aspirant. The best illustration of this is the 'Undetermined Questions', where the Buddha sets aside a set of questions. The set of these is found, amongst other places (although elsewhere often less in number), in the *Cūfilamālunkya Sutta* (M. 1.426) where, in response to questions about the eternal/non-eternal and finite/infinite nature of the universe, the Buddha is clear that he leaves such matters 'undeclared'. Explaining his reasons, the Buddha states:

> Why have I left that undeclared? Because it is unbeneficial, it does not belong to the fundamentals of the holy life, it does not lead to disenchantment, to dispassion, to cessation, to peace, to direct knowledge, to enlightenment, to Nibbāna. That is why I have left it undeclared. (Bodhi 1995: 536)

Philosophy of religion is, then, more than about extracting sets of answers to an identical raft of enquiries. Different religions are not different answers to the same questions. Now, some might query this and claim that the questions religions answer are ones fundamental to the human condition: questions of existential meaning and the cry in the wilderness of those suffering who seek purpose or explanation. This is a good objection – and in part useful. Some aspects of religions do answer key questions about the origins of suffering and the meaning and purpose of life – but often these are not the questions philosophy of religion asks, and they are so broad that they often need qualification before precise tradition-specific answers can be obtained.

It may also be the case that these existential questions are less amenable to the 'rational basis of belief' approach of the philosophy of religion than questions regarding, say, the logic of the ontological proof.

If we do take the view that different traditions do not, then, present a set of responses to the same questions, how are we to think of what they *do* represent and how might philosophy of religion as an activity address such a range of traditions usefully? While this is somewhat broad question, I want to make some suggestions with respect to how a Buddhist philosophy of religion might develop. The Western practice of philosophy of religion has been predominantly carried out from a theistic standpoint, and it may prove useful to, as it were, turn the tables. But how to do so? Perhaps we should consider how philosophy of religion emerges in theistic and Buddhist contexts.

It may be that much religious thought starts with an awe and wonder at the universe, and that theistic philosophy of religion begins for many with this (as well as the 'apologetics' motivation I mentioned earlier), moving on to consider the implications that might be drawn from such a universe. Perhaps it is instructive to reflect upon where Buddhism begins. I contend that Buddhism starts somewhere rather different – with the existential alone-ness and anxiety that marks the human condition. Such a contrast, however, does not preclude two useful interactions. One is brought about by the realization that these starting points can depart on journeys that lead towards each other. Theistic philosophy of religion, albeit often via theodicy, contends with the reality and scope of human (and sometimes animal) suffering. Buddhism, in at least some times and places, considers the rich multi-faceted universes with something rather like awe. Secondly, both theistic and Buddhist approaches seem, as I have suggested, to have their own sets of criteria for the assessment of religious claims. A task which philosophy of religion seems to have engaged in is to apply theistic religions' criteria to some Buddhist claims. A particular example of this might be John Hick and others wishing to use *Nibbāna* as an equivalent to the notion of 'Ultimate Reality' – somehow analogous to God or the 'Real'.[9] This always struck me as trying to get Buddhism to fit into a particular idea of what a religion should be like, and what it should be interested in. What might be more intriguing would be to apply the Buddhist criteria to theistic religious traditions.

Before moving on, I feel a word or two more is warranted with regard to Buddhist thought and religious pluralism. Much Christian philosophy of religion in recent decades has been concerned with how to negotiate the fact of other religious 'truth-claims' within the context of existing, and developing, understandings of Christian theology. While Hindu understandings have the most explicit role in informing pluralistic Christian ideas (most notably in Hick's, readily acknowledged, use of sections of the *Bhagavad Gita* that refer to 'many paths'), it is less immediately apparent in the case of Buddhism as to how pluralism is affirmed or embraced. We might argue that Buddhism is more exclusivist than many other traditions – asserting that *nirvana* is not achievable via the paths of other religious traditions. Maybe so, maybe not. While other religions are not likely to be rejected as wholly without merit, we might take two possible Buddhist routes to assessing their relative worth. One would be to evaluate the extent to which the teachings of other traditions approximate to the content of Buddhist traditions – as though the Buddhist has hit the truth-target in the bull's-eye. This is an approach that no doubt occurs in all religious traditions when they look sideways as the practices of their 'competitors'. The second is more interesting and relates to the ethical aspect of religion and the pragmatic focus of much Buddhist thought. That is: what practice does a religion lead to? I suggest that it is via the outworkings of belief that Buddhism might wish to assess truth-claims rather than on the extent to which they work as an accurate correspondence with an external metaphysical reality.

But, to return to the issues I briefly digressed from above, how might the Buddhist tradition engage with the philosophical aspects of a range of religions? This is a task that might help re-balance philosophy of religion – but it is one that has specific challenges. Firstly a Buddhist approach to theistic religious traditions might be said to be only philosophical in part. Much of such an undertaking might be best considered as psychological. To put it another way, it would be not to ask whether a belief or set thereof was rational, but rather to pose the question: what are the psycho-spiritual consequences of possessing certain types of belief? This is a different approach. It attends to the efficacy of belief, but also its risks and benefits. There is a widely known tradition in much Buddhist thinking that offers a critique of the belief in 'self' in such a way as to include within it, arguably, any belief in a permanent self that persists over time. What is less widely understood is that the way in which a self is defined, or more importantly the belief in such a self, is such that it can be read as including the belief in a theistic deity. Buddhism, certainly in the version we see in the Pali canon, seems to suggest that belief in an all-powerful, eternal and saving being has potentially dire consequences for the believer. Such a belief can lead to attachment and to an abandonment of one's own personal responsibility for salvation or enlightenment. Buddhism may consider belief in such a being as problematic not on grounds of the belief being necessarily irrational, but on grounds of being 'unskilful': having negative consequences, in terms of suffering (most notable mental or psychological) for the one who subscribes to such a belief. This claim – that the belief in the God of theism is 'unskilful' – may seem rather a bold one. Nonetheless, there seems some evidence for advancing it as representative of much Buddhist thought *if* we take theism as asserting a form of Deity which contradicts the Buddhist claim that three particular phenomena (the *tilakkhana*) characterize all existence. The three characteristics (sometimes called 'marks') are impermanence (*anicca*), unsatisfactoriness (*dukkha*[10]) and not-Self (*anatta*). All that we are able to experience is marked by these, and all seem opposed to the attributes given to a theistic God. However, that is merely, given what I have said before, a clash of truth-claims. For theistic belief to be *akusala* (unskilful[11]) it has to be seen as leading us to *dukkha*, to suffer. To cut to the quick of it, the God of theistic religion offers the danger of attachment. One may cling to it, grasp at it – and rely upon it to the detriment of one's spiritual progress. There is much, much more to be said on this topic, but I want to return to religious beliefs in general, rather than specific ones, at this stage.

As hinted at, Buddhism seems to have a concern with *how* we believe the contents of religious teaching. Given that philosophy of religion is concerned with the belief-aspect of religion or the belief-content component, a critical consideration of the way in which religious persons actually hold these seems exceptionally pertinent here.

The term usually used for 'views' in Buddhism is *diṭṭhi*. We find, as we might expect, a concern with 'right-view' in the Buddhist tradition. The Noble Eightfold Path, that widely known summary of the path to the Buddhist goal, contains *sammā-diṭṭhi* ('right-view') as something to be resolutely cultivated. However, we also encounter a number of places in the Pali canon which warn us of 'views'. In the *Cūḷasīhanāda Sutta*, we find:

> Monks, when ignorance is abandoned, and knowledge[12] arises in the monk, with the ending of ignorance and the arising of knowledge he clings neither to sense-pleasures, nor does he cling to views, nor to precepts and vows, nor to a Self-doctrine. Not clinging, he is not disturbed; not disturbed, he attains individually *nibbāna*. He understands 'birth is ended, the Holy life has been lived, that to be done has been done, there is no further coming to this world'. (M. 1.67)

This could be read as an injunction to abandon views generally, but also might be seen as referring only to 'wrong-view'. Often 'views' (*diṭṭhi*) without further qualification are presumed, in the texts, to be wrong views (*micchā–diṭṭhi*). Often this is ambiguous and requires interpretation, as in the *Sammādiṭṭhi Sutta*:

These are the four kinds of clinging: clinging to sensual pleasures, clinging to views, clinging to vows and precepts, and clinging to a doctrine of self. (Bodhi 1995: 137–38)

Here we see *diṭṭhi* as an object of attachment that ought to be abandoned, but it is not clear whether or not *diṭṭhi* here is shorthand for *micchā-diṭṭhi*. A number of writers have tried to disentangle any confusion here and the emerging position, when there is any agreement at all, is that it is not so much that the content-aspect of all views or beliefs is to be abandoned, rather it is that we must be attentive to the manner in which we possess beliefs/views themselves. Rupert Gethin identifies this strand of thought in the texts:

> In certain contexts what seems to be significant about *diṭṭhi* is not so much the cognitive content of a view, but the fact that we cling to it as dogma, the fact that it becomes a fixed view: this alone is true, all else is foolishness. Thus even so-called 'right views' can be 'views' (*diṭṭhi*) in so far as they can become fixed and the objects of attachment. (1997: 217–18)

Does this then indicate that we should reject all philosophical investigation? What does it mean to be unattached to views? Thanissaro Bhikkhu clearly sees a role for some kind of intellectual undertaking when he writes:

> An important point to notice is that attachment to views must be abandoned through knowledge, and not through skepticism, agnosticism, ignorance, or a mindless openness to all views. (T. Bhikkhu 1993: 62)

Here we see perhaps some progress – but there is no clarity as to what this 'knowledge' is like if it is not the possession of beliefs or views. I shall return to how we might have beliefs in an unattached manner shortly. However, some feel that Buddhism goes further than this – condemning all views in a fuller sense. The evidence advanced for this usually derives from the *Aṭṭhakavagga*. The *Aṭṭhakavagga* is part of the *Sutta-Nipāta*, and is one of the most interesting sections of the Pali canon with regard to views. This is most notable in the *Sutta-Nipāta* 786–87, where we find the following verses:

> For the person with spiritual excellence, nowhere in the world does he have any mentally-constructed view about the various spheres of becoming. As he has eradicated delusion and deceit, in what manner can he be reckoned? He cannot be reckoned in any manner whatsoever.

> He who is attached enters into debates about doctrines. By what and how can an unattached person be characterized? He has nothing to grasp or reject; he has purified all views here itself. (Saddhatissa 1994: 93)

In interpreting these, and other texts, Rupert Gethin seems to take a clear line that views are to be 'left behind' at some stage of the Buddhist path:

> Right view should not be understood as a view in itself, but as freedom from all views. This way of thinking is perhaps most clearly expressed in a series of poems found in the *aṭṭhaka-vagga* of the *Suttanipāta*, but is also implicit in the treatment of 'views' more generally in the Nikāyas. (1997: 218)

But not all experts agree with this position. Richard Gombrich takes what might seem like a more cautious approach when he claims:

> He [the Buddha] says that he does not dispute with the world; it is the world that disputes with him (Sn. III, 138). It seems but a short step from here to the statement that he has no viewpoint (*diṭṭhi*) at all; but this extreme position is found only, I believe, in one group of poems. (1996: 16)

One could become entangled in this debate,[13] but perhaps it is possible to achieve a better understanding for our current purposes by looking to the nature of *sammā-diṭṭhi* (right-view) as a way of seeing how we ought to relate to religious beliefs. The *Mahācattārīska Sutta* (M 3.72) gives us the notion that *sammā-diṭṭhi* (and indeed the other factors of the Eightfold-Path) can be understood as occurring in lower and higher forms:

> Right view, I say, is twofold: there is right view that is affected by taints, partaking of merit, ripening on the side of attachment; and there is right view that is noble, supramundane, a factor of the path. (Bodhi 1995: 934–35)

One way we might read this passage (and the text needs some interpretation here, as supramundane *sammā-diṭṭhi* is not explored in detail) is that lower *sammā-diṭṭhi* concerns the correction of inaccurate views, the content of the beliefs being moved from wrong ones which misrepresent reality to better accounts thereof. The higher form could then be seen as a realignment of the manner in which we do the believing itself. Buddhism can be seen here as acknowledging that changing our beliefs is only a beginning of a more radical transformation.

Human intellectual activity could, then, be seen as fraught with dangers. Many of these are more obvious – disputes can lead to conflict and being convinced of your own correctness is a possible source of smugness, a spiritual obstacle to change, and the source of dangerous dogmatism. Another danger is the belief that somehow the ever-changing, complex and open-ended reality that we exist as part of can be captured by the human artefact of analytic language – itself a product of that reality. This concern, over the abilities of language, most particularly applies to attempts to describe *nibbāna* – the final goal – but can also be seen to be a wider worry in Buddhist thought.

With respect to views, it seems we may see a typology of 'viewing' here. Worst is to hold an inaccurate belief in an attached manner, grasping our falsehood close – using it to justify intellectual and other forms of exclusivism. Best might be to have accurate views, perhaps, but not held at all – just something more akin to a direct seeing of the way things are – via the removal of ignorance and self-generated attachments to our own intellectual arrogance. This is more provisional, less 'my' belief than an attempt to experience the world less-mediated by a grasping desire to categorize and 'capture' the truth. But what of the two other possible belief-states? It seems altogether possible to hold an accurate view in a negative manner. For the Buddhist, this would be having adopted beliefs which better picture the reality of the universe, but doing so in a way that has potentially harmful consequences – and at some levels still implies a lack of true understanding of the nature of the beliefs themselves. Even when we are right, we can still be right in a wrong way – puffed up with pride and self-importance. What is most intriguing of all in this context is the combination of holding the wrong views, or inaccurate ones, in a good manner. By 'good' I here want to invoke the Buddhist positive evaluative term *kusala* – used to categorize things as 'good', but perhaps best translated as 'skilful'. Can I be wrong in the right way? I do not see why not – surely it is better to be wrong in a skilful manner than to have accurate beliefs badly held? Better from a Buddhist point of view, to be a considered, reflective, open-to-having-one's-mind-changed-in-the-light-of-experience Christian, than an unskilful Buddhist.

To conclude, the Buddhist philosophy of religion is one of radical alteration challenge. While it may call on us to analyse and to practise, what it asks is not for the practice of religion to sit alongside theory on parallel tracks that never intersect. Rather, Buddhism sees the two as deeply intertwined and suggests that philosophical analysis – without the benefit of the insights of meditative practice (such as those about the consequences of holding views in certain ways) – is not only unwise, or indeed unskilful, but also potentially dangerous. To be a Buddhist philosopher of religion is to practise it in one's life through compassion and meditation, and let the thinking flow from there – rather than the other way round.

Notes

1. For a strong account of some of the work being done in this very exciting and active area, see Nauriyal, Drummond and Lal 2006.
2. The extent to which it relates to Western philosophical endeavours remains open to question. This question is, at least partly, addressed in Ronkin 2005.
3. Unless otherwise stated, translations are my own. The Pali text derives from the CSCD digital edition of the Burmese version of the Pali canon, cross-referenced with the Pali-Text Society (PTS) editions. Where numbering variation occurs, the PTS version is given. The following abbreviations are used: A Anguttara Nikāya; M Majjhima Nikāya; SN Sutta-Nipāta.
4. In the *Simpasa Sutta* at SN 56.31.
5. There may also be an aspect here of an unseen critique of the use of logical reasoning in certain Brahmanical traditions popular at the time of this passage's composition – indicating this as part of a live debate, as much as pure speculation and consideration.
6. The *Milindapañha*. Possibly composed during the first century CE, but with possible later additions.
7. Buddhism sees itself – as a religious tradition which is a worldly phenomenon – as just as impermanent as anything else. It will persist for a while, then fade – until the path to enlightenment is rediscovered.
8. For an account of this *Sutta* and an engagement of its consequences for 'truth' in Buddhist thought see Jonardon Ganeri's valuable analysis in 'Why Truth? The Snake Sūtra' (2002). While he uses a particular approach in the piece, what is interesting is the claim that Buddhism's truth is established primarily by its efficacy.
9. A book which tries to tie Buddhist responses together to the traditional agenda of Western philosophy of religion is Sharma 1997. Whether it becomes necessary for Sharma to rather bend Buddhism to get it into the categories of the questions – or whether the questions are the aspects having to give – is a decision I will leave to individual readers.
10. This is a difficult to translate with any more elegance than this. Many choose 'suffering' but I here opt for the ungainly but accurate 'unsatisfactoriness' offered in Harvey 1990 and elsewhere.
11. Opinions vary regarding the translation of this term. See Webster 2005: ch. 3 for my defence of 'unskilful'. For a contrary opinion, see Keown 1992. For an overview of the term see Thich Nhat-Tu Bhikkhu 2006.
12. *Vijjā* – lack of ignorance. We might consider this as 'insight into the way things really are'. Ñāṇamoli (Bodhi 1995: 163) translates it as 'true knowledge', but this

grates somewhat for someone raised on the definition of knowledge as 'justified true belief' – to call something knowledge is to call it true. Nonetheless I can see their point, as they wish to demonstrate that *vijjā* is the absence of ignorance (*avijjā*). Perhaps 'genuine knowledge' would, in the light of this, be preferable.
13. See Webster 2005: ch. 4, or the exhaustive account in Fuller 2005.

Comparative Philosophy of Religion

David Cheetham

I want to suggest that the future of the philosophy of religion is going to be *comparative* in nature. This is not just a recognition of an inevitable widening of scope brought about by increasingly cross-cultural realities, but concerns the proper nature of the philosophy of religion itself. In what follows, I shall offer a brief discussion of comparative philosophy of religion and highlight some of the key areas of thought that have dominated the debate in this area. In so doing, I hope to bring out the purpose of the philosophy of religion as a discipline set within an ever expanding range of data (Ni, 2006). This, of course, reflects something of my own experience of working in a department of theology and religion at a British university that specializes in inter-religious studies.

The philosopher of religion is a properly comparative animal, not just in the sense of critically comparing religious beliefs, but also in the sense that comparison is a natural part of argument and understanding. In addition, the priority is *philosophical* rather than religious because there is a commitment to a process of thinking and open argument that remains in constant movement. Moreover, if philosophy can be characterized as an endeavour to get to the root of things – that is, to seek *deeper* meaning or comprehensive understanding,[1] then such a project is necessarily inclusive of as much data as there is available. Thus, whatever the personal commitments of the philosopher, it is a kind of enquiry that cannot be restricted to one religion alone. This might be contrasted with religious philosophy (or philosophical theology) where *religion* or theology is more the priority and which seeks to critically develop a more tradition-specific line of thinking or refine the articulation of a particular area of a tradition's beliefs. There is no doubt that both these types of philosophy of religion will continue to be developed in the future, but for those more concerned with what has been called the 'objective genitive' (which can be either the *philosopher* of religion or the *religious* philosopher), the parameters have broadened considerably over the past few decades. An additional question for us to consider is: what is the best practice for a constructive comparative philosophy of religion? There is no single answer to this question because it is connected to another enquiry about what constitutes a legitimate comparative practice: for example, should it be properly restricted to the articulation of differences, or is it search for a common account of religion? Towards the end of this chapter I want to suggest that the new broadened situation requires an experimental sense of *imagination*. That is, imagination for the task of comparison.

1. Talking about Philosophy and Philosophy Itself

A preliminary question concerns the nature of the field. Pierre Hadot draws attention to something important when he writes that 'it is perhaps necessary to have recourse to the distinction proposed by the Stoics, between *discourse about* philosophy and *philosophy itself*' (1995: 266). Hadot presents the ancient philosophical disposition as a *way of life* in contrast to what he discerns in much modern philosophy which 'appears above all as the construction of a technical jargon reserved for specialists' (1995: 272). Despite Hadot's comparison of ancient and modern, it is clear that his distinction is meant to apply to philosophers today concerning the intentions behind philosophy and its activity. The intentions behind the philosophy of religion might not be solely described as a logico-critical commentary on religious beliefs and systems. That is, it is too automatic to suggest that the philosophy of religion is properly a matter of subjecting religious beliefs to critical scrutiny from a detached perspective and that it makes no *a priori* judgement in favour of, or against, its subject matter. In this sense, I think Oliver Leaman is correct to say that philosophy of religion 'relates closely to the personal attitudes of philosophers themselves' (1998: 120). This is, of course, not just true of those philosophers working in the philosophy of religion, but perhaps indicates something about philosophers in general. Further, it is possible, as George Pattison has suggested, that philosophy's 'intellectual *eros*' is 'analogous to the aspiration of religion' because the concept of God 'coincides with what fundamental philosophy seeks to uncover as the ever-intended but ever-unthought presupposition of thought' (2001: 119). This intellectual *eros* is vivified in Bryan Magee's popular work, *Confessions of a Philosopher* (1997). Magee expresses strong opinions about the character of the true philosopher and the nature of philosophy itself. Throughout this autobiographical survey of Western philosophy he attacks (rather vehemently) the analytic 'Oxford' philosophy of his own student experience because, he argues, that it encourages a disinterest in (or distraction from) genuine philosophical problems. Moreover, if linguistic philosophers interpret philosophical dilemmas as mere epiphenomena of linguistic misapprehension or confusion – that is, as pseudo-dilemmas – then what remains of the problems of philosophy as such? Thus, tracing a genealogy of the (Oxford) analytic approach, he writes that: 'Philosophy, it came to be thought, just was the analysis, clarification and justification of our interesting and important beliefs' (Magee 1997: 529). It is not that Magee is unimpressed with the task of critical analysis and logical rigour or with exemplary practitioners of this approach, it is just that he does not expect great philosophy to be accomplished by analytic methods alone. For him, analysis is not built with *vision* in mind (1997: 529). Moreover, he perceives a danger in the preoccupation with analysis: 'if philosophy consists only in the analysis of problems ... then the problems themselves, and the theories themselves, are given to philosophy from outside itself' (Magee 1997: 529). Ostensibly, perhaps this might be related to an anxiety about the continuing relevance of *academic* philosophy and its desire to possess the 'philosophy' franchise. I am not sure that we should be at all worried about this. History is of course replete with examples of philosophers who have done their work outside the academy; in fact, the academic professional philosopher only really arrived on the scene from the eighteenth century onwards with university philosophers like Kant, Fichte and Hegel. No, what Magee is really concerned about is the idea that philosophy might become dominated or steered by purely linguistic, logical or social-scientific enquiries. True philosophy is drawn from different stock. For Magee, proper philosophical enquiry is recognized by its priorities: to understand, to get to the bottom of things, to explain ... Perhaps, then, with his passionate Kierkegaardian tone of voice, he is heading towards the notion of the religious nature of the philosophical quest? Nevertheless, this is at best *quasi*-religious because the philosopher's duty is not so much to provide definitive answers or solutions, but to instil a spirit of enquiry and on-going critical dialogue. Even if logical analysis does not completely epitomize the philosophical disposition, the philosopher of religion is someone who helps to articulate, understand, explain and critique the beliefs that are held up by religions for our acceptance. Unlike some religions, philosophy does not seek *arrival* as such but is an activity of continual critical questioning. Unlike *some* religions, but clearly there are many traditions that see the religious life as a journey towards higher stages of enlightenment or liberation. Here, then, the oft-used distinction between the assertive creedal character of religion and the persistent curiosity of philosophy becomes blurred.

Persuasion takes on a form, and has a purpose, different from logical demonstration. Thus Gilbert Ryle, at the beginning of his landmark work, *The Concept of Mind*, informs his readers that 'from time to time arguments of a less rigorous sort' are relevant, and that 'persuasions of conciliatory kinds ease the pains of relinquishing inveterate intellectual habits' (1990: 10). More typically, Richard Rorty protests against positivistic approaches and asks whether we might consider a kind of 'edifying' philosophy. He means the type of philosophy that prioritizes more fruitful ways of speaking rather than 'getting things right' (see Rorty 1979; 2003). It is our choice of words, or tone of voice, that is crucial in gaining the acceptance of ideas, and the importance of those ideas is located in their ability to enhance our experience and inject meaning into life. Here, the chosen method is a 'literary' one that seeks to develop an appropriate hermeneutical philosophy. Although the temptation might be to associate more hermeneutical styles with religious discourse, it would be a serious mistake to assume that the religious quest is well characterized by solely emotive styles or the rhetorical generation of meaning. In fact, there is a great deal in the analytic search for clarity of thought and correct understanding that has a deep resonance with religious discourse. However, the philosophical quest – analytic or hermeneutic – when understood as a thirst for asking deep questions about the meaning of life, nature of reality, knowledge or the 'good life' – already shares a deep kinship with more obviously religious concerns.

All this serves as a preliminary to the question of the comparative philosophy of religion. Thus, if there is a legitimate scholarly task to understand accurately the philosophies of different religions and cultures and to subject them to philosophical critique, I suggest (in agreement with Magee) that there is also a philosophical imperative to go beyond this: that is, there is a desire to understand or *explain* rather than just to describe or analyse. Furthermore, there will be a need for hermeneutical creativity when it comes to the construction of 'persuasive' *forms* of comparison.

2. Comparative Philosophy of Religion: Issues

In his comparative work, *Hindu God, Christian God* (2001), Francis Clooney sums up the comparative situation very well: 'religious people are moving about, ideas are shifting back and forth, and religions with their diverse claims are encountering, complementing and correcting one another' (2001: 7). Nevertheless, comparative philosophy of religion (CPR) is hardly a new issue. This is not just to state an obvious point about the facts of intercultural encounter down through history, it also refers to the attempt to claim it as a novel development in philosophy itself. Indeed, this would be a somewhat disingenuous claim, because it can surely be argued that *comparison* represents nothing substantially different from general philosophical practice and method anyway. Most philosophy has arisen from some kind of response to a competing idea, or a previous notion, or from a dialogue between rivals and interlocutors. The intellectual task of comparison is, as every student knows, a fairly common feature of many an examination paper which might ask them to 'compare and contrast' two philosophers' views on a given topic. The contemporary idea of CPR, then, might merely involve a broadening out or a *complexification* of the subject matter which has naturally resulted from the expansion of the experiential, historical and contextual information which feeds the philosophical imagination (Ni 2006). But to recognize the increased complexity or diversity of the area under investigation (religion) does not mean that something new has emerged in terms of intellectual practice and method. In the future, scholars might come to see the interest in CPR in the latter part of the twentieth and early twenty-first centuries as something that merely represented a transition to a more global perspective which resulted from philosophers feeling that the milieu of their experiencing had been influenced by a new *proximity* of different religions and cultures. Perhaps once the monoliths of East and West have been eroded by the forces of globalization, the idea of comparison as a cross-cultural challenge will have morphed into the problem of the sheer *volume* of material at the philosopher of religion's disposal. Thus, a new danger might emerge: a sort of intellectual malaise – philosophers getting punch drunk with conceptual overload.

It is not that the practice of comparison itself is controversial, rather it is the subject matter that makes things problematic. Thus, with CPR the problem centres around the rather obvious issue concerning the universal extent of *both* religion and philosophy as recognizable concepts or activities. The recent broadening out of philosophy of religion's concerns is historically linked to the emergence of *religion* as a (pseudo-)generic in the Enlightenment: a disengagement from the authority of the church and the turn to the subject made humanity the centre of enquiry and reason the guiding light. Under Kant's influence, it was reasonable religion supported by the morality of the categorical imperative that gained credence. In addition, Hegel's lectures in the philosophy of religion presented a huge vision of the dynamic movement of history with religion as 'the highest object that can occupy human beings ... the region of eternal truths and eternal value' (Hegel 1988: 75). Whereas European philosophy of religion might have largely originated as a philosophizing about Christian beliefs, I would suggest that it was inevitable – due to the sheer *philosophical* scope of writers like Kant and

Hegel – that it would become concerned with religion as a wider concept. What we see in the contemporary cross-cultural expansion of the subject is not so much a disruption of philosophy of religion but a realization of its true compass. This is not something that is primarily a feature of the Enlightenment 'categories' either, but arguably reflects a basic philosophical *method* which seeks to look at ideas apart from their contexts in order to consider the merit of the ideas in themselves.

The familiar criticism is that all this assumes that philosophers of religion are looking at a fabricated *genus* – religion – that is instantiated in various forms in global human experience. However, it is questionable whether this should be an issue at all. Philosophers of religion are not looking at religion as a definite category in the sense of a distilled notion that succinctly epitomizes a variety of family resemblances. Admittedly, some may seek to arrive at such a notion after exhaustive investigation, but this does not have to be a complete notion that is *already* in place before legitimate philosophizing about it can begin. Further, not all the aspects of religion are going to be of equal interest and the primary concerns will probably centre on beliefs, worldviews, 'ultimologies', language and so on. A *total* definition of religion which includes all the various Smartian dimensions is not necessary, rather it is those aspects that trespass on the territory of primary philosophical interests that will be the main concern. However, philosophers of religion might be attentive to the many different expressions or *types* of belief, for it seems clear that in the Western academy the notion of religion as a broadly conceived cultural phenomenon is gaining acceptance and this means that the philosophy of religion with its 'traditional' problems will have to evolve as well. In my own philosophy of religion classes many students are keen to learn about philosophies, like Eastern philosophies, that have not formed part of the traditional 'philosophy of religion' curriculum until quite recently. Moreover, in Western cultures the changes brought about by globalization, postmodernity, recent events and even by what some have called 'the turn to the aesthetic', have created a new agenda. The anticipated decline of religion (with the concomitant increase in secularization) has been confounded by the resurgence of religion and new spiritualities, and this has already begun to influence contemporary philosophical and theological reflection. Thus a philosopher of religion working in these contexts increasingly finds that her terms of reference have become much more diverse. Graham Ward has called attention to the changing nature of religion and its meaning in the contemporary Western world.[2] He writes that 'modes of believing and the structure of sensibilities are morphing following the new visibility of religion in the public sphere' (2006: 179). The kind of religion that is visible is no longer 'old' religion, but a new type that is not well captured by traditional descriptions, categories or even *problems*. Instead, for Ward, *religio* as a concept should be extended to include a wide range of lifestyles and aesthetic dispositions. Thus, speaking of the differences between the traditional, cohesive, social impact of organized religion and the new *religio*, he writes:

> Rather than functioning as an integrating factor in the life of a society, religion will develop forms of hyper-individualism, self-help as self-grooming, custom-made eclecticism that proffer a pop transcendence and pamper to the need for 'good vibrations'. (Ward 2006: 185)

So, despite the view of *religio* as an invented category that represents a European imperialism, Ward advocates its continued use for two reasons.

Firstly, we cannot ignore the fact that 'religion' is part of the linguistic currency of our culture. Thus, Ward argues that 'words do not disappear. They may go out of use for a time, but they always remain potentially employable because they are part of the vocabulary of the language' (Ward 2006: 185). The term is still being used, but the difference today is that 'its semantic field' is changing. Although Ward is happy to re-habilitate a transformed meaning of religion, he is clearly not intending to endorse the Enlightenment's version of it.

Secondly, we can ask what would be accomplished by abolishing a word? We cannot impose a more neutral framework of understanding by linguistic manipulation alone and 'the idea that by dropping the term we become less ideological is nonsense' (Ward 2006: 185).

Whilst we might acknowledge that the term itself still possesses a strong cultural *presence*, enlarging our understanding of the term is a future task for CPR.[3] As we indicated a moment ago, the comparative philosopher of religion will be particularly interested in the different readings of the human predicament and the solutions offered, the cogency of the various ontologies that are presented and so on. The definition of religion will probably remain unsettled, but this only means that philosophers *of religion* are encountering the same ambiguities as those who look at other fields like the 'philosophy *of mind*' or the 'philosophy *of art*' and so on.[4]

If there is a problem defining religion, then when we look at philosophy we find similar issues. Thus, here again, the question is whether there is an activity called 'philosophy' that has the same character around the globe. This relates to identifying the sort of practice that was highlighted earlier: a spirit of enquiry, an *on-going* critical dialogue and so on. Nevertheless, attempts at tightening the definition of 'philosophy' means that certain reflective discourses are excluded. For example, until recently, some

Indian philosophies were stereotypically held to represent religious modes of thinking and therefore not of the same ilk as more logically rigorous types of Western analytic enquiry. Only recently are non-Western philosophies being seriously considered by the Western academy as being of equal (or surpassing) merit to Western counterparts. Underlying the sense of reservation on the Western (analytic) side is the perceived danger that extending the description of 'what philosophy is' to include a variety of discourses – life-policies, worldviews, mystical experience, asceticism and so on – means that the more logically rigorous methodologies will be dissipated. Moreover, if there is a disparity in terms of analysis and rigour, or in terms of the aims and goals of philosophical activity and argument, then cross-cultural philosophical discourse will be at cross-purposes. The result is that the practice of comparative philosophy can be a matter of carefully selecting those aspects of the other discourse that seem to *connect* substantially and methodologically with the interests of the host discourse. This is not just a feature of Western appropriations of non-Western thought in recent times, but can be a practice seen historically in many philosophical and cultural traditions that seek to dialogue with or include aspects found in rival narratives. However, this leads to a hetero-reading of other traditions that considers them through a particular lens. For example, the validity of 'other' philosophies might be weighed according to the extent to which they mirror or embellish concerns found in Western thinking. Moreover, viewed from the other side, there is the temptation among non-Western thinkers to adopt Western or dominant styles or models of thought and argumentation in order to bestow a certain legitimacy.

Another approach is to strongly affirm *culture-specific* philosophies coupled with the assertion of incommensurability between traditions. The motivations for this stem from a political distaste for cultural and intellectual imperialism and/or a basic postmodern scepticism about the possibility of universal categories of thought. In light of this, the proper task becomes one of the articulation of particular philosophical traditions rather than any sort of global project. Although, ostensibly, this seems to suggest that CPR is ill-advised or is attempting to do the impossible, the comparative task can nonetheless be morphed into one of expressing the differences between traditions. Or else, incommensurability is something that merely suggests the limitations that may govern such projects. However, in some cases this 'critique' might not just result from an epistemological scepticism, but also constitute a form of romantic pseudo-protectiveness about the other's cultural sanctity. Thus, Martha Nussbaum has called attention to the problem of seeing the other 'as untouched by the vices of one's own culture' (1997: 134). Moreover, there is a peculiar sense that incommensurability entails that the turbulent seas of philosophical contestation and critique have been *stilled*. Analogously, the various ships and crafts (beliefs and worldviews) have become strangely becalmed – they can perhaps still see each other from a distance but there is no chance or danger of meaningful encounter or confrontation.

There is no doubt that cultures display differences which mean that cross-cultural discussions present challenges, but given our common humanity (if only as a biological notion) it is unlikely that these differences amount to a total lack of comprehension of the other. Moreover, it appears that the 'problem' of incommensurability is selectively applied depending on the kind of comparisons being undertaken or the political agendas that lurk in the background. Thus, for example, if there are incommensurable cultural traditions then there are presumably incommensurable comparisons across historical periods also (Holder 2006: 41). However, it is paradoxical that the latter comparisons often seem less controversial than the former. It is commonplace for scholars to dialogue with thinkers of the past as if there was a meaningful exchange of ideas taking place. John Milbank is one who argues for 'the end of dialogue' between religious traditions on the basis of their incommensurability. Yet, despite this, it does not stop him from stretching across the centuries, peeling away secular aberrations, in order to discern what Augustine *really meant*. Nevertheless, perhaps with historical comparisons a special case can be made for dialoguing with past thinkers if they are in the 'same' tradition? (Thus, it is possible to have a dialogue with Augustine if one is located in an Augustinian tradition.) But this seems hardly different from saying that one can compare traditions across different cultures on the grounds of similar 'problems' (e.g., suffering). That is, if it is possible to claim a similar tradition that validates one's cross-historical conversations, it is arguably possible to trace similar themes or concerns across cultures in order to build a meaningful exchange and dialogue.

For John Clayton, the problem of incommensurability is rather set up by 'an unimaginative and flat-footed theory of public reason' (2006: 78). That is, ironically, the charge of incommensurability is parasitic on the assumption that there has to be a single overarching universal meaning for public discourse to take place and it is this assumption (rather than its denial) that in fact overrules the possibility of meaningful exchange across cultures. Instead, public debate between differing positions requires only a willingness to be a 'reasonable partisan' (Clayton 2006: 78). The prerequisite for entry is not an agreed neutrality but a *contestability* (Clayton 2006: 72) – an openness to interrogation. In this way, CPR is made possible not because it is underpinned by universalist assumptions but because there is a basic willingness to debate cross-culturally. In a way, the conclusion is obvious:

the exemplary practice of CPR is not just about individual philosophers thinking in isolation and formulating grand systems, but is a *dialogical* activity or 'contest' between two or more philosophers from different religious traditions.

3. Comparative Philosophy of Religion: Types

One of the features of this field is that there appear to be many different intentions behind comparative work. Thus, at the grandest end of the spectrum, CPR may be motivated by and caught up in a *vision*. Here one outstanding example is Hegel's concept of *aufhebung* and the historical development and progress of *Geist* towards the Absolute Self-Conscious Spirit. Then there is John Hick who, contrary to some misconceptions, is not really following Hegel's lead. Hick's ambition is to be *explanatory* rather than visionary.[5] That is, he has deliberately characterized his comparative philosophical project as a second-order discourse that does not make first-order claims in the same way that the religions do. Nevertheless, he offers his pluralistic hypothesis as a religious interpretation of religion. He means to take seriously the ultimate claims that religions make and how these might be understood in light of one another. Thus, his comparative project is an attempt to construct something that offers a satisfactory meta-theory of *religious* aims and intended goals. Here the goal of CPR becomes almost wedded to religion itself – to provide some sort of account of how the contradictory ultimate hopes of the various religions can still be said to have a *real* referent and therefore constitute legitimate responses to 'reality' as it is. Although many may shy away from Hick's global project, one of the virtues of his approach is the sheer boldness of its conception. His is not a purely descriptive craft that is preoccupied with 'knowing about' the many different philosophies. Instead, he engages in a higher enquiry: Hick is *philosophizing*.

A less comprehensive agenda is what John Holder has called the *problematic* approach (see Holder 2006). Here the intention is to use comparative methods in order to shed new light on particular problems in the philosophy of religion. Holder offers an analogy of a baseball player who seeks to improve her batting technique by appropriating aspects of cricket batting techniques. (2006: 42). He asks if the critic would cry foul – protesting that each technique is an inextricable part of a particular 'game'. Here the focus is not on obtaining a comprehensive understanding of religions in general, but on particular problems. In which case, many conceptual devices and strategies are marshalled and the precise comparability of culture-bound ideas becomes a secondary concern. Admittedly, it is not entirely clear how prioritizing problems is going to overcome the need to assume a certain comparability, but this depends on what the nature of the problem is and how much conceptual or cognitive comparability is required to channel what might be discrete cultural discourses in roughly the same direction. However, if we take the problem of evil as an example, there might be a more hermeneutical or rhetorical strategy in view where ideas are appropriated by the philosopher looking for a better way of talking about the issues.

Similarly, there is what Paul Griffiths has called *constructive comparison* (see Griffiths 1997). Griffiths's own example of this is Lee Yearley's comparative look at the virtue of courage in the work of Mencius and Thomas Aquinas (see Yearley 1990). Francis Clooney's book, mentioned earlier, is also a good example of constructive comparison. He seeks to bring Hindu and Christian views to bear on the topic of God. This, he argues, leads to an 'integral theological conversation where traditions can remain distinct although their theologies are no longer separable' (Clooney 2001: 8). Moreover, the common denominator seems to be 'human reasoning'; for this, he argues, is a feature that characterizes *understanding* between peoples and forms the basis for those who seek to 'think through, probe and explain what they believe' (Clooney 2001: 8). Moreover, even if there are differences of emphasis evident in the comparative exercise, there is at least a sense of *arguability* (similar to Clayton's contestability) that underpins the encounter between the intellectual traditions of different religions (Clooney 2001: 8).

Alternatively, Clayton stresses the 'clarification of difference' as a 'legitimate end of argument' (2006: 309). Or further, CPR might be kind of *craft* – the scholarly comparison of ideas. In a recent introductory text, Gwen Griffith-Dickson suggest that 'we can only give specific, scholarly accounts of how particular cultures or traditions have interacted in particular historical periods and places' (2005: 10). Nevertheless, whatever their legitimacy as scholarly pursuits, both 'clarification' and 'craft' as comparative practices might be labelled as discourses *about* philosophy of religion rather than being philosophy of religion itself. Historical contexts should always inform the philosopher's task, but there is the worry (for the philosopher though perhaps not for the social scientist) that ideas become frozen into their cultural contexts and historical periods and assume the status of museum curiosities. In this sense, is the *comparative* emphasis actually a distraction? As we indicated earlier, although it reflects a broadening-out of the field of 'religion', the activity itself might indicate the rather uninteresting practice of compiling a wider range of data, contexts and material. At its most anodyne, the method of CPR is similar to a 'history of ideas' approach that philosophers have sometimes suspected of not being philosophy itself. That is, it is possible for the historian of ideas to approach the topic by providing detailed accounts of how certain philosophical questions concerned particular figures in their particular cultural and historical contexts, without considering the questions themselves. And so the protest by the philosopher is that if we are concerned with *living* philosophical problems then why should we be occupied with surveying intellectual cultural items and putting them on display in a 'cabinet of ideas'? Of course, understanding how problems have preoccupied people of other eras and places is often the key to helping contemporary thinkers unlock them. Similarly, as we have said, historical and comparative practices introduce new perspectives to solve familiar problems that have been approached from a single-tradition perspective. Nevertheless, comparison may become a matter of looking at, say, the problem of suffering or the question of the afterlife and considering the various perspectives and contributions of the different religious philosophies – a sort of tokenism. So, such problems become resolved into a variety of cultural oddities – numerous versions and options are supplied – but we all leave with a sense that the *problems* themselves have been bypassed. CPR is a risky enterprise – not just because it is a political problem that might unwittingly involve imperialistic chauvinism (see Nussbaum 1997) – but, from a philosophical perspective, because it risks *missing the point*.

4. Comparative Imagination

Our interests might not just be concentrated on the practice and method of CPR but also on the comparative philosopher herself. Another way of saying this is that the task of being an effective comparative philosopher of religion is both analytic and hermeneutic: if there is a virtue in the pursuit of clarity and accuracy, then there is also a call for hermeneutical courage and ambition. Moreover, it may be that the differences and incommensurables that exist between traditions require a new adventurism that goes beyond the critical comparison and analysis of problems and ideas. This is the need for imagination: the philosopher as mystic or aesthete.

Although there are notable counter-examples, CPR does not necessarily have to entail an interfaith vision which envisages comparative dialogical work as leading towards a greater sum total of harmonious truth or, even, a greater good. This does not imply an inherent recalcitrance in its discourse, rather it is a way of saying that philosophy is always moving forward in the pursuit of truth or greater understanding – *palatable or otherwise*. It is paradoxical that the thinker that is most associated with the denial of truth as a meaningful notion turns out (in later life) to be one of its staunch defenders. Thus, Nietzsche, in a striking passage, writes: 'We have arranged for ourselves a world in which we are able to live... But that does not prove them. Life is not an argument; the conditions of life might include error' (Nietzsche 2001: 121). Moreover, *'Fundamental Insight*: There is no pre-established harmony between the furthering of truth and the well-being of humanity' (Nietzsche 1995: 517). The starkness of Nietzsche's account of truth in these quotes may actually resonate very much with the subject matter of our focus: religion. Any thoroughgoing (and interesting) comparative philosophical discussion about religion cannot responsibly avoid the issue of truth. Thinking of educational virtues, Andrew Wright comments that honesty and the inclusion of questions of truth are an aid towards 'cultivating ... freedom for a proper relationship with the *order-of-things*' (Wright 2004: 223).[6]

If a 'realist' CPR has a pedagogic value then, rather than avoiding the collision of various truth-claims, it should be aiming towards strategies that foster a mature sense of encounter with claims that conflict or compete with one's own. Whilst not arguing for a realist perspective, George Pattison has suggested that the philosophy of religion, or the kind of enquiry it represents, has an important role to play in religious studies faculties as a vehicle for 'mutual interrogation and clarification' (2001: 128). This must surely involve an encounter of the *real* kind with the other. For how much mutual interrogation or clarification can there be if we are safely cocooned in our own non-real readings of the other (which is really to say that there is not any *otherness* at all)? Nevertheless, this collision of beliefs is the kind of thing that some comparative philosophers of religion have instinctively sought to avoid. Thus, an anti-realist epistemic option presents itself as a tempting solution to the problem of different religious claims and comparative difference. The idea that our beliefs are *myths* that do not correspond to the outside world means that their incompatibilities are softened and that there are virtually unlimited narratives which can be advanced. No longer constrained by the problem of what is real, anti-realist theological language enjoys, in the words of Peter Byrne, 'a renewed licence for speculation' (2003: 169). Of course, it is possible to overstate the 'licence' here because anti-realists are just as concerned to *construct* 'reality' as to engage in free hermeneutics. It would also be misleading to typify anti-realists as ones who, epistemologically speaking, are entirely libertarian.

Nevertheless, whatever the virtues or discipline of a 'proper relationship with the order-of-things' and with encountering the *real* other, there is a constructive purpose in a certain disengagement in order to review, imagine and model the differences and commonalities between the various systems and objects of belief. Here we are not simply talking about a disengagement from reality, but also a kind of intentional forgetfulness regarding the problem of cross-cultural incommensurability. That is, we deliberately choose to temporarily ignore the 'collision of differences' in order to liberate the imagination. One possibility is suggested by Clayton (2005). Citing Wilhelm Halbfass as an influence, he seeks to pursue a 'dialogic comparison by *constructing imaginary conversations* between major thinkers of the European and Indian traditions on philosophical topics' (Clayton 2005: 102; emphasis mine). Clayton's imaginary comparison is between Ramanuja and David Hume concerning their criticisms of natural theology in the *Sribhasya* and the *Dialogues concerning Natural Religion* respectively. Clearly, although the conversation between these two thinkers is an imaginary construction taking place in the mind of a single scholar, the scope and limitation of the dialogue is controlled by the topic under discussion and the problematic (natural theology) being addressed.

Nevertheless, we might take things a stage further and seek to engage in a freer form of comparative hermeneutics. Such a free hermeneutics is not an irrelevant conceptual idleness, but could be characterized as a form of play which, as during childhood, has an important role in apprehending and understanding reality. Put simply, there is a significant role for a *kind* of anti-realist strategy, not so much as a full-blown epistemic policy about the world and the other, but re-appropriated as an aesthetic type of imaginative exploration and world-making. However, coupled with this must be a clarification of the roles that both realism and anti-realism play in the construction of fruitful ideas. Thus, the possibility of a free hermeneutics – if you like, a quasi-Kantian 'purposiveness without purpose' – is dependent on there being an assent to *both* what is real and unreal. Analogously, to distinguish the *unreal* nature of the events in a play at the theatre from what is real is crucial for our enjoyment. So, in the words of Roger Scruton, the audience lives 'for a while on a plane of pure untroubled sympathy, laughing or crying without the slightest moral or physical cost' (1992: 215). Translated into our purposes, such an epistemic spaciousness has the advantage of allowing the comparative philosopher to be less concerned about the real incommensurables between traditions and more able to engage in the exploration and modelling of possibilities by experimenting with likenesses and differences that exist in the philosopher's own 'theatre'. Indeed, comparing the philosopher to an artist, Bergson asked: 'Would not the role of philosophy ... be to lead us to a completer perception of reality, by means of a certain displacement of our attention?' (1965: 138). Perhaps this connects with Ryle's acknowledgement of 'persuasions of conciliatory kinds', or Rorty's 'edifying philosophy', operating alongside more logically rigorous methods? We should not be bashful about presenting (performing?) the *form* of our comparisons: forms of similarity and likeness (or forms of contrast and difference) which help to suggest new models for the comparative task. Ostensibly, this is to propose nothing more sophisticated than the kind of use of the imagination that assists the normal everyday task of perception and understanding. However, my point is that it seems that the opportunity for hermeneutical freedom is potentially lost when cross-cultural comparison is forbidden by strict epistemological embargos (like incommensurability). It is here, ironically, that imagination is most needed.

5. Summary

In summary, I said at the beginning of this chapter that the future of the philosophy of religion is going to be comparative. This is something that I suggest has emerged from the very nature of philosophy itself as an interrogative and dialogical activity *between* thinkers, but it has recently been intensified by cross-cultural realities. If philosophy is concerned to get to the heart of the matter, then it seems inevitable that the scope of its task must include the widest possible range of information. Moreover, the future context of the philosophy of religion will be a discipline that finds itself located within an ever-expanding range of data and if it is at all *curious* then it will want to consider this data. Nevertheless, the purposes of CPR may be interpreted variously – thus, for example, it might be properly restricted to the articulation of differences between culture-specific traditions or, again, it may be characterized by the search for a common account of religion. This is not something that is necessarily the concern of *method*, but perhaps reflects certain philosophical (or other) viewpoints or 'positions' that are adopted. Nevertheless, I have argued that CPR should be something more than a scholarly craft of comparing ideas. This is because I have suggested that the practice (or motivation) of philosophy is not just a discourse that seeks descriptive accuracy and rigour but also strives for understanding and explanation. Finally, this might not just be a challenge for the practice and method of CPR, but a rethinking of the kind of philosophical disposition necessary for the task. That is, the challenge for philosophers of religion to be imaginative people who engage in hermeneutical exploration.[7]

Notes

1. Here I share an affinity with Schellenberg and Golding (see their chapters in this volume).
2. Some parts of this discussion of Graham Ward are also found in Cheetham 2006: 39–41.

3. Quinn (2005) makes similar observations.
4. A similar point is made by Victoria Harrison; see her discussion of 'vague concepts' (2006: 144–45).
5. Paul J. Griffiths also draws attention to Hegel and Hick and presents them as examples of a 'definition and classification' approach to comparative philosophy of religion. Griffiths notes that Hick is much more 'anti-hierarchical' than Hegel in his classification of religions, however he argues that both share the assumption that there is an 'objective genitive' that is the focus of the philosophy of religion (see Griffiths 1997: 617).
6. Some parts of this paragraph also appear in Cheetham 2005: 32.
7. I am grateful to Rolfe King for his comments on an earlier draft of this paper.

'Thinking Differently' in the Context of Sikh Religion

Nikky-Guninder Kaur Singh

For feminist philosophers of religion the effort to develop ways of 'thinking differently' is not a luxury: we are forced to do so if we are to survive as (female) gendered philosophers of religion. It is an 'absolute necessity' which is laid upon us if we are to find ways for the philosophy of religion to facilitate our becoming divine, rather than deadening us in its moribund ways. (Jantzen 1999: 26)

The hegemony of the phallus cannot be disrupted only by criticizing it, important though such a critique is; a transformation of the imaginary is required. (Jantzen 1999: 193)

In Dr. Sher Singh's classic *Philosophy of Sikhism* we get an informative account of the many different scholars who studied the Sikh religious tradition analytically and critically. But as it happens, the Vedantic nirmalas, the Sikh gyanis, the Singh Sabha writers, the namdharis, and the Western trained scholars are all men. The author himself admits that 'the prejudices and the inclination of a writer are cleverer than his "censor" and they enter into his writing so imperceptibly and unconsciously' (S. Singh 1944: i). Western philosophers like Nietzsche, Hegel, and Croce also warn us not to assume the 'innocent eye' of the author (See White 1978: 53). In spite of every effort, any writing will have the slant and inclination of its author. Since theologians, exegetes and translators in the Sikh context have primarily been elite males, their malestream perspectives have constructed a worldview that is fundamentally patriarchal. Their one-sided scholarship has been terribly detrimental for their society and needs to be balanced urgently by a feminist perspective. We must develop ways of 'thinking differently'.

I see three major areas in which we need to have an alternative approach.[1] The first pertains to Sikh metaphysics. The Sikh ultimate reality is the infinite One, transcending space, time, gender, and language. But whenever it is imagined or expressed, the ontological being is invariably modelled on the male gender. I want us to shift our focus to the female side. The dominant image of the 'father' in Sikhism must have a feminist counterpart: we must imagine the divine as the 'mother' too.

The second pertains to Sikh Scripture, the Guru Granth. It is the quintessence of Sikh metaphysics, ethics, and aesthetics. Revered as the Guru Eternal, the book is the centre of all Sikh ceremonies and rituals. But somehow the palpable textual reality is regarded as the 'soul' of the Gurus. It is important that we retrieve the Sikh sacred text as the 'body' of the Gurus.

Finally, we must change our thoughts on the five symbols that Sikh men and women wear. Popularly called the five *K*s (since they all begin with the letter *K*), *kesha* (long hair), *kangha* (comb), *kara* (bracelet), *kirpan* (sword), and *kacha* (long underpants) are markers of Sikh identity. For the most part however these multivalent symbols have been reduced to patriarchal signs. Sikh identity, which has been monopolized by the masculine, must be shared by the feminine. We must think about the vital female associations of the five *K*s as well.

My endeavour, though certainly different from the androcentric perspective of male scholars of Sikhism, is in tune with the male Sikh Gurus (1469–1708), who themselves were thinking quite differently in their religiously and politically insular milieu. Now my feminist friends might critique me for not applying the 'hermeneutics of suspicion' lens to the words of the Gurus (See see Doris Jakobsh's important work [2003]). But the voice of the Sikh Gurus – unsullied by male hermeneutics and translations – encourages me to develop ways of 'thinking differently' that shatter male hegemonies. The views of the Sikh Gurus are extremely relevant to us in our dangerously divided and polarized world. Rather than equip ourselves with suspicion, we need to open ourselves so that we feel their transparent and spontaneous verse. Sure enough, the Gurus were men of their times. Living in a patriarchal, mediaeval India, they may not even have been aware of all the liberating implications of their passionate poetry and egalitarian actions. But they set them in motion, and that momentum must be carried on.

My overall goal is to bring about a change in the androcentric structure of Sikh society and culture. I do not want us to think differently just for the sake of mental gymnastics. The divine, the Scripture, the symbols are essential elements of the Sikh religious tradition, and the way we think about them has a profound impact on the everyday life of the people. As feminist philosophers have been urging, by transforming our imagination, we can transform our everyday reality. Different images can stir our psyche and enable us to open ourselves to new dreams, new possibilities, new actions. Since images integrate the intellectual faculties with our aesthetic, axiological, and emotional self, I hope a different imaginary from the Sikh sacred text will vibrate in the conscience and consciousness of Sikh men and women so that their habits, customs, and attitudes will be in harmony with the voice of their Gurus.

1. Sikh Ultimate Reality as Mother

The Sikh Gurus envisioned the ultimate reality as a singular infinity with no contours, no limitations whatsoever: *Ikk Oan Kar* (One Be-ing Is) proclaimed the founder Guru Nanak (1469–1539), and his successors reaffirmed his singular infinite. At the same time, they intimately related with this One and charged their readers to experience it in countless ways – male and female, lotus and ocean, Allah and Ram. Extremely close relationships with the divine overflow in the Guru Granth:

'You are my father and you are my mother!' (GG 103)

In such breathtakingly beautiful verses, the divine is embraced as father, mother, brother, sister, friend. A sense of plenitude strips off patriarchal stratifications and blots out masculine identity as the norm for imaging the transcendent. It stretches our imagination. We feel new emotions. We see new vistas. We experience joy in so many different ways. Sadly however Sikh scholars have elaborated upon the *father* dimension and utterly neglected the empowering *mother* imaginary.

What is lost then is the serious way that female genealogy is taken up. The processes of menstruation, birth, and lactation that feminist thealogians,[2] philosophers, and psychologists of our own times find so critical are fully affirmed in the Sikh sacred book. The divine as mother directs our gaze towards our primal home – her body. With 'her' we begin to gather our thoughts on our entry into this variegated world. Affirming the equality of male and female in the creative process, Sikh Scripture reminds us that we are organically formed from *both* father and mother. The unity of *bindu* (semen) and *raktu* (blood) is the source of life: 'mother and father together form the fetus, and with blood and semen they make the body' (GG 1013); 'the union of mother and father earns us the body' (GG 989); and Kabir categorically states, 'without mother or father there can be no children' (GG 872). Feminist scholars have noted how Aristotelian doctrine attributes the father with the agency to create, and so the maternal womb is only a container of inert and cold matter to which the warm sperm gives life. Against androcentric perceptions of a temporary 'little oven in which the paternal gene was nurtured and cozily leavened' (Cavarero 1995: 74), the womb (*garbh* or *udar*) is claimed as the source of life in Sikh Scripture: 'in the first stage of life, O friend, you by the divine will, lodged in the womb' (GG 74). In the Sikh metaphysical scheme, both parents are equally important in the gift of life, and the whole person is created by and in the womb.

The sacred verses resonate with many positive memories of our lodging in the mother's creative organ: 'in the mother's womb are we taken care of' (GG 1086). This maternal space is honoured as a social utopia in which the foetus is free from patriarchal designations of class, caste, and name: 'in the dwelling of the womb, there is neither name nor caste' (GG 324). The embryo in the womb is the scriptural paradigm for one rapt in meditation and contemplation; its upside-down posture graphically represents spiritual love since 'each breath is that of the true name' (GG 1026). Womb is the locus where mind and body together grow and feed on the elements partaken by the mother. It is in *her* body, with *her* body, that we begin our immediate connections with the cosmos and come into the world.

As the maternal continuum, the mother retrieves the primacy of birth over death. *She* offers new openings to feminist perspectives that are underscored by scholars in their own and different ways. *Her* body connects each one of us with the two sequences of infinity: the past and future of every being, male or female. In her provocative book, *In Spite of Plato*, Adriana Cavarero notes: 'Both infinities, past and future, origin and perpetuation, always exist through the feminine' (1995: 60). At the outset of her study on Freud, Madelon Sprengnether makes the observation: 'Whatever our other differences, as human beings we have one thing in common: we are all born of woman'. Sprengnether (1990: 1) finds a vivid testimonial to the power of the mother's mother's body in Freud's observation that, 'after a protracted labor, it [the baby's skull] takes the form of a cast of the narrow part of the mother's pelvis' (Freud 1974: vol. 1, 169). Sikh Scripture illuminates the views of contemporary feminist scholars that we are rooted in female genealogy, and returns meaning to the basic fact that we are all born of woman. Rather than an abstraction, the foetus is firmly lodged and reveals to us a palpable portion of infinity in which each of us from every species becomes embodied and exists authentically.

The powerful image of natality pulls us into the realm of the present-day world. The horizon of the physical, so severely severed by the patriarchal metaphysical order in which death functions as the fundamental paradigm, is protected by the mother's sexual and maternal powers. Feminist scholars criticize metaphysics as a form of matricide, and, in Luce Irigaray's words its soil has become culture, history, which successfully forgets that anything that conceives has its origins in the flesh' (1993: 109). For Cavarero, 'man, with a masculine – universal – natural valence, is a term from a language that has turned its gaze away from the place of birth, measuring existence on an end point that bears no memory of its beginning' (1995: 69). Grace Jantzen argues that the obsession with death is connected to an 'obsession with female bodies, and the denial of death and efforts to master it are connected with a deep-seated misogyny' (1999: 132). For Jantzen, the various forms of dominance – racism, capitalism, colonialism, homophobia, ecological destruction – are manifestations of the need to conquer death. In contrast with the necrophilic imagery of the male symbolic, the pervasive womb imagery in Sikh Scripture affirms life and living in diverse forms. The maternal power with her paradigm of natality overturns the male death-ideal as its fundamental paradigm. Indeed, 'the womb of the mother earth yokes us together' (GG 1021). Birth becomes the absolute possibility of orienting ourselves in the physical world so that we experience fully the Absolute within the natural and social fibres of our being.

Our mother imaginary not only affirms the cosmic processes of conception, gestation, and birth, but also gives us an appreciation for lactation. Mother's milk is deemed very nutritious for it satisfies all hungers, and, for me, Sikh scriptural poetry overflows with mother's milk. I can hear the language of the Gurus joining in with the words of contemporary French feminist scholar Hélène Cixous (1986:93), 'Voice: milk that could go on forever. Found again. The lost mother/bitter-lost. Eternity: is voice mixed with milk' (Cixous and Clément 1986: 93). The Guru Granth reminds us that every individual is formed from the physical and psychological sustenance provided by the mother. Her milk is inexhaustible. Not only does she feed her foetus with her nutrients, she also suckles the new-born with her life-giving milk. 'The child's original attraction is to the mother's breast-milk' (GG 972), acknowledges the founder Sikh Guru. The fifth recalls the experience of 'her milk poured into the baby's mouth' (GG : 987), and claims that satisfaction and fulfilment come from the mother pouring milk into her child's mouth (GG 1266). The Gurus compare the intensity of saintly devotion to that of an infant's love for the mother's milk (GG 613). In an unforgettable juxtaposition of analogies, the divine is likened to a 'cane for the blind' and 'like mother's milk for the child' (GG 679). In another tender passage: 'says Nanak, the child, you are my father and my mother, and your name is like milk in my mouth' (GG 713). Throughout the Guru Granth, the Guru–poets unabashedly express their attachment to the divine through an infant's attachment to the mother's breast: 'my mind loves the divine, O my life, like a child loves suckling milk' (GG 538). In a plurality of sounds and rhythms, in a collage of artistic images, Scripture replays the first Guru's effervescent mnemonic, 'that One is the calf, She is the cow, and She is the milk' (GG 1190). The sacred text is intrinsically written in 'white ink', and we must absorb the maternal element in order to derive total nutrition and full benefit.

Clearly we establish our authenticity not in opposition to, but pulling toward the mother. Our return to our mothers would not constitute acts of regression, as our phallocentric psychoanalysts may speculate, but a real progression toward new forms of subjectivity and new avenues for discovering our human potential. Sikh Scripture resonates with the views of feminist thealogians and object-relations psychoanalysts, who posit the maternal-infant relationship at the heart of a person's psychological and social development. Instead of the Freudian oedipal conflict, castration complex, and individuality, feminist thealogians, like Naomi Goldenberg, and object-relations psychoanalysts, like Melanie Klein and D.W. Winnicott, shift the focus to the maternal–infant relationship. Both thealogy and object-relations theory 'derive their insights into the matrices that support human life from an image of a woman-in-the-past' (Goldenberg 1995: 155). The voice of the Gurus displaces the father from his dominating symbolic and cherishes the body of the mother, the love of the mother, the care of the mother, the caresses of the mother, the transverbal communion with the mother. The male Gurus remember her prebirth and postbirth creativity, and our re-memories in turn can help us improve the individual and social fabric of our lives. 'Just as the mother takes care of her children, so the One sustains us' (GG 680). The abundant joy of envisioning the ultimate is 'like the look between a child and its mother' (GG 452). Attaining divine bliss is like 'the heart blossoming when it beholds the mother' (GG 164). When we feel the divine arms around us – 'like a mother tightly hugs her child' (GG 629) – we cannot but recharge the innermost batteries of our own selves, and renew our relationships with our families, friends, and community.

2. Sikh Scripture as the Body of the Gurus

Intersecting space and time, Sikh scriptural text is the very *body* of the Gurus. For me, a Sikh woman scholar, the identity between the Granth and the Gurus is a radically feminist affirmation of the unity of mind and body, sacred and material, form and formless. As such, the body of the Gurus visibly, aurally, sensuously, boldly subverts patriarchal assumptions.

The Guru Granth has 1430 pages. Its skeins, tissues, and membranes are made up of the poetic utterances of the Sikh Gurus, Hindu bhaktas, and Muslim sufis. It germinated in the literary matrix of the founder Sikh Guru Nanak, and over the course of history grew into the body that has become the nucleus of Sikh belief and conduct. In 1604 Guru Arjan (Nanak V) compiled the Granth. In 1708, Guru Gobind Singh (Nanak X) invested it with Guruship. So crucial was the corporeality of the sacred word for Guru Gobind Singh that just a day before he died, he made the Granth the Guru forever. Amidst political and religious turmoil, amidst wars and battles, the physical presence of the Granth sustained, nurtured, and centered the Gurus and their devotees.

In public worship and privately at home, Sikhs revere their Guru ardently: they perform *prakash* (opening the Guru Granth in the morning) and *sukhasan* (putting it in bed at night), and verbally communicate with the Ultimate through *vak* (reading of the passage on the top left page as the Granth is opened at random). The holy text is carried on the head, it is fanned with a whisk, and men and women with their heads covered and barefooted bow in front of it. Daily the book is dressed in beautiful brocades and silks. Sikhs seek its presence for all their rites and ceremonies. They marry by circumambulating the Guru Granth four times. In naming children, parents pick a name beginning with the first letter from the page that the Guru Granth fortuitously opens at. Sikhs conduct all their rites as though the book were the body par excellence of the Gurus, which indeed is a very unique and innovative phenomenon. The Hebrew Bible, the Vedas, the New Testament, the Quran, are absolutely significant in their respective traditions. But in no case do they embody the Jewish prophets, or the rishis, or the evangelists, or the Prophet Muhammad. In the Sikh instance the Granth is literally the Guru. During all their liturgical prayers Sikhs commemorate the identity between the Guru Granth and the manifest body (*deh*) of the Gurus as the congregation recites in unison:

Guru granth ji manio pragat guran ki deh
ja ka hirda sudh hai khoj sabad mahi leh

Know Guru Granthji as the manifest body of the Gurus;
Those whose hearts are pure find it in the word.

It is from this body that generations of Sikhs are begotten, aesthetically honed, and psychologically, socially, and spiritually sustained.

Ironically, at some ineffable level, Sikhs deny the physicality of the Guru Granth. They view the 'body' pejoratively, and refuse to see the Granth as the body of their Gurus. There is thus a terrible incongruity between what we hear Sikhs recite and how they actually put those words into practice. The centuries-old taboos against the body in their patriarchal milieu inhibit them from recognizing the new and liberating vision of their Gurus, with the result that the body–spirit dualism and its drastic corollaries dominates Sikh society. It is out of 'respect' then, that Sikhs do not wish to associate their holy book with any notion of the body. In my own experience, whenever I happen to mention the corporeal aspect of the sacred text, I meet with a lot of hostility from male Sikhs. I am told loudly and clearly that the Guru Granth is the 'soul' of the Gurus, which must not be confused with their 'body'. It surprises me that even in the academy the issue of the 'body' is not broached. There are some excellent works coming out on Sikh Scripture that fill in a lot of gaps on the formation and canonization of the text, but the unique Sikh phenomenon of the book as the *body* of the Ten Gurus does not 'matter' much to our scholars.

It is important that we address this critical phenomenon. We must not fear, deny, or ignore it. Indeed, as the Sikh Gurus intended, this powerful example of body–spirit unity should inspire us to think about our selves and the world around us in new and wholesome ways.

The tenth Guru did not pass on the Guruship to any of his male disciples; he passed it to the Granth. There were to be no battles of ego against ego to climb patriarchal ladders. After his death, Sikhs looked up to Mata Sundari (his second wife) for guidance, and she emphatically stressed the physicality of the Guru Granth. (For more details on the life of Mata Sundari, see: Singh, H. 1992: 277.) When schismatic groups tried to claim succession to the Guruship with the aim of setting up their own leaders, Mata Sundari boldly rejected any such move. In a strong voice she issued the following pronouncement:

> Khalsaji, you must have faith in none other except the Timeless One. Go only to the Ten Gurus in search of the word. 'Nanak is their slave who obtain their goal by searching the Word.' 'The Guru is lodged in the Word. That One Itself merged with the Guru who revealed the Word.' The Word is the life of all life: through it we meet with the ultimate One.[3]

Clearly, the attributes and properties of the physical Guru are embodied in the word; the 'Guru is lodged in the word – *Guru ka nivas sabad vich hai*'. So the word is not a formless 'logos' but 'the life of all life – *jian andar ji sabad hai*'. At a politically and socially unstable time for Sikhs, Mata Sundari draws their attention towards life and living. She reaffirms the book as a concrete reality of the Timeless One (*akal*). Containing the divine–human encounter of their Ten Gurus, Sikhs henceforth were to derive their guidance and inspiration from the Guru Granth. There would be no other Guru. The reality of the ten was embodied in their verse. However, Mata Sundari exhorts that the 'word' has to be actively searched (*khoj*). Sikhs cannot passively accept the Guru = Granth identity. Each person has to dynamically see, hear, touch, feel, imagine their way through the sacred verses of their Gurus to gain their access to and intimacy with the timeless One.

So each of the devotees, male and female, has to relate with this body personally. The body of the Gurus allows no room for any mediums or mediations. Priestly authority has no place in the direct encounter. Scholars or commentators, rituals, philosophical doctrines, or any sort of societal or gender hierarchies must not come in between the Sikhs and their sacred poetry. Bestowing Guruship on the textual body, Guru Gobind Singh clearly mandated that every Sikh have a meaningful dialogue with the Granth. Nobody is barred from engaging with the Guru Granth. Men and women, married or unmarried, all are welcome to hear, recite, touch, and see their Guru – all the time. No period is profane. The Guru Granth does not carry any phallic rules or regulations. The sacred verse does not set up a strict deontology or draw up a list of rituals. It is not prescriptive; nor is it proscriptive. The Gurus do not try to convince the non-believer that the One exists or argue for proofs that may be ontological, epistemological, moral or teleological. Their words are divinely inspired – and as they express a longing for the matrix from which all of us came, they recharge us to rediscover that source for ourselves.

This body of the Gurus becomes a mirror for each of us. It reflects that our senses and organs are sacred. That our bodies are the home of the infinite One. That our flesh is the source for attaining religious wisdom. How can we suppress and reject or hate that which houses the divine? 'Whatever lies in paradise beyond can be found in the body here – *jo brahmande soi pinde*', proclaims the Guru Granth, loud and clear (GG 695). The body is our marvellous possession. Its structure is spiritual: 'Body is the home of the divine One and by the divine One is the body maintained' (GG 1059). How can we denigrate our physical selves when 'all hope and wisdom are this body, illuminated by the divine light'? In the tissues of the Granth, we find many different terms used for the body – *tanu, deh, kaia, pind*, but in each case it is made up of the transcendent; after all 'in every pore dwells the divine – *rom rom mahi basehi murar*'! (GG 344). The integration of the physical and spiritual self is openly expressed in Sikh sacred literature.

The corporeality of the book most definitely resists, however, any theory of incarnation because that would only be another way of rejecting its distinctive physiognomy. As a physical body, the Guru Granth attests to the fact that the Gurus are not incarnations who descended down from a supreme being above. Guru Gobind Singh, who conferred Guruship on the Granth, was the one who loudly denounced such a view: 'If anyone calls me the supreme being / They shall fall into the pit of hell'.[4] In contrast with the theory of *avatarvad*, the body of the Gurus attests to the wonderful phenomenon of birth: each of them is birthed by their particular mothers. The flesh and blood of the Gurus was conceived in the mother's body, fed on her placenta, issued forth from between her legs, and was cut at the umbilical cord. The Sikh Gurus were born of mothers, and foremothers, and it is their real selves that we encounter in the Guru Granth. When we think of the sacred text as the body of the Gurus, Mata Tripta, Mata Khivi, Bibi Bhani, Mata Ganga, Mata Nanaki, Mata Gujari, and the other mothers of Sikhism flash before our eyes, and our lips utter the Granthian exaltation '*dhan janedi mata* – blessed are the mothers!' Our respect goes to all the mothers from all the species, and so the Guru Granth fills us with pride in our own bodies, and charges us all, men and women, to savour the transcendent One – experienced by the Gurus in their own bodies – here and now.

Actually, is it not idolatrous to think of the book as the 'soul' of the Gurus? In that case, bedecking and bowing to and reading from the Guru Granth become formal ritual and empty worship. Without the body, the message of the Gurus is ossified; we hold and touch something immaterial that we have never known or touched, we see and recite but letters on a page. Memorized perfectly, read out perfectly, the disembodied words can have no possible meaning for our human selves. They serve merely as the type of incantations the Gurus vigorously denounced. By removing its physicality, we reduce the Guru Granth to an icon, an image, a recitation of mere letters; but by relating to it as the body of the Gurus, our discourse and engagement acquire meaning and vibrancy.

So when we encounter this body intimately with our heightened senses, we get in touch with the transcendent One and open ourselves to a world of difference and diversity. The scriptural body is made up of Sikh Gurus, Hindu Bhaktas, and Muslim sufis from different religious, ethnic and geographical backgrounds, but only when we *see* the same crimson colour flowing in all its veins and arteries, do we become aware of our essential humanity. We read and recite the names of the divine written out in Arabic or Sanskrit, but only when we *hear* the body of the Gurus pulsating with universal passion do we recognize our common religious, cultural, and linguistic origins. Not by numbing but by honing our senses do we get to *enjoy* the enchanting beauty of the Gurus' body. After all, the founder Guru said, 'only the person who can smell a rose can appreciate its fragrance'.

We proudly announce the social equality promoted by the Gurus but only when we actually treat our daughters like sons do we *touch* their body. The Gurus' body flushed out ancient notions of female pollution attached to the natural processes of menstruation and childbirth – but Sikh culture has not gotten rid of them in daily practice. By denigrating our girls and women, and aborting female foetuses, we are only hurting the Guru's body. When we *taste* the transcendent substance connecting the cells and molecules in the body of the Granth, we nurture our own bodies – male and female alike. We may sumptuously dress and garland the Guru Granth and pay utmost respect by bowing and sitting on the floor in front of it, but it is when we respect people of all sexes, castes, complexions and religions that we truly respect our Gurus.

By activating our sensory faculties we intimately partake in the Gurus' presence during moments of personal or corporate piety. And so in their words we meet with them in person – *khoj sabad mahi leh* – just as we recite in the liturgical couplet. We solicit their advice, share with them our angst and joy. The Guru Granth is not the abstract words. It is the living Guru. From the Gurus' body Sikhs are born and on the Gurus' breast they are fed.

3. Sikh Symbols as Female Modality

Sikhs firmly believe that during the spring festival of Baisakhi in 1699, Guru Gobind Singh introduced a new physical identity for his community, and no matter what part of the globe they may migrate to, Sikh men and women proudly continue to maintain their five *K*s. However, from the traditional codifiers of the ethical manuals to contemporary theoreticians, the five *K*s have been claimed and studied and perpetuated solely in male terms. And so the long hair curled with all of Samson's might is an inversion of Hindu *mundan* (the shaving of heads for boys); the comb is its polar device, for it controls the long hair and signifies social interaction (unlike the unruly hair of ascetics); the sword symbolizes heroic power; the bracelet is some form of weapon of control and self-defence; and the undergarment is an abandonment of the Brahmin's *dhoti* (worn by Hindu priests), or an antithesis to Muslim circumcision, or a useful device for 'male protection'. As I have discussed in depth in my recent work (N. K. Singh 2005: ch. 4), such macho interpretations uphold macho moods and motivations. Instead of symbols of self-respect and mutuality, as Guru Gobind Singh intended them to be, the five *K*s operate as tools of male domination, with women excluded as the 'other'.

The range and subtlety of the male interpretations are bewildering. My own intellectual training and cultural codes had trained me so well in the male and militant puissance of the five *K*s, that I could not even imagine that long hair, combs, bracelets, underwear, or swords could be viewed from a female perspective. The thought of their being female never crossed my mind! But what sounds so radical is in fact the most natural. Indeed, what could be more commonsensical than the idea that long hair, comb, bracelet, underwear, and even the grammatically feminine *kirpan* (sword), have a female identity? If symbols that are intrinsically paradoxical and multivalent can be masculine, why can't they not be feminine as well? By unfolding their message we 'live' our symbols, which, according to Eliade (1965: 208), 'implies an opening towards the Spirit and finally access to the universal' (1965: 208).

For me now the five *K*s belong to an interlaced pattern, which is reproduced entirely from Sikh Scripture. All five are drawn from Guru Gobind Singh's own memory of his sacred text, and are fashioned on the articles idealized by his predecessors. They are all about a passionate experience of the divine in our daily life. Each of them endorses the scriptural expression of spirituality through women's activities and embellishments. Female accessories from his metaphysical text are appropriated by the male Guru and are made three-dimensional requisites for his followers, both men and women.

Over and over, the Guru Granth evokes the figure of the bride and her dressing-up as the mode, which makes the divine accessible to the human experience. Woman is 'privileged' in Sikh Scripture because she is the one who is psychologically and spiritually honed. Her various bodily adornments are imbued with profound significance. Her hair is neatly braided (GG 558), and *her* braids are held together by embroidered tassels (GG 937). The long hair of women is an expression of the sanctification of the human personality in the Sikh holy writ. Clearly, it is *her* braids and not *his* top-knots that are so highly valued in the Guru Granth. She is ever the *suhagan*, the 'fortunate wife' who is never abandoned. Her hair is not shorn, for that was a cultural mark of the 'unfortunate widows' (*duhagan*).

Similarly, the comb has special religious significance. The Sikh Scripture assigns regularly a transcendent value to female activities and accoutrements. Throughout the text, female toiletry is highly valued: women's necklaces, ribbons, jewels, clothes, cosmetics, perfume are all imbued with metaphysical significance. The woman is extolled for the mental tenacity with which she uses her items. We can see the comb in her hands as 'the woman with patience gets her braid knotted – *dhiraj dhari bandhavai kaman*'

(GG 359). The poetically charged alliteration of '*Ds*' evokes a rhythmic application of the comb, its teeth turning and returning, smoothing and arranging her hair. Another verse from the Guru Granth further qualifies: 'It is with Truth that the woman braids her hair' (GG 54). The quintessential philosophical ideals of Sikhism are reproduced in this daily female activity. The truth with which she braids her hair is not an abstract mathematical conception; it is not a 'reified noun', 'out there' as Mary Daly would say. Truth is a dynamic activity. It is a subjective and existential engagement with the ultimate reality that pours out organically into our self-understanding, and our relationship with our families and society. Profoundly captured, truth is the woman's hands holding her long hair, and, with the help of her comb, weaving the different strands together. The harmony and wholeness of immutable truth is recreated daily by her combing and braiding.

The *kangha* is not an antithesis to the *kesha*; there is a synchronicity, a close relationship between them. Both together release, redesign, retrieve infinite human potential. The comb is the instrument for attending to oneself, and so combing the hair becomes a self-reflective process, which leads to a life of beauty, imagination, and truth for both men and women.

The steel/iron *kara* also evokes the female ornaments and mode of dressing up treasured in the Guru Granth. Sensuous poetry and sublime philosophy delineate the Granthian precedent for the khalsa's bracelet: 'by wearing the bracelet created by the Creator, consciousness is held steadily' (GG 359). Since the texture of her bracelet is literally the divine creatrix, by wearing it on our bodies, the chasm between the material and the divine is suspended. The bracelet around our wrist lays our consciousness still and bare – ready for a passionate experience with the transcendent One. All narrow, discriminating, self-centered, self-serving actions, and all heavy-handed masculinist operations are discarded by the hand that wears this bracelet. The *kara* formulated by Guru Gobind Singh for his Sikhs is modelled on this Granthian bracelet.

The prototype for the sword is distinctly found in the Guru Granth as well, and it is made up of literally 'divine wisdom' (GG 235, GG 938, GG 1072). Unlike a phallic weapon, the sword is conceived as an essential instrument for the development of human consciousness. Importantly, the paradigmatic person utilizing the sword is a woman: 'by taking up the sword of knowledge, she fights against her mind and merges with herself' (GG 1022). It is the strong and intelligent woman who leads us to the authentic self that lies beneath all our superficial differences and conflicts. Unlike our media images in which the 'overt glorification of the female body' are only 'covert operations' that depreciate this body, making women feel deficient and ashamed (Bartky 2002: 248), our scriptural paradigm is perfectly aligned within and without.

And like the rest of the *K*s, the *kacha* fits in with typical female norms and patterns, which enables us to gather our humanity rather than divide male from female, Sikh from Hindu or Muslim. It is modelled on the meta-physical garments worn by the female figure in the Guru Granth. Not those 'who take off their clothes and go naked like Digambaras' (GG 1169), but she who 'wears the clothes of Love' (GG 54) is prized in the Sikh sacred text. As a covering for the genitals, *kacha* becomes a signifier of self-affirmation. Sewn by the virtues of modesty and sexual restraint, it is the symbol for cultivating morality at a fundamental level. Like his predecessors, the tenth Guru urged people to observe sexual morality within the context of normal family life instead of pursuing celibacy. Home, family, marriage, and children, are a part of the natural life cycle and should be fully respected.

In fact this marker of Sikh identity is a unique phenomenon in the history of religion. With our habit of studying our subject in the heavens, it might give some scholars a pain in the neck to study something so close. But the *kacha* draws our attention to our fundamental human identity in a most meaningful way. It really discloses an unusual foresight and wisdom on the part of Guru Gobind Singh, for the more I think about it, the more radical implications this '*K*' seems to carry for living our lives as men and women today. Whereas the other symbols attend to the construction of the individual and that of the communal identity, this '*K*' forces us to think about personal relationships between partners, be it man and woman, man and man, or woman and woman. Thus it even establishes an *'ethics of the couple'* desired by modern feminists. The place that Irigaray searches for between the morality of an individual (locked up in the family) and the morality of a whole people (*sittlichkeit*), a place 'where the two halves of the natural and spiritual world can be and change' is precisely the space of the Guru's symbol (1993: 132).

The five *K*s flow out and represent the metaphysical values enshrined in the Guru Granth. Each of the five symbols is clearly a 'coincidence of sensible appearance and suprasensible meaning', and this coincidence, Gadamer says, is the original significance of the Greek *symbolon*, 'the union of two things that belong together' (1989: 78). Because it fosters a strong sense of identity both at the individual and communal levels, wearing the five *K*s conforms to Foucault's 'true social practice' (1988: 51). The art of existence is refined through them. As they enable each Sikh – male or female – to cultivate their physical and psychological self, the five *K*s intensify a communal identity amongst them. In this true social practice Guru Gobind Singh made the 'past' of his Sikhs 'present again' in a radically new and palpable way.

The 'coincidence' between the five *K*s and their scriptural prototypes is particularly important for women. The five *K*s are foreshadowed throughout the Guru Granth in the hands and on the body of a female, the quintessence of womanhood. By recognizing the ontological equivalence between the items of the paradigmatic woman and the five *K*s worn on their own bodies, Sikh women can reconstruct their lost identity. That they are not patriarchal symbols construed just for the bodies of men, but human archetypes revealed in their holy book by a woman, is most validating and self-affirming. Women can ontologically share in the being of *her* physically and spiritually refined body, they can physically and psychologically receive the direct flow of *her* energy from *her* symbols to the five they wear on their own bodies. Thus they can wear the five items as *naturally theirs* – not as inversions or divisions from men of other faith, nor as hand-me-downs from fathers, brothers, and uncles. The five *K*s are *hers* as much as they are *his*. Guru Gobind Singh dispelled all conventional taboos against female pollution, menstruation, and sexuality by giving the five *K*s to both men and women – without any exceptions whatsoever against widows or menstruating women, against women who are pregnant or in childbirth, against single or married women. We need to think again and again that these are symbols of sexual equality, and continually struggle to overturn their construction as symbols of phallogocentric subjectivity and spirituality.

4. Conclusion

I must say, our thinking differently about these three vital phenomena is an exciting and liberating process. Imagining the divine as mother, relating to the sacred text as the *body* of the Gurus during all rites and ceremonies, and wearing physical adornments cherished in Sikh metaphysics should prove to be empowering for both men and women. Our thinking is not meant to denigrate men. Thinking through the female dimension only helps us include *her* resources and add to our fundamental humanity. Thus we escape the imprisonment of a gender polarization, which has left all of us insecure, suppressed, homogenized, and painfully split. By 'thinking differently' we join Sikh metaphysics with Sikh practice, just as we join together all the aspects of our lives – personal, psychological, institutional, and moral. But because of the androcentric worldview that we have absorbed for so many centuries, we really have to work hard at thinking differently right now and make it our daily practice. I hope very soon we will not even have to worry about thinking differently – we will all be thinking together about us.

Notes

1. I have been thinking about these three areas for quite some time. For a detailed discussion regarding number 1, see N. K. Singh 1993: ch. 2. For number 2, see N. K. Singh 2004. For number 3, see N. K. Singh 2005: ch. 4.
2. *Thea* means 'goddess', so *thealogian* (spelled with an 'a') is the preferred term for feminist scholars in religious studies.
3. Quoted in the original by Harbans Singh (1983: 108–09). According to Harbans Singh, this letter sent by Mata Sundari is in the possession of Bhai Chet Singh, of the village of Bhai Rupa. It was addressed to his ancestors (H. Singh 1983: 108). See also Deol 2001: 28.
4. In Guru Gobind Singh's autobiographical '*Bacitra Natak*' (1973: 6.32–33).

Philosophy of Religion Takes Practice: Liturgy as Source and Method in Philosophy of Religion

James K. A. Smith

Introduction: Limits of the 'Renaissance' in Philosophy of Religion

There has been much discussion of the 'renaissance' in the philosophy of religion in the last several decades of the twentieth century. After the last gasp of positivism and the final attempt to police philosophical discourse through ordinary-language philosophy, there emerged the space for a renewed consideration of religion within the halls of philosophy in two senses: on the one hand, religious themes and questions once again became legitimate topics for philosophical reflection; on the other hand, and perhaps more radically, a critique of the supposed neutrality and objectivity of philosophical reason opened the space for *religious* philosophy – that is, philosophical reflection undertaken from a perspective and orientation that was unapologetically religious and confessional. The 'of' in this renewal in philosophy *of* religion was both an objective and subjective genitive: religion was re-introduced as a legitimate mainstream topic of consideration (objective genitive), and religion was admitted as a legitimate orienting perspective for philosophical research and reflection (subjective genitive).

Work along the former lines included renewed interested in religious phenomena such as miracles, the perennial problem of evil, as well as the conditions of possibility of religious language or 'God-talk'.[1] This developed into a more robust renewal of 'philosophical theology' now exemplified in the work of Eleonore Stump, Marilyn Adams, Stephen Davis, Brian Hebblethwaite, Brian Leftow, and many others.[2]

Developments along the latter lines of a *religious* philosophy were closely connected with the development of 'Reformed epistemology' as articulated by Nicholas Wolterstorff and Alvin Plantinga – a distinctly non-foundationalist epistemological project that sought to contest the criteria of 'rationality' that had been marshalled to exclude religious belief from both the halls of philosophy and the sphere of public discourse.[3] Articulating a critique of the supposed neutrality and autonomy of reason, Wolterstorff and Plantinga argued that religious belief was *just as* 'warranted' as other presuppositions in philosophy that, in fact, shared the same epistemic status.[4] Thus Reformed epistemology undercut the foundationalist rationalism of philosophy and thereby opened a path of legitimacy for philosophical reflection oriented and informed by religious presuppositions.[5] This critique of foundationalism and neutrality resonated with other developments in philosophy, including Alasdair MacIntyre's account (1988) of the 'traditioned' nature of rationality, as well as the tradition of 'hermeneutic' philosophy associated with Heidegger and Gadamer which also emphasized the constitutive role of presuppositions in shaping rationality – anticipating the shape of a 'postmodern' critique of foundationalist reason.[6] This other, 'Continental' critique of secular reason could be seen as culminating in the work of John Milbank (1990).[7] While these different schools of thought are not often associated (indeed, Reformed epistemology remains virulently allergic to 'postmodernism'), I would suggest that, in fact, these tensions represent a kind of sibling rivalry.[8]

These developments represent a flourishing renaissance in philosophy of religion, and the work of this generation has made it possible for us to further imagine what the future of philosophy of religion might look like. In this chapter, I want to offer an appreciative critique of these developments in philosophy of religion. Recognizing my own indebtedness to this earlier work, I nonetheless want to suggest a significant lacuna or blind spot, viz. the absence of any rigorous attention to worship, liturgy, or the *practices* of religious communities. In sum, one could argue that philosophy of religion has been attentive to *beliefs* but not *believers*. It has been characterized by a kind of epistemological fixation that myopically focuses on either the epistemic status of religious belief, or an explication of the propositional content of specific beliefs (e.g., the goodness of God, God's eternity, or resurrection). But philosophy of religion has spent very little time being attentive to how embodied, flesh-and-blood believers experience religion primarily as a form of life. A formative and usually central aspect of that form of life – across religious traditions – is participation in corporate worship, liturgical practices, and other forms of shared spiritual disciplines. In other words, believers tend to focus on faith as a way of life ('what we *do*') whereas contemporary philosophy of religion tends to treat faith as a way of thinking ('what we *believe*').

In this chapter I will sketch a way forward for philosophy of religion that seeks to overcome this blind spot and direct the attention of philosophy of religion to *practice*, and liturgical practice in particular. The chapter will hover somewhere between a report on the current state of affairs and a manifesto which envisions a different future for philosophy of religion. As such, it will be necessarily programmatic; my goal is to sketch an agenda for new research trajectories in philosophy of religion which, I hope, will be taken up by others. But since this work remains to be done, my account will be given from this side of the Jordan, as it were – looking ahead to possibilities across the river that need to be explored.

More specifically, I want to consider liturgy[9] as both a 'source' and 'method' in philosophy of religion. This roughly correlates with the two trajectories of philosophy of religion I have sketched above in terms of two modes of the genitive 'of': on the one hand, worship and liturgical practice needs to be made a more central object of philosophical consideration; on the other hand, in league with the critique of secularity sketched above, liturgical participation might be understood as a unique condition of possibility for philosophical reflection.

1. Cartesian Ghosts: The Lingering Rationalism in Philosophy of Religion

Levinas (1969: 134) famously remarked that *Dasein* is never hungry. And yet, does *Dasein* ever eat? In the same vein we might ask: Does *Dasein* ever worship? Or more pointedly, do the believers countenanced in contemporary philosophy of religion ever kneel or sing?[10] Do they ever pray the rosary? Do they ever respond to an altar call, weeping on their knees? In fact, do *believers* ever really make an appearance in philosophy of religion? Is it not most often taken up instead with *beliefs*? Judging from the shape of the conversation in contemporary philosophy of religion, one would guess that 'religion' is a feature of brains-in-a-vat, lingering in a particularly spiritual ether but never really bumping into the grittiness of practices and community. Indeed, one wonders whether such 'believers' really even need to go through the hassle of getting up on Sunday morning. Once the beliefs are 'deposited', it is hard to see what more is needed to be faithful.[11]

The renaissance in philosophy of religion in the past 30 years has been beholden, I would contend, to a lingering rationalism which remains at least haunted (if not perhaps *governed*) by a Cartesian anthropology that tends to construe the human person as, in essence, a 'thinking thing'. Because it assumes a philosophical anthropology that privileges the cognitive and rational, philosophy of religion thus construes religion as a primarily epistemological phenomenon. As a result, the 'religion' in philosophy *of religion* is a very cognitive, 'heady' phenomenon – reduced to beliefs, propositions and cognitive content, which are the only phenomena that can make it through the narrow theoretical gate that attends such rationalism. Believers, insofar as they appear, seem to be little more than talking heads. The result is a reductionism: religion, which is primarily a 'form of life' and lived experience, is slimmed down to the more abstract phenomena of beliefs and doctrines. The rich, dynamic, lived experience of worshipping communities is reduced to propositions that can be culled from artefacts produced by these communities (e.g., documents, creeds, Scriptures). If philosophy of religion pays any attention to liturgy or other religious practices, it is usually only in order to mine the 'artefacts' of liturgy for new 'ideas'.

Thus philosophy of religion as currently practised tends to reflect a working (or at least functional) assumption that doctrine is prior to liturgy, and thus ideas and propositions trump practices. Practised in this rationalist mode, philosophy of religion finds a ready-made proportionality to theological doctrines, ideas, and propositions. Hence what has flourished in philosophy of religion has been philosophical theology of a particular sort.[12] At best, this amounts to a reduction of 'religion' to propositional thinking, a narrowing of the richness of religious lived experience. At worst, the result is not just a 'thinning' of religion, but a falsification of it, insofar as religion construed as primarily a cognitive or propositional or epistemological phenomenon fails to discern the heart of religion as practice. What one works on is often a reflection of one's tools. If all I have is a hammer and nails, I am not equipped to work on an electric circuit. In that vein, contemporary philosophy of religion is equipped with a tool-belt made for thinking about thinking – analysing concepts of a certain sort. As a result, the philosopher of religion is only equipped to 'work on' religion insofar as it can be made (and thus cut down) to the measure of conceptual, cognitive thinking.[13] Attention to aspects of religion as a form of life and set of practices would require a different, or at least expanded, tool-belt.[14]

A new renaissance in philosophy of religion could be sparked by reversing this assumption and taking seriously the priority of liturgical practices to doctrinal formulations. Otherwise, we would be in a situation akin to theatre studies which is absorbed with texts and forgets that these are scripts for performance.[15] It should also point us to the priority of liturgy and practice vis-à-vis the artefacts of religious traditions (e.g., the priority of the kenotic hymn in Phil. 2.5–11, etc.). Before the creeds were 'creeds', and thus documents to be mined, they were *prayers* enacted by a community in the context of confession in worship.[16]

If we are going to reverse the assumption, and recover the priority of liturgy to doctrine – that is, recover a sense of religion as a form of life and embodied experience – this will require challenging the rationalist philosophical anthropology that underlies contemporary philosophy of religion. And in fact, religion itself does this: religious faith – and the ways of life associated with religious communities – resist rationalist reduction and exhibit a way of being-in-the-world that manifests the fundamentally affective nature of the human person. In sum, it is precisely the phenomenon of religious life that points up the paucity and thinness of the Cartesian 'thinking thing' as a very *un*-natural beast. It is not that a cognitivist philosophical anthropology is just too narrow or selective, but that it actually falsifies the engaged, embodied character of our being-in-the-world. So attention to religion *as* a form of life and nexus of liturgical practices brings us up against a phenomenon that challenges and deconstructs the lingering rationalist anthropologies that continue to shape method in philosophy of religion. There is, one could say, a very different, non-rationalist philosophical anthropology implicit in liturgical practice such that liturgy becomes a catalyst, even a 'revelation', that unsettles overly cognitivist pictures of the human person. In sum, it is the very phenomenon of religion as liturgical practice which functions as a 'shot in the arm' to philosophy of religion by calling for a philosophical anthropology that honours our primarily affective, pre-cognitive, communal and practised' mode of being-in-the world. Thus there is a dialectical relationship envisioned between philosophy and liturgy: on the one hand, the lived religious experience embodied in liturgical practice points to the necessity of an affective (non-rationalist) philosophical anthropology; on the other hand, the development and assumption of an affective philosophical anthropology enables philosophy of religion to be primed for dealing better with the more fundamental phenomena associated with religion, viz. practices rather than doctrines.

In fact, it was just this impetus – this interjection of embodied, lived religious experience as a 'shock' to regnant philosophical method – that was the prompt for the young Heidegger's critique of the lingering Cartesian rationalism that characterized Husserl's early phenomenology.[17] Thus we can find the resources for this retooling of philosophy of religion by considering an analogous critique in the rudimentary elements of Heidegger's critique of Descartes and Husserl. A central aspect of Heidegger's project in *Being and Time* was to call into question the rationalist anthropology assumed by Husserl, who still tended to construe human beings as primarily perceiving things – as if we inhabited the world as observers and spectators who spend time *thinking* about the world. In contrast, Heidegger argued that primarily and for the most part, we do not *think* about a world of objects; rather, we are *involved* with the world as traditioned actors. The world is the environment in which we swim, not a picture that we look at as distanced observers.[18]

Careful phenomenological attention to the dynamics of religious life – that is, religion as a way of life (Hadot) or form of life (Wittgenstein) – manifests something about the nature of human being-in-the-world that is missed by the overly cognitivist paradigms that currently govern philosophy of religion. In particular, the communal practices that shape religion show us that human being-in-the-world is oriented more fundamentally by desire than thinking, and manifests itself more in what we do than what we think.[19] As such, it is precisely religious life that calls for a revision of the *philosophy* at work in 'philosophy of religion'.

2. Critique of Secular Reason

The Heideggerian critique of Cartesian rationalism – a critique that was directly generated by engagement with religious sources – yields a more supple philosophical anthropology that is primed to think about religion as a lived, embodied phenomenon rather than merely a set of beliefs, doctrines or ideas. A philosophy of religion that methodologically adopts this affective philosophical anthropology will be poised to consider 'religion' in a way more proportionate to how it is lived 'on the ground', so to speak. In short, it will be a philosophy of religion that will be enacted as a philosophy of liturgy, a philosophy of lived religious practices.

However, that is only half of the methodological revolution I am advocating. In arguing for a more robust engagement between philosophy and liturgy, I am not only advocating that philosophy of religion make liturgical practice an object of more sustained reflection; I also want to make the further suggestion that liturgical practice and formation does and ought to function as the condition of possibility for properly *religious* philosophy. So the complete picture will include not only a philosophy *of* liturgy, but a liturgical philosophy.

On this score, the vision of a liturgical philosophy is simply a more radical development of existing models that advocate for the integrity of religious philosophy – that is, philosophical reflection that unapologetically begins from and is informed by a specific religious worldview. As such, it extends existing critiques of foundationalism and Enlightenment dreams of a 'secular reason' as neutral, objective, and autonomous. This has been articulated in several different ways over the past century:

- A philosophical tradition stemming from the Dutch Reformed tradition, embodied in Abraham Kuyper's vision of Calvinism as a 'world-and-life view' – which included the claim that all thinking about the world begins from *some* world-and-life view and that such worldviews have the same epistemic status as identifiably 'religious' worldviews.[20] This was further developed in Herman Dooyeweerd's critique of the pretended autonomy of theoretical thought, articulated in explicit dialogue with the phenomenological tradition of Husserl and Heidegger.[21]

- A related, but somewhat different development of this Kuyperian critique of Enlightenment objectivity is articulated in the 'Reformed epistemology' of Alvin Plantinga and Nicholas Wolterstorff. Rejecting the foundationalism that would rule out religious presuppositions as a contamination and compromise of objectivity, Reformed epistemology is a non-foundationalist account of rationality which secures warrant for religious starting points for thought. Furthermore, Reformed epistemology argues that all rational reflection begins from *some* ultimate presuppositions, though it is pluralist about this, arguing that theoretical thought can begin from very different, and even incommensurate 'control beliefs'.[22] In any case, there is no such thing as a 'neutral' or presuppositionless reason of the sort promised by Enlightenment accounts of rationality.
- The same critique of Enlightenment models of rationality – particularly Cartesian and Kantian – was articulated by Heidegger (as already discussed above) and further developed by his student, Hans-Georg Gadamer who pointed out the 'Enlightenment prejudice against prejudice' (1993: 270). A similar mid-century critique of objective (scientific) rationality was articulated by Michael Polanyi.
- Alasdair MacIntyre offered an allied critique of 'secular' or supposedly 'objective' rationality with a specific attention to ethics. In particular, MacIntyre has been concerned to point out the way in which reason is always already *traditioned* – indebted to and shaped by particular narratives generated by particular communities. Thus there is a significant sense in which rationality is 'relative to' these stories, communities, and traditions – and there is no rationality which is not tethered to *some* story, community, and tradition.[23]
- Building on the work of MacIntyre and Hauerwas, and marshalling the resources of post-Heideggerian continental philosophy (while also offering a trenchant critique of the latter), John Milbank's critique of supposedly 'secular' social theory is a dense microcosmic challenge to the very notion of a neutral 'secular reason' as the basis for theory of any sort, philosophy included. Milbank radicalizes MacIntyre's critique by suggesting that so-called 'secular' reason always assumes a covert theology, and that in the context of Western modernity, the

operative 'theology' undergirding secular reason is a kind of bastardized, heretical version of Christianity.[24] As such, theorizing about any sphere of human life and culture – including sociology, economics, and philosophy – always already begins from an operative, albeit covert, theology. As such, it is no longer possible to exclude explicitly Christian theological starting points from the space of the academy on the grounds that such 'theological' presuppositions contaminate the purity of secular theory. There is no pure secular reason; there are just certain theologies which get to pass themselves off as universal and objective. Once the emperor's nakedness is pointed out, however, then other theological starting points should be admitted to an academic space which is pluralist, not secularist.[25]

While I have not reproduced the arguments here, cumulatively these diverse critiques of secular reason and the myth of objectivity opened the space for the legitimacy of *religious* philosophy – philosophical reflection that is informed and oriented by explicitly confessional starting points (whether Jewish, Christian, Muslim, Hindu, etc.). Having debunked the 'myth of religious neutrality' (Clouser 2005), religious starting points could no longer be ruled as violations of academic orthodoxy. (It is perhaps an irony that American departments of 'religious studies' are often the last bastions for this passé secular orthodoxy!)

However, while these critiques of secular reason spawned much distinctively religious philosophy, the 'religion' that informs such philosophy still tends to be a religion of *ideas*. The way religion contributes to philosophy is by means of a conceptual jump-start: distinctive special revelations give to philosophy concepts and propositions that would not otherwise have been available for reflection. We might describe this as a 'revelational' or 'illuminative' model of religious philosophy whereby what religion provides is a unique storehouse of ideas and concepts that would not otherwise be available to philosophical thought. Religious revelation offers a unique deposit of wisdom that is then mined and refined by philosophical reasoning. This revelational model characterizes otherwise diverse modes of religious philosophy, from Gilson's understanding of Catholic philosophy to Plantinga's account of Reformed epistemology to Levinas's account of the genius of the Torah.[26]

But such a model for the influence of religion on philosophy continues to reflect the rationalism criticized above. It still takes religion to be a set of beliefs which provide content for propositional thought, a result of assuming believers are primarily 'thinking things' or 'believing animals' for whom faith is more about the right propositional content than an embodied comportment to the world and the neighbour. Religious philosophy just argues that such 'ideas' are not only legitimate *objects* of philosophical reflection, they constitute legitimate *starting points* for philosophical reflection. But whether under the microscope (objective) or in the mind of the perceiver (subjective), 'religion' in this picture remains a largely conceptual, heady phenomenon. In sum, though the critique of secular reason that underwrites contemporary religious philosophy has challenged the myth of neutrality associated with Enlightenment reason, it has not properly countered the rational*ism* that attended this, construing human beings primarily as thinking things and solitary[27] 'perceivers' of the world. In short, believers are construed as if they were more down-to-earth versions of academics, and religious faith is treated as the sort of thing one does at academic conferences. In this picture, religion is reduced to a matter of seeing, not loving.

The versions of this critique of secular reason offered by MacIntyre and Milbank, however, point toward another more integral understanding of religious philosophy precisely because they recognize the central place of practices and liturgy in the formation of human identity, and thus the role of both in the very shaping of rationality. In sum, one can already see in MacIntyre and Milbank an alternative philosophical anthropology that understands human persons not as thinking things, but practising animals – even liturgical animals of a sort. This is both a result of and feeds into a more fulsome post-liberal understanding of religion as a set of communal practices – a 'form of life'.

3. A Way Forward: Philosophy of Liturgy and Liturgical Philosophy

I would suggest that the renaissance in philosophy of religion stands in need of another renaissance – and that Reformed epistemology stands in need of further reformation (*semper reformanda!*). In particular, the future of philosophy of religion – while agreeing that religion is both a legitimate *topic* and *starting point* – must also contest the reductionism and lingering rationalism that remains operative in philosophy of religion. I suggest that the future for a properly post-foundationalist, post-liberal, and post-secular philosophy of religion requires that philosophy turn to liturgy – both as topic and fount for reflection.

This requires a two-fold methodological reorientation. First, as I have been arguing, philosophy of religion must eschew philosophical anthropologies of the Cartesian variety which still tend to construe even religious believers as thinking things. This leads to a second reorientation, viz. recovering a sense of 'religion' as a way of life or form of life. By 'religion' I do not mean some universal phenomenon or generic type (I am not advocating a return to 'phenomenology of religion' as articulated by Otto, VanderLeuw and others); rather, attention to religion as a form of life will require grappling with religion as inescapably *particular* and thus tied to particular practices. This shift in orientation should then give us a new angle of vision, putting a different set of phenomena in our philosophical sights, particularly the communal practices of religious communities and traditions that constitute the formative liturgies of the faith. We will then be in a position to appreciate that, for the faithful, religion is a matter of practice.

What is at stake here is a refusal of still lingering theory/practice dualisms. While contemporary philosophy of religion has recovered religion as a legitimate topic of philosophical investigation, and even recovered religious faith as a warranted starting-point for philosophical reflection, it still tends to assume a priority of ideas over practices, and thus a priority of doctrine over liturgy. It thus gives the impression that doctrines are not inextricably tethered to practices. So philosophical theology distills the 'doctrines' of, say, Christian faith and then sets them under the philosophical microscope with little if any consideration of their origins in a confessing, worshipping community. Before the Trinity was crystallized as a doctrine, it was expressed in prayer, and the liturgical milieu out of which doctrine emerges is crucial for understanding what is at stake for the religious community. For instance, the community's baptismal confession that 'Jesus is Lord' is not a matter of merely theoretical knowledge and 'getting it right'. It is a political *act* that contests the reigning practice of confessing Caesar as Lord (N. T. Wright 2000: 161–62). As such, conversion to Christian faith and baptismal profession was not seen as the adoption of merely a new 'paradigm' or set of propositions, but rather a transformation of one's allegiances embodied in a unique set of practices inscribed by participation in the liturgy. There is an irreducibility of faith's liturgical enactment that cannot be simply translated or exhausted by articulation of doctrines. Thus, if we are to try to do justice to religion philosophically, we will need to honour this irreducible and primary liturgical moment of religion.

We might find a way to conceptualize this in Charles Taylor's notion (adopted from Benedict Anderson) of the 'social imaginary'. Taylor emphasizes that all societies and communities are animated by a social imaginary, but this does not mean that all are oriented by a 'theory'. The social imaginary is 'much broader and deeper than the intellectual schemes people may entertain when they *think* about social reality in a disengaged mode' (Taylor 2004: 23; emphasis added). Rather, the social imaginary is meant to indicate 'the ways people *imagine* their social existence, how they fit together with others, how things go on between them and their fellows, the expectations that are normally met', etc. (Taylor 2004: 23; emphasis added). Taylor describes this as an 'imaginary' in order to refer to 'the way ordinary people "imagine" their social surroundings' which is 'not expressed in theoretical terms, but is carried in images, stories, and legends' (2004: 23). Most importantly, Taylor emphasizes a dynamic relationship between understanding and practice: 'If the understanding makes the practice possible, it is also true that it is the practice that largely carries the understanding' (2004: 25).[28] Or, to put it otherwise, the understanding is 'implicit in practice'. As Taylor remarks, 'humans operated with a social imaginary well before they ever got into the business of theorizing about themselves' (2004: 26). I am suggesting that philosophy of religion could attend to the richness of religion as practice if we considered it in terms of a social imaginary. By analogy, then, we could say that humans were religious well before they ever developed a theology, and for most 'ordinary people', religion is rarely a matter of theology. Rather, there is an understanding of the world – a horizon for inhabiting the world – that is carried in and implicit in the practices of religious worship and devotion. These rituals form the imagination of a people who thus construe their world as a particular kind of environment based on the formation implicit in such practices. If philosophy of religion is going to take religion seriously, then it needs to attend to religion as a social imaginary – a set of liturgical practices in which a unique understanding is implicit.

We can see examples of this sort of reorientation of philosophy of religion in current work associated with 'Radical Orthodoxy'. For example, the work of Catherine Pickstock and Graham Ward has paid close attention to Christian liturgy, specifically the Eucharist. Pickstock's *After Writing* (1998) is an extended analysis of the distinctive ontology and philosophy of language embedded in the Roman rite. Similarly, Ward (2001: esp. 81–96) has taken seriously the words of institution ('this is my body') to generate a unique participatory or analogical ontology. These are clear examples of a shift in *topic*, looking to liturgy as a *resource* for philosophy. However, one could suggest that this mode of philosophical engagement with liturgy still remains within the 'illuminative' model described above. In both cases, the liturgy is taken to be a resource for new *ideas* which can generate a distinctly Christian philosophy. The liturgy is construed as a space for a thought project. This is significant and legitimate; however, it still tends to treat liturgy as a fund for ideas rather than a practice of formation. Thus engagements with liturgy tend to be mining expeditions for ideas and concepts otherwise unavailable.[29]

A further reorientation of philosophy to liturgy would not just look to liturgical practice as another place to find ideas, but would be attentive to the central dynamics of *formation* that are at the heart of liturgical practice. And an even further radical reorientation would then consider how liturgical participation would contribute to the formation of philosophical imagination itself – not just philosophical reflection on how liturgical practices shape our comportment to the world, but how liturgical practices shape our *philosophical* comportment to the world. On this account, the condition of possibility for a properly *religious* philosophy is not just access to a unique set of ideas unveiled by revelation, but participation in the liturgical practices of the community as a means of shaping the philosophical imagination and what constitutes 'rationality'. One can see something like this anticipated in MacIntyre's account of rationality as traditioned, but the explicit link to liturgy is only beginning to be developed.

Such a thorough reorientation of philosophy of religion can be seen in a couple of promising examples. The first is recent work by Jewish philosopher Peter Ochs on Jewish morning prayer. In particular, Ochs (2006a) carefully explicates the way in which immersion in the ritual of Jewish morning prayer is a mode of 'training in how to make judgments' (2006a: 50). More specifically, he shows how participation in Jewish morning prayer is a practice of redemptive thinking which 'redeems the way we ordinarily misjudge the world' – a way of undoing our socialization into propositional ways of judging the world which tend to be absolutized, and thus fail to do justice to the richness of the world. Jewish morning prayer, then, is a way to 'nurture actual, everyday habits of thinking that are not dominated by this logic' – which translates into a new *philosophical* orientation when they are undertaken by the philosopher (Ochs 2006a: 50).[30] Second, I find William Abraham's articulation of 'canonical theism' to be an example of a 'thicker' philosophical vision that draws on the liturgical specificity of Catholic confession and liturgy as both resource and condition for insightful philosophical reflection. Abraham emphasizes the importance of drawing on the 'deep content' of Christian belief – the canonical theism 'dispersed in the scriptures, the Nicene Creed, the iconography, and the liturgy' – in contrast to the 'minimalist theism' of current philosophy of religion which cannot 'do full justice to the way in which a host of Christian believers actually believe' (Abraham 2006: 14–15).

In this space I have been able to provide only a programmatic survey of the current landscape and sketch a suggestion of further agendas for research. Promising developments give an indication and hope that a new renaissance in philosophy of religion is possible – one in which we finally appreciate that philosophy of religion takes (liturgical) practice.[31]

Notes

1. As an example of this development, consider, for instance, the work of Antony Flew (1961; 1966; Flew and MacIntyre 1955).
2. For just a sample of representative work in this vein, see Clark 1992; Stump 1993; Adams 2000; Hebblethwaite 2005; Davis 2006.
3. There is also a European and Catholic story to be told here associated with Blondel and later Gilson's claims regarding a 'Christian philosophy'. As usual, at stake here is how we receive the legacy of Thomas Aquinas – a debate that has come to the fore again with contemporary retrievals of *nouvelle théologie*. However, I cannot do justice to these issues here. For relevant discussion, see F. A. Murphy 2004; Long 2006; English 2006.
4. Most famously, Plantinga (1967) pointed out the analogy between the epistemic status of belief in 'other minds' and belief in God.
5. For classic statements of this project, see Wolterstorff 1976; Plantinga and Wolterstorff 1983; Plantinga 2000. For a succinct introduction to Reformed epistemology, see Clark 1990.
6. For a summary of this related to philosophy of religion, see Smith 2000; 1997.
7. In Smith 2004 I have tried to suggest some overlap between the project of Reformed epistemology and radical orthodoxy.
8. Much work remains to be done on this score, and I cannot pursue it further here. Suffice is to say that Plantinga's critique of 'postmodernism' (2000: s. III) is a rejection of a straw man, and that, in fact, his non-foundationalist account of warranted belief has much in common with Heidegger, Rorty and perhaps even Derrida. For some recent hints along this line, see the discussion of Plantinga and Rorty in Dann 2006.
9. I will employ the term 'liturgy' in a broad and generous sense (in order to see some kind of 'liturgy' as integral to different religions), without diluting its meaning (such that any and all 'ritual' would constitute liturgy). As a baseline definition, liturgy could be said to include not all ritual, but specifically *rituals of ultimate concern*: rituals that are *formative* for identity in a way that trumps other ritual formations. Admittedly, this might include rituals not associated with 'traditional' religions (e.g., rituals of Nazi fascism, other rituals of totalizing nationalism). I want to leave the door open for a consideration of these 'secular' liturgies, but will not consider them in this chapter. Here I will be assuming liturgies associated with identifiable religions. And while I will tend to privilege examples of Christian liturgy, I think my account provides a framework for considering Jewish, Muslim, Buddhist and other liturgies in the same way. (This is not Tillichian [or Hickian] insofar as it is informed by a genuine pluralism; I do not mean to suggest that all rituals of ultimate concern are, at the end of the day, concerned with the same ultimate. Rather, embedded in the practices are very different, antithetical understandings of the ultimate.)
10. To his credit, it should be noted that in the later Heidegger, believers dance and pray (see Heidegger 1969: 72; for further discussion, see Westphal 1999: 146–63).

11. One might legitimately wonder whether this is an indication of the overwhelmingly Protestant influence in contemporary philosophy of religion.
12. For instance, when philosophers of religion turn to a consideration of prayer, it is primarily the epistemological challenges that are focused upon, or issues of how prayer can be reconciled with the doctrines of God's omniscience and omnipotence (see, for example, Stump 1979; Masek 2000). For a contrasting philosophical engagement with prayer, see Ochs 2006a.
13. I do not think this is a phenomenon unique to 'analytic' of Anglo-American philosophy. Much 'Continental' philosophy of religion also exhibits an epistemological fixation.
14. In *Speech and Theology* I argue that this was precisely the project of the young Heidegger: to come up with a new 'concept' that could do justice to the richness of lived experience, and *religious* lived experience in particular (see Smith 2002: 67–113).
15. For a related discussion, see Faber 2006: ch. 11.
16. One could perhaps describe my approach as a 'post-liberal' philosophy of religion (see Lindbeck 1984).
17. Another impetus was the messiness of lived ethical experience as analysed by Aristotle. For a discussion of Aristotle in these terms, see Heidegger 1992.
18. I have unpacked this in more detail in Smith 2002: 67–82.
19. Religion as a form of life ('what we *do*') also confirms important developments in philosophy of mind, cognitive science and neuroplasticity, which emphasizes the ways and extent to which our comportment to the world happens at the level of the bodily, tactile and pre-conscious. Philosophy of religion has yet to engage these conversations, but a turn to liturgy provides the catalyst for such explorations. For relevant discussions, see Wilson 2002 and Gallagher 2005. This just comes down to requiring that philosophy of religion take embodiment seriously. For an important beginning, see Coakley 2003.
20. For a succinct statement, see Kuyper 1943 presented as the Stone Lectures at Princeton Theological Seminary in 1898. Thus Malcolm Bull (1992) once described Kuyper as 'the first postmodern'.
21. See Dooyeweerd 1999. For exposition, see Clouser 2005 and Smith 1999.
22. See Wolterstorff 1976. As such, Reformed epistemology could be read as a kind of 'standpoint' epistemology and thus would be akin to recent developments in feminist epistemology. For a discussion, see Harrison (forthcoming) and Wesselius 1997.
23. This is most fully articulated in MacIntyre 1988, but for a succinct statement, see MacIntyre 1977: 453–72.
24. The boldest statement of this remains Milbank 1990. For an exposition of this project, see Smith 2004: esp. chs. 4–5.
25. This sort of critique is not just offered by Christian theologians. See, for instance, Connolly 1999. For a Christian theological engagement with Connolly's non-Christian anti-secularist pluralism, see Johnson 2007.
26. See Gilson 1993, which is a series of meditations on truths shown to philosophy by revelation; Plantinga 1992a; on Levinas's conception of the relation between religion and philosophy, see Robbins 1991: 100–32.

27. This aspect of the regnant paradigm should not be underestimated. A survey of the literature in philosophy of religion will yield a picture of religion as something that one does largely on one's own (again, I think there's a certain Protestantism at work here). If philosophy of religion stands in need of a turn to liturgy, it also stands in need of a communitarian shot in the arm via a more robust ecclesiology. Indeed, one might suggest that ecclesiology is one of the theological loci most ignored by the renewal of philosophical theology.
28. It should be noted that 'understanding' here refers to something akin to Heidegger's notion of 'understanding' (*Verstehen*) which is not to be equated with theoretical or propositional 'knowledge' (See Heidegger 1962: s. 31). This 'understanding' is still distinct from, and irreducible to, 'theoretical' or propositional knowledge. So not even the 'understanding' implicit in practice is to be identified with the sorts of 'ideas' that tend to be the currency of contemporary philosophical theology.
29. George Vandervelde (2005) offers a nuanced critique of Ward's tendency to see the Eucharist as a 'privileged ontological site'.
30. Ochs's work is indicative of a promising developing practice in post-liberal philosophical theology called 'Scriptural Reasoning' (see Ochs 2006b; as well as the essays collected in Pecknold and Rashkover 2006).
31. Research for this chapter was supported in part by the Philosophy and Liturgy Research Initiative funded by the Calvin Institute of Christian Worship at Calvin College. My thanks to fellow team members Nicholas Wolterstorff, Sarah Coakley, Terence Cuneo, Reinhard Hütter, and Peter Ochs and John Witvliet for helpful conversations along these lines.

Knowledge of God, Knowledge of Place and the Practice and Method of the Philosophy of Religion

Mark Wynn

One standard account of the nature of the philosophy of religion supposes that it is occupied above all with two questions: what meaning is to be assigned to religious claims concerning for example the reality or existence of God, and secondly, to what extent are those claims plausible? These two questions pick out two broadly defined routes into the subject matter of the discipline: one concerned basically with conceptual issues (in analytic philosophy of religion, it is of course the concept of God that is pre-eminently of interest), and the other focused upon the epistemology of religious belief. These two routes are of course intimately connected: a certain method for establishing the plausibility of religious claims will naturally presuppose some account of what kind of reality is under investigation. Hence Aquinas's argument from motion, for example, issues famously in a conception of God as immutable, impassible, immaterial, and so on. Similarly, a conception of God as perfect being, for example, will issue in a certain mode of investigation of God's reality, the most celebrated example of which is perhaps the ontological argument.

In recent analytic philosophy of religion we also find this correlation of themes – various conceptions of the nature of God help to define, and are defined by, various epistemologies of religious belief. I would like to begin by offering some comment on two such combinations.

Analytic philosophers of religion have been much interested in the analogies between the epistemology of religious belief and that of other kinds of belief. Two analogies have proved to be particularly fruitful – first the idea that the canons of explanation which operate in the natural sciences, and which give scientists good reason to infer the existence of as yet unobserved entities, provide an analogy for the sort of case that can be made for the existence of God, in so far as God constitutes a 'simple' explanation for various phenomena that would otherwise be at most only partially explained. The work of Richard Swinburne (2004) is I suggest the most fully developed and most cogent example of this sort of strategy.

Other philosophers have been impressed by the analogy between ordinary perceptual belief and religious belief. Swinburne's case also depends upon reference to religious experience, but one might think of, for instance, William Alston's work (1991) on 'perceiving God' as a paradigmatic example of this sort of approach. Of course, Alston's claim is not that ordinary sensory experience and religious experience are precisely analogous from an epistemic point of view: indeed some objections to religious experience depend, he thinks, upon an inappropriate extension of the epistemic standards that properly apply in relation to sense experience to the domain of religious experience. This sort of move he regards as 'epistemic imperialism'. But the other side of his case is to maintain that often enough the grounds which are taken to discredit religious experience would also, if applied consistently, discredit sensory experience – this is the basis of his 'double standards' objection to scepticism about religious experience. And this strand of his case clearly implies that on certain central points sensory and religious experience stand or fall together, especially in so far as both are embedded within doxastic practices which incorporate various checks upon the veridicality of individual experiences.

Of course these two approaches – one grounded in scientific explanation and the other in ordinary perceptual experience – are importantly different from one another. Most obviously perhaps, the scientific analogy implies that religious belief rests upon an inference, rather than being 'properly basic'.[1] But on certain fundamental points, the analogies are in agreement: both issue most readily in a conception of God as a particular individual, to be construed by analogy with unobserved theoretical entities in science, or by analogy with the objects that impress themselves upon our senses in ordinary perceptual experience. And both imply that it is possible to apprehend God's reality, at least in principle, independently of any deep-seated evaluative commitment. It is noteworthy, for example, that while Alston acknowledges that religious experience is very often affectively toned, he is also eager to suppose that the 'phenomenal content' of such experience is not simply affective – on the grounds that its being purely affective would call into question the objective reference of the experience (Alston 1991: 49–50). Similarly, both these models for knowledge of God imply that our ethical, aesthetic and otherwise engaged response to the world is not directly relevant to our knowledge of God – since God can be inferred from, for example, the findings of the sciences concerning the law-governed nature of the universe, or apprehended by way of some supra-sensory encounter.[2]

So the 'method' or 'practice' of at least one significant strand within recent philosophy of religion has involved combining (1) an epistemology of religious belief which is rooted in various secular analogies with (2) a correlative conception of God. The epistemology implies bypassing our engaged practical response to the material world; and God is then conceived as a kind of individual entity, by analogy with the objects of sense experience or the theoretical entities of science. Both of these lines of enquiry, the broadly Swinburnean and the broadly Alstonian, have proved I think immensely fruitful: both have thrown various aspects of the epistemology of religious belief into new relief, and helped us to see how the grounds that might be cited in support of religious belief are in many ways continuous with those which we take to operate, unproblematically, in other contexts.

However, this kind of approach to the method and practice of the subject does not of course exhaust the possibilities. Here I want to sketch another kind of approach – one which gives a larger role to our practical engagement with the material world as a route to knowledge of God, and which is less inclined to assimilate God's reality to that of individual entities. For this purpose, I shall also appeal to a secular analogy, but rather than perceptual or scientific knowledge I shall be concerned with our knowledge of place.

Let us begin with the conceptual route into our topic, before turning to some epistemological implications. I am going to argue that the concept of God is in various ways reminiscent of the concept of place, and that this gives us reason to assimilate the epistemology of religious and 'placial' belief.

It is a commonplace of philosophical theology that God's reality has a supra-individual character. And the same sort of idea is implied I think in popular religious consciousness when it is supposed that God is not so much an individual entity as a context, in the light of which we can make sense of individual entities. This kind of conception is found in the writings of, for example, John Paul II and Rowan Williams, who together can speak authoritatively for two central strands of the Christian tradition. John Paul remarks for instance: 'In the incarnation of the Son of God ... the Whole lies hidden in the part' (John Paul II 1998: s. 12). And Rowan Williams observes similarly that talk of God 'is structurally more like talking about some "grid" for the understanding of particular objects than talking about particular objects in themselves' (R. Williams 1984: 15).[3] So on these accounts, it is the world as a whole, or some overarching 'grid' or frame of reference applied to individual entities, that supplies our clearest clue to God's nature, rather than individual entities themselves. The same kind of perspective is apparent in, for example, Aquinas's teaching that God is subsistent existence, and in his associated proposal that it is the world as a whole that offers our best image of God:

God planned to create many distinct things, in order to share with them and reproduce in them his goodness. Because no one creature could do this, he produced many diverse creatures, so that what was lacking in one expression of his goodness could be made up by another; for the goodness which God has whole and together, creatures share in many different ways. And the whole universe shares and expresses that goodness better than any individual creature. (Aquinas 1989: 1.47.1)

This conception of God's reality as supra-individual suggests a first analogy between that reality and the reality of places. For places too are not simply individual entities. Nor of course are they mere conglomerations of individual entities – since to speak of a place in normal usage is to suppose that a given region of space exhibits some genuine unity. As Edward Casey (1996: 32) comments, place 'is situated between the Charybdis of sheer singularity and the Scylla of contingent commonality' – that is, places are supra-individual, yet not mere collections of things.

One consequence of this feature of places is that a place is best imaged not so much by individual entities that fall within it, but by the sum of such entities, considered as an integral whole – just as God, on the view we have been considering, is best imaged not by individual creatures so much as by the world considered as an integrated whole. To this extent then, there is a parallel between the relationship of God to creatures and that of a place to its parts.

Of course, this analogy invites the objection that God's transcendence of the world involves a deeper ontological distinction than any which is implied in the distinction between a place and its parts. It may be that a place is not just a conglomeration of individuals, but if the parts of which it is comprised were to cease to exist, then so would place. By contrast, on standard accounts, of the kind endorsed by Aquinas as well as John Paul II and Rowan Williams, creatures could cease to exist without God ceasing to exist. To mark this point of disanalogy, we might suppose that it is not so much the bare concept of a place that presents a useful analogy to the concept of God, as the concept of a *genius loci* – where the *genius* of a place is taken to be a power that inhabits the place and gives it structure. Of course in the traditional idiom, even a *genius loci* cannot exist apart from its place – but in so far as the idea of the *genius* involves the thought of a kind of power which gives unity to the place, the concept can in principle be extended, I suggest, to include the case where the existence of the *genius* is not dependent logically upon that of the place.

So to this extent it is the *genius loci* concept rather than the bare concept of a place that presents a closer analogy to the concept of God. Moreover, like a place, a *genius* is best imaged by the parts of the relevant locus considered as a unity – rather than by any individual entity. So for example the '*genius*' of Dartmoor (the English national park) is revealed most clearly not in individual stretches of heath, but rather in the prevailing colours, scents, geology and meteorological conditions of the moor as a whole, together with its history and architecture – where these various elements of our appreciation of the moor are not simply added together, and considered as a conglomerate, but instead fuse to produce a unitary sense of place. The architecture of Dartmoor, for example, would present a different appearance in a different place, so our appreciation of this feature of the moor is conditioned by our appreciation of its other features, and vice versa. Of course, I am not maintaining here that there 'really' is a power that inhabits the moor, and which communicates its likeness to the moor – I am bracketing that question, to consider simply what is involved in the concept of a *genius loci*.

Suppose we grant then that, for these reasons, the supra-individuality of a *genius loci* in its relation to the parts of a place is analogous to that of God in relation to creatures. Why should this proposal matter religiously? Williams, John Paul II, Aquinas and others all affirm the doctrine of divine supra-individuality not least because it offers a way of rendering unintelligible the idea that my relationship to God might somehow stand in competition with my relations to creatures. If God's reality is akin to that of a 'grid' (to adopt Williams's phrasing of the point) then I cannot find value apart from God – because it is only by reference to God that I can see my relationship to creatures in proper perspective, so that it is only through God that I can properly access the values that are realized in individual things. By contrast if God's reality is conceived by analogy with that of an individual creature then, in the absence of elaboration, the possibility of competition between God and the goods represented by creatures will seem to be at least in principle admissible.

If the doctrine of divine supra-individuality has some religious significance for these reasons, then we might infer that on this point anyway the *genius loci* model offers a helpful correction, or extension, of the conception of God implied in the idea that knowledge of God is akin to scientific or perceptual knowledge. In brief, to speak of God by analogy with a *genius loci* is to suggest, as these models do not, that God is known not so much as another individual entity, whether inferred or not, but as the context, or frame of reference, in light of which we can see the significance of individual things in proper perspective.

It is perhaps worth adding that one standard objection to accounts which emphasize the divine supra-individuality is to suppose that thereby they are committed to an attenuated conception of God's personhood. (Compare for example Charles Hartshorne's criticism of Aquinas's doctrine on this basis, e.g., Hartshorne 1968.) On this point, the *genius loci* model may, arguably, fare better than some other formulations of the idea of divine supra-individuality. For the *genius* of a place is typically represented in personal terms – and typically conceived as a kind of conversation partner, in so far as we identify the character of a place by reference to the prevailing moods and habits of thought that it tends to evoke in us, just as we determine the character of human beings on this basis. Of course, the sense in which a place, or even a *genius loci*, is 'personal' is not quite that in which a human being is personal – but it is striking even so that personal categories seem to lie at the root of our engaged appreciation of particular places.

Let us look more briefly now at two other respects in which the current model proves consonant with standard accounts of the divine nature. If God is conceived by analogy with a theoretical entity in science, or an everyday perceptual object, then unsurprisingly it is natural to think of God's agency as a kind of efficient causation. But of course theological tradition has also insisted that God acts as a final cause. Here again the *genius loci* analogy can have some use in helping to bring into new relief a familiar theological affirmation.

A recurring theme in the philosophical literature on place is the idea that the agency of places is story-mediated. The history of a place, or in general the stories associated with it, provides a context which helps to fix the sense of behaviour at that place – and thereby the place can elicit certain kinds of behaviour, in so far as people seek to act in ways which are congruent with its storied (and otherwise defined) identity. There are of course many examples of this phenomenon in everyday life – such as the laying of flowers at the scene of a fatal accident; there are also larger scale examples, concerning for instance the question of the use to which the site of the 9/11 attacks should be put. In all these cases, the place exercises a kind of agency, by shaping human behaviour in ways that respect its storied identity. (For an extended illustration of these ideas see Mandoki 1998.) Of course this is not an instance of efficient causation but more like final causation – our behaviour in these cases is shaped by the goal of congruence with the storied identity of the place. In theological ethics, God's agency is often treated similarly. For example it may be said that what makes a certain kind of sexual behaviour illicit is not so much the fact that there is a specific injunction in Scripture condemning such acts (even if there is such an injunction), but rather the fact that such acts do not fit their storied context, where the story in this case concerns God's activity in creation, reconciliation and redemption.[4] Here the world is being treated as a kind of 'place', whose storied identity is given by its relation to God, who in turn acts therefore not simply as an efficient cause, but by revealing and constituting the storied meaning of the world — and in this way God establishes the appropriateness of, and on occasion actually elicits, some kinds of behaviour (those which fit their storied context) rather than others.

Extending these connections we might therefore think of God as the *genius* whose locus is the world.[5] In general, the *genius* of a place communicates its likeness to the place, and thereby gives the place a unitary character. And as the source of the world, God confers upon it a unitary, storied (and otherwise defined) identity, which bodies forth the divine identity. (Logos language is of course one way of making this point: the world partakes of a unity and sensefulness that is God's own.) It follows then that human behaviour is called to be congruent not only with the place which is the world, but also with God, as the *genius mundi* — so that God acts as a final cause.

The philosophical literature on place has also examined at length the related question of how human identity, variously conceived, may be grounded in place. My 'identity' in the everyday sense of the term is given in significant part by the story which I tell of myself.[6] If asked to introduce myself to someone at some length, and in this sense to explain who I am, I am likely to rehearse various significant episodes from my past — concerning the development of various formative relationships and allegiances, or the acquisition of various professional and other skills. And given that the storied and otherwise defined identity of a place bears on the meaning which attaches to the behaviours enacted at that place, we might add that I can only properly rehearse my life story if I can also specify the identities of the places which provide the setting for the things I have done — for it is only in the light of their placial context that particular stretches of behaviour can be assigned a determinate sense. For example, to put the point crudely, the act of applying paint to a surface carries a very different meaning if I am at home and helping to decorate, rather than at a school which I am defacing.

It is of course a commonplace of theological tradition that human identity cannot be specified apart from God. And in some writers we find the idea that reference to God is required as a condition of the coherence of my life story, and in this sense in particular serves as a bulwark of my identity. As Augustine comments:

> You are my eternal Father, but I am scattered in times whose order I do not understand. The storms of incoherent events tear to pieces my thoughts, the inmost entrails of my soul, until that day when, purified and molten by the fire of your love, I flow together to merge into you. (Augustine 1991: XI, xxix, 39)

The model of God as the *genius* whose locus is the world is also nicely consonant with these reflections. Just as it is not possible to tell my life story independently of reference to the character of the particular places which provide the setting for various episodes of that story, so ultimately it is not possible to tell my life story independently of reference to the storied and otherwise defined character of the locus which is the world – because once again, it is only so that the various stretches of behaviour which form my life can be assigned a determinate sense (consider again the example of sexual behaviour). And in turn this implies that a truthful telling of my life story will depend on knowledge of the *genius* of the locus which is the world – which is to say that whatever deep knowledge I may have of myself will turn out to be inseparable from my knowledge of God.

I have been exploring various ways in which the concept of God is analogous to that of a place or, better, to that of the *genius* of a place – with particular reference to the ideas of divine supra-individuality, God's status as a final cause, and the divine grounding of human identity. On this basis we might suppose that knowledge of place presents a religiously richer analogy for knowledge of God than do analogies which appeal to perceptual or scientific kinds of knowledge. I am not suggesting that perceptual and scientific models are incompatible with the idea of God as supra-individual, final cause and ground of human identity, but they do not throw these themes so directly into sharp relief – whereas the place model, I think, does draw our attention to precisely these matters, and helps to show how they are not just discrete proposals, but aspects of one and the same underlying conception of the divine nature.

Of course just as the perceptual and scientific models issue in a somewhat distinctive conception of the epistemology of religious belief, so will this placial approach. To know a place (or, equally, its *genius*) depends upon a sensuous, storied and conversational appreciation of relevant points of salience. Applying this model, we might suppose similarly that knowledge of God does not rest fundamentally upon a disengaged apprehension of general features of the cosmos, or upon a supra-sensory perception of a particular entity, but is rooted in our practical engagement with the place which is the world. Indeed, on this view knowledge of God is not just analogous to knowledge of place – for an integrative knowledge of the character of particular places will be partly constitutive of knowledge of God considered as the *genius mundi*.

To return to the question of the 'practice' and 'method' of the philosophy of religion, one implication of these remarks is of course that while recourse to secular analogies is certainly of assistance in bringing into focus the nature of knowledge of God, we need to be aware of the larger existential or theological resonances of particular models – and to develop further models where our current accounts fail to be sensitive to the embodied, placial context of religious knowing. If this were done, some 'problems' in the discipline might seem less pressing. For example, the discussion of why God's existence is not more evident (the so-called problem of divine 'hiddenness') often trades implicitly on the perceptual or scientific models of what knowledge of God might involve. Given these models, the question arises: why are standard inferential arguments for God's existence not more persuasive, or why do more people not report encounters with God? But if knowing God is a matter of knowing the *genius* of the world, and if knowledge of particular places is therefore partly constitutive of knowledge of God, then these issues will have to be at any rate differently conceptualized.

In this chapter I have explored one way of giving closer attention to the practical, engaged character of religious knowing. Another approach, with the same kind of practical focus, would be to scrutinize particular religious practices, and consider what conception of God, or what model of religious knowing, is implied in such practices. One very obvious (place-relative) practice which might be examined in these terms is pilgrimage. Pilgrimage is particularly suggestive because it has itself been a source of theological controversy, and the self-understanding of pilgrims is therefore often informed by relatively theoretical theological commitments. (For further discussion of this practice, see Wynn [forthcoming].)

The case of pilgrimage throws light on two other questions of relevance to this volume: 'Is philosophy of religion a universal discourse?', and 'Is it a second-order discourse?' Pilgrimage practices do seem to be universal across the major faith traditions, notwithstanding the objections to the practice posed by some of the founding figures of these traditions (see Brown 2004: 216–17). So a study of this practice could well proceed across cultural or faith boundaries, since it is plausible to suppose that in at least some fundamental respects pilgrimage is motivated by similar concerns, regardless of religious or cultural context – for example the concern to achieve an embodied relationship to founding events or figures within a given tradition. And no doubt philosophers of religion (rather than philosophical theologians, who are writing along confessional lines) have particular reason to take an interest in practices which do cross faith boundaries.

The example of pilgrimage also makes clear, I suggest, that the philosophy of religion is not just a second-order activity. Pilgrimage practices are often saturated with philosophical kinds of assumption, not least because, again, such practices have long been the subject of theological critique – for instance on the grounds that they rest upon a crude idea of divine localizability, or a superstitious belief in law-suspending events. So here philosophical discussion need not be concerned simply with bringing out the implicit sense of practices – it can instead criticize their philosophical assumptions or, equally, free some practices from the appearance of confusion, by vindicating the philosophical commitments of their exponents. Closer examination of particular religious practices, and the conceptions of divine presence and activity, for example, that are embedded within them, is another respect I suggest in which the method and practice of analytic philosophy of religion might be extended.

Lastly, why suppose that the philosophy of religion is important? There are of course many reasons for thinking the discipline important – one of which would be its bearing upon religious practice. To some extent, the importance of the discipline today is evident in the fact that it appears worthwhile to pose this question. In earlier times, the importance of religious claims would have seemed simply obvious (how could a well-ordered human life be possible apart from an informed acquaintance with such claims, one might have wondered), and in turn the importance of investigating such claims with whatever rational methods were to hand would also have seemed obvious. In this earlier context then, this question would not have had the force that it does for us. In our time, by contrast, the main challenge to the religious point of view is posed not so much, I suggest, by evidential difficulties as by a problem of indifference: we fail to see why it should matter, to the questions of practical living that we need to address here and now, whether or not one adopts a religious point of view. And if that is so, then one respect in which the philosophy of religion may prove to be important is by helping to restore our sense of the mattering of (at least some forms of) the religious point of view.

Of course, a philosophy of religion which aims to recover our sense of the importance of a religious point of view is not likely to take the epistemic route into the discipline's subject matter that I distinguished earlier. It is more likely to begin with the concept of God (or the sacred otherwise conceived), and to try to show how various ideas of God can be brought to bear upon our everyday concern to achieve an appropriate practical orientation in the world. And a place-based analogy for God may well prove more useful in this regard than analogies which theorize God as an individual entity knowable independently of our practical engagement with the world – just because if God is so knowable, then to that extent knowledge of God will appear to be sealed off from the kind of knowledge that most obviously matters to our contemporaries, namely knowledge of how to order our lives practically in the world here and now. By contrast, placial knowledge is obviously and crucially relevant to this practical kind of knowledge – because it is only in light of sensitivity to place that the real significance of our behaviour (and therefore its fittingness or otherwise) can be determined.

A good deal of philosophy of religion concentrates naturally enough on the abstractly creedal dimension of what it is to believe in God – so even when philosophers of religion do take the concept of God as their starting point (rather than epistemological matters), the issues they debate may not carry any very direct implication for religious practice. This suggests that the other strategy I have commended in this chapter of beginning with particular religious practices, and considering the connections between those practices and various conceptions of God – may also have some merit for a contemporary formulation of method in the philosophy of religion. Such practices will not typically exhibit the developed theoretical understanding that is found in philosophical treatments of the concept of God but, even so, they can involve a genuine taking stock of the nature of the world and the possibilities which it affords for human life. Analogously, my appreciation of the nature of a particular place, and of the demands and opportunities it affords, will often be mediated by way of my embodied apprehension of its significance, and independently of any more abstract, theoretical investigation of its character.[7]

An example can be found in pilgrimage practices again – for instance in the recognition implied in such practices that standing in a relationship of physical proximity to the relics of a saint can count for something religiously. It is not an entirely straightforward exercise to explain, from a theoretical point of view, why standing in such a relationship should matter, and it is easy to imagine various over-generalizing or in other ways false accounts being offered – for example it may be said that the significance of the practice is solely to offer a stimulus to thought, by providing an occasion to recall the saint; or on the other side that the significance of the practice depends on some metaphysical belief concerning the enduring, quasi-magical efficacy of the bones of the saint. Alternatively, it could be argued that what we recognize in our embodied response to the post-mortem body in general (and to the relics of a saint in particular) is the enduring ethical significance of the body, in so far as it was the vehicle for the realization of a certain kind of meaning. These are points I have developed elsewhere, but I mention them here just to suggest how our embodied responses may involve a genuine yet pre-discursive insight into the world and the kinds of ethical and other claims which it may make upon us.[8] Giving an account of this kind of insight will very often involve keeping clear both of reductionist (for example, psychologizing) and of overly metaphysical treatments of the conditions of the sense of such practices.

So the philosophy of religion could well seek to draw out the kind of knowledge that is implied in such religious practices – by attention to what we might call the phenomenology of the practice, that is, the particular felt significance that is assigned to a given place, in light of which the practice makes sense or with which it appears to be congruent. On the view I have been expounding, this exercise would also count as an examination of the concept of God, as it would provide one route into the question of the identity of the *genius* of the larger place which is the world.

It is striking that many discussions in the philosophy of religion could in principle be transferred en bloc to a world whose phenomenology was quite different from that of our own world – such as a world which was ordered according to natural regularities, but without generating the sensuous and practical possibilities that are characteristic of a human life. If we think of God as the *genius* of the particular locus that is our world, and if we want some account of how a concept of God might mesh with questions of how to orient ourselves practically in this world, then we may well wish to supplement these kinds of discussion with some of the strategies that I have touched upon in this chapter.[9]

Notes

1. The idiom of 'proper basicality' derives of course from Alvin Plantinga. See, for example, his essay 'Is Belief in God Properly Basic?' (1981).
2. It is worth noting that in *The Existence of God*, Swinburne does allude to an argument from the beauty of the natural world, but it is above all temporal regularity which provides the basis for his argument from design (2004: 190–91).
3. In this remark, he is expounding a comment of Wittgenstein.
4. For an exploration of these connections see Banner 1999: 21–26.
5. A similar claim is implied of course in the idea that God's supra-individuality in relation to creatures is like that of a *genius* in relation to the parts of its locus.
6. Of course philosophers have often been occupied with a rather more narrowly defined notion of 'identity' – according to which 'I' would still be me even if I had done none of the things that in fact constitute my life story. Compare Saul Kripke's treatment of proper names as 'rigid designators' in *Naming and Necessity* (1980). The further sense of identity that I am discussing here is perfectly serviceable, even if less precisely defined.
7. Compare David Seamon's account (1980) of the kinds of understanding that are implied in our embodied interaction with the world.
8. For fuller discussion of these matters, see Wynn (forthcoming).
9. I am grateful to Peter Byrne for his helpful comments on an early draft of this paper.

Reformed Epistemology and the Recontextualizing of Natural Theology

Michael Sudduth

Introduction

Contemporary Anglo-American philosophy of religion continues to exhibit significant interest in the epistemology of religious belief. Roughly stated, religious epistemology is an area within philosophy of religion concerned with the positive epistemic status of religious belief. More precisely, it designates inquiry into whether, in what sense, and under what conditions beliefs with religious content, especially belief in God, can have epistemic properties such as rationality, justification, warrant, and knowledge. In other words, the epistemology of religious belief is concerned with the epistemic integrity, appraisal, or evaluation of religious belief.

One dichotomy within contemporary religious epistemology is between what I will designate *evidential* and *non-evidential* approaches to religious epistemology. According to the former, religious belief possesses positive epistemic status only if there is sufficient evidence for it. For this reason the evidential approach is usually allied with natural theology, the project of developing rational arguments for the existence and nature of God. By contrast, the latter approach attempts to ground religious belief in intuition, religious experience, or some other ostensibly direct (as opposed to inferential) process of belief formation, where the process is taken to be an epistemically efficacious one. Since the 1980s this approach has been commonly associated with the *Reformed epistemology* movement represented by prominent American philosophers Alvin Plantinga, Nicholas Wolterstorff, and William Alston.

In the present chapter I will examine the implications of these two approaches in religious epistemology for a central methodological question concerning philosophy of religion. How should philosophical reflection on religious belief be carried out within the perspective of faith? I will focus on one particular but very important expression of philosophical reflection on religious belief, namely natural theology. The 'perspective of faith' here will designate the Christian faith, though much of my argument will be applicable *mutatis mutandis* to other religious traditions whose doctrines are grounded in an ostensible divine revelation and systematized by way of something like dogmatic theology. Restated, then, what do these contrasting epistemologies of belief in God entail about the role of natural theology within the perspective of the Christian faith? I argue that the distinctive contribution of Reformed epistemology at this juncture is not the exclusion of natural theology from the Christian's rational reflection on God, but a critique of a particular way of carrying out this activity, the so-called pre-dogmatic conception of natural theology.

1. The Evidentialist Approach to Theistic Belief

The evidentialist approach to belief in God maintains that belief in God is rational only if there is sufficient evidence for it. This evidence must be drawn solely from human reason, from what we know or rationally believe by way of sense perception, induction, intuition, and our other natural cognitive faculties. Clearly not everyone who accepts this claim believes that there *is* sufficient evidence for belief in God. Quite a few people in fact explicitly deny it, or at least are agnostic about it. Some of these people nonetheless believe in God, but the majority of them do not. I will understand a 'theistic evidentialist' to be someone who (1) believes in God, (2) accepts the evidentialist requirement for belief in God, and (3) believes that there is sufficient evidence for belief in God. Assuming the value of rational beliefs, characteristics 1 and 2 together sanction the project of natural theology, and characteristic 3 entails the objective validity of that project.[1]

On my understanding of theistic evidentialism, theistic evidentialism entails the endorsement and objective validity of natural theology, but it does not entail that theistic belief must be based on the arguments of natural theology.

First, suppose we take a slightly stronger formulation of theistic evidentialism according to which belief in God is rational only if it is *based on* sufficient evidence, not merely that there *is* such evidence. We should not conclude from this that theistic belief is rational only if it is based on the arguments of natural theology, or any explicitly formulated argument. If a person, S's, belief, b, is based on evidence, then S has what he takes to be truth-indicating reasons for b. The person takes it that some of his other rational beliefs, b^*, provide evidential support for b. We might also suppose that b^* are causally responsible for generating or sustaining b. In this case, b is based on reasons, which he would presumably cite if he were asked why he thinks b is true. The 'supports relation' can be explicated in terms of rational argument, and a sufficiently reflective person might do just that. But prior to this, b need not be based on any explicitly formulated argument.

The point here is not to deny that the evidentialist forges a tight connection between rational belief and argument. The point is rather that logical arguments are often best taken as attempts to formally articulate more implicit grounds or evidence for belief. So the theistic evidentialist can plausibly view the arguments of natural theology as a way of *showing* the rationality of belief in God, rather than making theistic belief rational. In this way, natural theology would allow the theistic evidentialist to reflectively confirm, elaborate, and develop a more natural or spontaneous reasoning about God.[2] This kind of reflection may be important to theistic apologetics or to improving the epistemic credentials of belief in God, especially in the face of various objections to characteristic 3. It is certainly necessary to the theistic evidentialist's position, for there is no good reason to believe characteristic 3 unless one has worked though natural theology arguments.

Second, suppose we adopt a more modest version of evidentialism according to which the rationality of theistic belief requires simply the *availability* of sufficient evidence, presumably somewhere in the person's intellectual community. In this case, a theistic evidentialist need not claim that belief in God ordinarily originates from *any* kind of reasoning or inference. He might suppose that belief in God originates from testimony, religious experience, or is produced directly by God. As long as there *is* sufficient evidence, belief in God is rational. The theistic evidentialist is not committed to the further claim that this evidence must have been causally operative in producing his belief in God. Of course, an evidentialist might want to make this additional claim (and some have), but given that many of our ostensibly rational beliefs are in place prior to the consideration of evidences and the development of arguments, it may be more sensible simply to require the availability of evidence (see Wykstra 1989).

The above points highlight the fact that the evidentialist approach to belief in God is logically compatible with a variety of different accounts of the causal origin of belief in God. Belief in God may originate from argument, but it may also originate from a more spontaneous kind of inference, or it might not originate from any kind of inferential cognitive process. Thus, contrary to a common criticism (e.g., Clark 2000: 271), evidentialism does not necessarily place an unrealistic demand on our actual doxastic practices. It does, however, place an important demand on the theistic evidentialist. If someone rationally believes maintains characteristic 3, it would seem to require having reasoned to this conclusion from an examination of the arguments of natural theology.

2. Reformed Epistemology and Natural Theology

Reformed epistemology began as a critical response to the tradition of theistic evidentialism, specifically the evidentialist requirement for belief in God. In a variety of publications stretching from the 1970s to the present, Alvin Plantinga (2000), Nicholas Wolterstorff (1983), and William Alston (1991) have each challenged the idea that the positive epistemic status of belief in God depends upon argument or evidence. Reformed epistemologists have defended the *proper basicality* of theistic belief, the idea that belief in God can be rational (or possess some other sort of positive epistemic status) even if it is not based on evidence, indeed even if there is no evidence available for it. The general logical architecture of this defense defence has been to argue that there is no plausible epistemological theory that excludes taking theistic belief as properly basic. Of course, Reformed epistemologists have also presented a number of positive arguments *for* the proper basicality of belief in God. These have been largely based on the analysis of positive epistemic status and analogies between theistic belief and other kinds of ostensibly properly basic beliefs (e.g., belief in other minds, belief in the external world, sensory perceptual beliefs).

While Reformed epistemologists have relied on recent developments in general epistemology to launch their non-evidentialist approach to religious epistemology, the idea of properly basic belief in God is by no means a novel idea in philosophy of religion. In *Our Knowledge of God* (1939), John Baillie defended the idea of immediate knowledge of God over against the tradition of natural theology associated with both St. Thomas Aquinas and the Protestant scholastic tradition. In the latter part of the nineteenth century and early twentieth century, William James's 'Will to Believe' (1970 [1896]) contained a defence of the right to hold religious beliefs in the absence of evidence. In his famous *Varieties of Religious Experience* (1902), James argued that all rational discourse about God is ultimately grounded in religious experience, a direct sense of the presence of the divine. In the nineteenth century Charles Hodge, Samuel Harris, William Shedd, George P. Fisher, and Augustus Strong all argued that there is a natural knowledge of God that is immediate or intuitive and does not originate from any process of reasoning.

So Reformed epistemology must be seen as continuous with an older tradition in American philosophy of religion, indeed a tradition that arguably stretches back through Protestant scholasticism and mediaeval philosophy to ancient Greek philosophy (see Caldecott 1901; Hoitenga 1991). This continuity is particularly important from the vantage point of assessing Reformed epistemology's stance toward natural theology. There has been a strong temptation to interpret the claims of Reformed epistemology as a critique and rejection of natural theology.[3] This interpretation is mistaken. Reformed epistemology opposes theistic evidentialism, not the project of natural theology. While theistic evidentialism entails an endorsement of natural theology and its objective validity, the converse is not true.

The proper basicality thesis amounts to the claim that theistic belief has positive epistemic status for some (perhaps many) people under some circumstances in the absence of propositional evidence. While this entails the negation of the classical evidentialist requirement for theistic belief,[4] it does not entail the negation of the claim that there is evidence for theistic belief. It also does not imply that evidence cannot contribute to the positive epistemic status of belief in God in various ways. Indeed, the proper basicality thesis is compatible with there being strong evidence for theism and this evidence, at least on some occasions, playing a significant role in conferring positive epistemic status on belief in God. So there is nothing intrinsic to the proper basicality thesis that leads us in the direction of rejecting the project of natural theology. Reformed epistemology simply denies that either natural theology or the evidences it develops are necessary for the positive epistemic status of belief in God.

It is worth noting that many of the defenders of immediate knowledge of God in nineteenth-century philosophy of religion (e.g., Hodge, Shedd, Harris, Strong) also did not reject natural theology. Many of them presented a variety of theistic arguments. Although they contended that the knowledge of God is intuitive or immediate, it may nonetheless be systematically clarified, augmented, and defended by way of inference and argument. These thinkers objected to the idea that the natural knowledge of God is based solely on inference or that the knowledge of God originates from theistic proofs. Natural theology is important, as it is a scientific or reflective expression of theism, but it is grounded in the intuitive or direct awareness of God. Knowledge of God is analogous to our knowledge of the external world and other minds. Rational argument here always presupposes a more fundamental knowledge of the realities in question. Our immediate knowledge does not render inference and argument superfluous, but the latter always presupposes the former and functions as their ultimate ground.

3. Natural Theology and the Perspective of Faith

I have argued, then, that theistic evidentialism entails the endorsement and objective validity of natural theology and that there is nothing intrinsic to the idea of properly basic theistic belief that would render it incompatible with natural theology. So there can be a constructive dialogue between theistic evidentialism and Reformed epistemology concerning natural theology. Among other things, each can ask how we should view natural theology from the perspective of faith. Up to this point I have simply been considering the logical relationship between these two approaches to religious epistemology and the project of natural theology. The crucial question is how each respectively sees, or ought to see, the place of natural theology as an activity of reason within the context of faith. So let us first examine the idea of 'perspective of faith'.

A theist is rarely *just* a theist. He or she will typically belong to a particular theistic religious tradition, be it Judaism, Christianity, Islam, dualistic Vedanta Hinduism, or some other brand of religious theism. Theistic religious traditions involve both religious practices and systems of belief. With regard to the latter, theistic religious traditions make more claims about God than are included within the province of natural theology. These claims, while shaped in various ways by the experiential and practical tier of religion, are usually the deliverances of authoritative sacred texts. As such they are allegedly beyond the power of human reason to demonstrate or otherwise prove. These religious claims are divinely revealed and form the content of so-called revealed theology.

In the Christian tradition, Thomas Aquinas is well known for having distinguished between the *articles of faith* and the *preambles to the faith*. The latter are truths about God that can in principle be demonstrated by human reason. These truths include the existence, unity, goodness, and wisdom of God. The articles of faith are truths about God that reason could not even in principle demonstrate, for example, the doctrine of the Trinity, the incarnation, Christ's passion and bodily resurrection from the dead. Aquinas provides one way of drawing the lines of demarcation between natural and revealed theology, but Christian thinkers have disagreed about precisely where to draw these lines. Anselm, for example, thought that he could prove the necessity of the incarnation, and Richard of St. Victor and Bonaventure tried to prove the doctrine of the Trinity. Others, recognizing the limits of natural theology, have sought to supplement natural theology with various historical evidences of the Christian faith, especially evidences that purport to show that the Bible is a divine revelation, thereby lending indirect support to the doctrines of Scripture. Invariably, though, the Christian theist is someone whose theism is informed by a range of sources other than human reason. The two interrelated primary sources are Scripture and church tradition, which are codified in the system of dogmatic theology. So to situate natural theology within the perspective of faith involves placing natural theology in this larger doxastic context.

4. Two Rival Versions of Natural Theology

I want ultimately to argue that Reformed epistemology rejects a particular way of thinking about natural theology within the perspective of faith. But to see this in its clearest relief, I will consider in this section two rival versions of natural theology articulated in the Protestant scholastic tradition.[5] These represent different ways Christian theists have tried to relate rational reflection on the existence and nature of God to their faith perspective.

a. The Dogmatic Conception of Natural Theology

The presentation of arguments for the existence and nature of God first unambiguously appear in the Protestant tradition in Philip Melanchthon's *Loci Communes* (1535, 1543–44) and *Commentary on Romans* (1532, 1540). In the latter they appear as an elaboration and development of Romans 1.19–20, which affirms that God can be known from the created order. In the former they appear under the heading *de creatione*, a biblically based discussion of creation. In each case, it is clear that theistic arguments are directed to the Christian as a means of rationally reflecting on the data of Biblical revelation. Melanchthon develops theistic arguments in the course of articulating aspects of revealed theology, with the stated goal of strengthening the Christian's knowledge of God.[6] There is no attempt here to construct a theology of God based solely on reason.

In sixteenth-century and many seventeenth-century Protestant dogmatic systems theistic arguments were typically presented under theological prolegomena or the *locus de Deo*.[7] In these systems, though, neither theological prolegomena nor the *locus de Deo* was pre-dogmatic in nature. Both exhibit a dependence on and integration with Scripture and the correlated Christian doctrine of God, even where the dogmatic system begins with the *locus de Deo*. This explains the reliance on Scripture in the *locus de Deo*, as is illustrated in the use of the 'divine names' as a point of departure for articulating and systematizing the divine attributes (e.g., Muller (2003b: 254–72). It also explains the inclusion of the doctrine of the Trinity under the *locus de Deo* (e.g., Hyperius 1568; Musculus 1560; Danaeu 1583; Turretin 1679–85). In some instances the *locus de scriptura* is prior to the *locus de Deo* (e.g., Polansdorf 1617; Leigh 1654, and Turretin 1679–85) so it is clear that the doctrine of God rests on scriptural revelation as its foundation, not reason. Not surprisingly, we find no independent locus on natural theology, either within or prefaced to the theological system.

To be sure, we do find an apologetic use of theistic arguments among these Protestant scholastics, though in this context theistic arguments are not used to establish either theism or the Christian faith but simply to refute atheists and remove objections to the faith within the larger logical architecture of revealed theology. Francis Turretin and Edward Leigh, for example, used the proofs to refute atheists, but these arguments appear subsequent to the doctrine of Scripture under a biblically informed doctrine of God. This is, of course, entirely consistent with the instrumental use of reason in theology. There is a reasoned defence of the faith but no apologetically motivated theological prolegomenon in which natural theology is used to lay the foundations for subsequent claims about God derived from Scripture.

b. The Pre-Dogmatic Conception of Natural Theology

The influence of Cartesianism on Protestant theology in the seventeenth century contributed to an expansion of the role of reason in theology.[8] With this expansion, there was a progressive detachment of natural theology from revealed theology. Natural theology became an autonomous system of rational theology that was intended as a pre-dogmatic foundation for the Christian faith.

Some illustrations of this from the Protestant scholastics help clarify this evolution of natural theology. Jean-Alphonse Turretin presented natural theology as a system of purely rational truths accessible to reason apart from any supernatural revelation (see Klauber 1994: ch. 3). For Salomon van Til, natural theology was a prolegomenon in which a purely rational discourse on the divine existence and attributes, separated from Scripture, prepared the way for the system of revealed theology (1704, 1719: s. I. i–iii, II. i–iii). The idea of a distinct rational-theological locus upon which the biblical doctrine of God could be based further evolved during the eighteenth century under the influence of Christian Wolff and Wolffian rationalism.[9] In the works of Johann Friedrich Stapfer and Daniel Wyttenbach, a detailed discussion of the existence and attributes of God is the first port of entry to the doctrine of God, only subsequently followed by a discussion of Scripture and the Christian doctrine of God (Stapfer 1756–57).

In England, the Protestant response to Deism led many to erect a supernatural theology on the basis of a limited natural religion that encompassed the existence and attributes of God, as well a range of moral duties accessible to reason, as is illustrated in Richard Fiddes's *Theologia Speculativa* (1718) and Joseph Butler's *Analogy of Religion* (1736).

The nineteenth century would inherit this pre-dogmatic conception of natural theology, adjusted in various ways to counter the Kantian and Darwinian critique of traditional cosmological and design arguments. This arguably reached its culmination in the famous Gifford Lectures established by Lord Gifford in 1888. Gifford's goal was to provide a platform for a purely scientific or rational treatment of the existence and nature of God, independent of any claims originating from an ostensible divine revelation. Such a project, while indicative of the character of post-Enlightenment natural theology, marks a significant departure from the early Protestant scholastics.[10]

5. Evidentialism, Reformed Epistemology, and the Pre-Dogmatic Conception of Natural Theology

The dogmatic and pre-dogmatic conceptions of natural theology represent two significantly different ways in which Christian theists have tried to relate rational reflection on the existence and nature of God to their faith perspective. How should we think of evidentialism and Reformed epistemology in this regard?

a. Evidentialism and the Pre-Dogmatic View of Natural Theology

We might suppose that the pre-dogmatic conception of natural theology entails evidentialism, for it supposes that revealed theology needs to be based on a more fundamental kind of theology accessible to human reason and grounded in evidences. There is little doubt that some theologians have taken this model to imply that faith must be grounded in evidence, or that the distinctive doctrines of Christianity can be reasonably believed only on the basis of natural theology or its evidences.[11] On this view, natural theology is a prerequisite for reasonable belief in both God and the Christian revelation. However, it is not clear that the pre-dogmatic foundations model has this implication. Theistic evidentialism involves a claim about what is required for *anyone's* belief in God to be rational. The pre-dogmatic conception of natural theology entails a more restricted evidentialist requirement, a requirement for the systemic or scientific development of theology. This is a demand placed on the theologian's implicit claim to be engaging in rational discourse about God. One can be an evidentialist in this domain without being an evidentialist about rational belief.

There is of course a positive correlation between theistic evidentialists and advocates of the pre-dogmatic conception of natural theology, but this is better interpreted as a case of classical foundationalism and evidentialism in philosophy exerting causal influence on Christian dogmatics. Evidentialism, when applied to theology, led to the pre-dogmatic conception of natural theology. At any rate, situated in the context of the Christian faith, the evidentialist principle seems to entail the pre-dogmatic conception of natural theology. First, if the rationality of belief in God requires evidence, then *a fortiori* the rationality of belief in the Christian God requires evidence. While evidences of revelation play a role here, the force of such evidences arguably presupposes natural theology. So we return to natural theology foundations, which must be supplemented by Christian evidences. But secondly, theology, revealed or natural, is ostensibly *rational* discourse about God. Given the evidentialist principle, though, we can only understand the rationality of theological discourse in terms of some form of external validation. So when the Christian attempts to reflect on his belief in God in the light of the evidentialist principle, he will find in natural theology the starting point of an epistemic validation of his larger doctrine of God. In the systematic articulation of the doctrine of God, natural theology must come first and provide the basis for subsequent claims made about God from divine revelation. So there is an important evidentialist argument for the pre-dogmatic conception of natural theology.

b. Reformed Epistemology and the Pre-Dogmatic View of Natural Theology

While Reformed epistemology does not reject natural theology, its critique of evidentialism does provide, at least indirectly, a challenge to the pre-dogmatic view of natural theology. There are two considerations from Reformed epistemology that reinforce this challenge and critique.

First, according to the Reformed epistemologist, there is no *need* for a pre-dogmatic conception of natural theology because there is no need for revealed theology to be epistemically validated by natural theology, which is ostensibly the point behind the pre-dogmatic view of natural theology. Reformed epistemology defends externalist theories of knowledge, according to which knowledge is understood in terms of reliable processes of belief formation or the proper functioning of our cognitive faculties.[12] Externalist theories allow for religious knowledge independent of evidence or argument, whether of the sort found in natural theology or in Christian evidences. As long as the religious belief in question was reliably engendered or produced by properly functioning cognitive processes or faculties, the belief will have the kind of positive epistemic status sufficient – along with truth – for knowledge. This means that religious experience, tradition, and the Scriptures can be epistemically efficacious sources of belief on their own, without assistance from reason.

If one adopts an externalist epistemology, then at the reflective level it will not be necessary to do natural theology to validate the positive epistemic status of one's belief in the doctrines of revealed theology. This is not to say that natural theology will not be necessary for some other reason. It is simply to note that a shift in one's epistemological assumptions, specifically the introduction of externalism, removes the primary motive for construing natural theology as a foundation for revealed theology, namely the need for an epistemic validation of revealed theology from outside the sphere of revealed theology. For the Reformed epistemologist, the Christian is right to begin with revealed theology in his rational reflection on God.

Second, from the perspective of Reformed epistemology it is not *possible* for natural theology to constitute a rational foundation for dogmatic theology.

(1) A foundation gives a guarantee, and in the context of modern philosophy this guarantee has been understood in terms of certainty or some other powerful epistemic credential. Along with many others, Reformed epistemologists have argued that theistic proofs do not constitute rationally compelling arguments or logical demonstrations.[13] Hence, they cannot confer on belief in God the kind of epistemic credentials necessary for a foundation for revealed theology, at least not in the way envisioned historically by advocates of the pre-dogmatic model of natural theology. However strong the arguments of natural theology, they cannot confer on religious belief a greater certainty than such beliefs have on other grounds, which ostensibly involve genuine human–divine interaction (e.g., God presenting himself to us in our experience, the inward testimony of the Holy Spirit). Indeed, it would seem that in this regard, inference is inferior to other grounds for religious belief. Making the former the basis for the latter seems methodologically wrongheaded.

(2) The force of theistic arguments plausibly depends on antecedent assumptions about God and God's purposes and interactions with the world, in much the same way that our inferences about other minds and the external world depend largely on assumptions about these that we derive from a multiplicity of sources. The strength of theistic arguments is

arguably affected by what we take ourselves already to know about God from Scripture, religious experience, and church tradition. In that case, theistic arguments do not have the necessary theological neutrality required for being *pre*-dogmatic foundations for revealed theology. For example, theistic arguments seem to underdetermine God's *unlimited* power, knowledge, and goodness. However, if I already know that God is perfect, it is easier to infer with some show of plausibility God's unlimited power, wisdom, and goodness from the spatial and temporal regularities of the world. Also, the force of theistic arguments depends in part on how much weight is given to 'evil' as alleged evidence against the existence of God. The doctrines of divine providence and an afterlife taught in Scripture, however, play an important role in reducing the force of the problem of evil.

(3) Even if natural theology could produce a logical demonstration of the existence of God in a theologically neutral manner, this would woefully underdetermine *Christian* belief in God. The Christian theist is someone who believes that God is Father, Son and Holy Spirit, who became incarnate in the person of Jesus of Nazareth for the redemption of the world, and who is intimately involved in the details of our lives, guiding the church and so forth. To complete the vision of the pre-dogmatic view of natural theology, the latter would have to be supplemented by various historical evidences that support the claim that the Bible is a divine revelation. But this returns us to points 1 and 2. Are these evidences strong enough to be foundations for revealed theology?

Now the preceding considerations do not entail that natural theology has no value, but they do undercut the contention that natural theology can play the role envisioned by the pre-dogmatic conception of natural theology. Hence, Reformed epistemology must be interpreted as rejecting this particular view of natural theology.

6. Conclusion and Future Prospects

In this chapter I have examined the implications of two approaches in religious epistemology for rational reflection on God within the perspective of faith. I have argued that theistic evidentialism when employed as a principle of reflection on Christian belief in God – entails a particular conception of natural theology, namely as a rational foundation or basis for dogmatic theology. This view of natural theology as an independent system of theology separate from the theology of Scripture has dominated post-Enlightenment philosophical theology. This conception of natural theology, I have argued, stands in sharp contrast to how many of the early

Protestant scholastics thought of natural theology, namely as a rational exploration of the doctrine of God revealed in Scripture. The distinctive contribution of Reformed epistemology at this juncture is a challenge, not merely to the philosophical tradition of evidentialism, but to those segments of the post-Enlightenment Christian theological tradition that inherited from evidentialism a particular way of relating faith and reason.[14]

I have not argued here that Reformed epistemology entails an endorsement of the dogmatic view of natural theology, though the prospects for this are interesting and should be an issue of future focus for Reformed epistemologists. To what extent can the distinctive epistemological features of Reformed epistemology support a dogmatic recontextualizing of natural theology? What *is* clear, though, is that Reformed epistemology's implicit critique of the pre-dogmatic view of natural theology has opened up the possibility of a genuine re-evaluation of the relevance and function of natural theology within the perspective of faith.

Notes

1. Whereas a 'sanction' authorizes or provides a reason to pursue the project, 'objective validity' entails the success of the project.
2. A position maintained by several prominent Catholic and Protestant theologians at least since the latter part of the nineteenth century (Joyce 1924: 8–9; Maritain 1954: 2–10; Flint 1893: lecture 3; Hodge 1878: 32).
3. Plantinga perhaps unwittingly contributed to this impression in some of his earlier material, for instance his criticisms of natural theology in *God and Other Minds* (1967) and his linking the defence of properly basic belief with objections to natural theology within the Calvinistic streams of the Protestant theological tradition in 'The Reformed Objection to Natural Theology' (1980).
4. I have argued elsewhere (Sudduth 1999a; 1999b) that Reformed epistemology is compatible with various evidentialist constraints on positive epistemic status. Reformed epistemology affirms that belief in God (or, some range of theistic beliefs) often has enough warrant for knowledge independent of propositional evidence. This is compatible with the claim that (1) some *types* of theistic belief need evidence to be sufficiently warranted for knowledge and (2) there are some *circumstances* in which any kind of theistic belief requires evidence to have the degree of warrant needed for knowledge.
5. A detailed discussion of these two concepts of natural theology may be found in M. Sudduth, *The Reformed Objection to Natural Theology* (forthcoming).
6. For a detailed discussion of natural theology in Melanchthon and Melanchthon's influence on subsequent Reformed dogmatics, see Platt 1982: ch. 2.
7. For a detailed discussion of theistic proofs in Reformed scholasticism, see Muller 2003b: esp. 48–52, 153–95.

8. On the modern transformation of natural theology in Catholicism, see Broglie 1953. On shifts in Protestant orthodoxy, see Bavinck 2003: 87–89, 104–08, 183–92, 287–89, 512–17; Muller 2003b: 138–50, 193–95.
9. See Muller 2003a: 82–84, 174–76, 305–08, 396–98; 2003b: 121–29, 141–50, 193–95.
10. For a discussion of Gifford's view of natural theology in contrast to Aquinas's, see Hauerwas 2001: ch. 1.
11. 'It [natural theology] provides the rational basis on which belief in supernatural revelation can rest. For if we did not first know from the exercise of our natural powers of knowledge that there is a God, how could we accept as the Word of God anything that was claimed as a revelation from God? How could we believe in God, unless we knew first of all that there existed a God to be believed? From a religious standpoint, then, the knowledge of God such as natural theology provides is necessary as a preliminary to faith' (McCormick 1943: 5–6; see also Vos 1985: ch. 4).
12. 'Reliability' and 'proper function' are externalist conditions because we do not have introspective access to whether these conditions obtain or not.
13. See Plantinga 1992b; 1998; Clark 2000: 273, 282–84.
14. Reformed epistemologists must be viewed here as resurrecting the critique of natural theology at the heart of Dutch neo-Calvinism beginning in the latter part of the nineteenth century and represented by thinkers such as Abraham Kuyper, Herman Bavinck and Cornelius van Til. For further discussion on this, see Sudduth (forthcoming).

The Role of Trust and the Practice and Method of Philosophy of Religion

Rolfe King

Contemporary analytic philosophy of religion has seen much concentration on the grounds for *belief*, but less focus on *trust*, or on the relationship between trust and discipleship. Yet trust and discipleship are important features of religious practice. Questions such as: 'What is the relationship between trust and evidence?' or 'What is the relationship between trust, discipleship and growth in faith?' seem insufficiently explored. Work on trust has been done, particularly on the relationship between trust and faith (e.g., Swinburne 1981: 104–24; and Schellenberg 2005: 107–26), but not, as far as I am aware, taking the approach adopted here. Most deeply, there seems to have been insufficient examination of the question: 'Is it a simple matter for God, if there is a God, to win our trust?'

My approach is to focus particularly on this question, starting first with wider issues about trust and religious discipleship generally. Roughly speaking, I take belief to be belief that x is, or is not, the case (or was/will/might be, etc., where x relates to God, beings, entities, or states of affairs), and trust to be about relying on x in connection with a particular act, desire or goal. I argue that light may be shed on notions of evidence and belief in God, as well as on discipleship more generally within theistic and non-theistic religions, if the practice of philosophy of religion includes a greater focus on trust. My method is partly to use thought-experiments and the role of imagination to explore how religious trust might be formed. My primary suggestion is that trust is the pivotal turning point for the concept of 'evidence for God'.

Trust seems to be particularly relevant to discipleship and religious epistemology. Religious epistemology seems to be a *journey-epistemology*: a journey-oriented epistemology with trust required to take steps along the way. Imagine, for example, that I decide that I want to be an 'Andrewite' – a committed follower of Andrew. Andrew's words would become the rock of my life; the *foundation* on which I build my ethics, my goals and so on. I become a disciple and place my trust in Andrew. Why might I decide to do this? For any religious disciple it would seem that the reason for putting trust in Andrew (one can substitute a range of religious leaders here) is that I believe that Andrew has been to a 'place' I want to go to. Or if he has not been there at least he has learnt much from those who have. But ideally he will have at least experienced something about the place I want to go to. This seems to apply across a wide range of religious traditions – the 'place' is clearly different for each, but it is a place which is distinct from this world, the world that we see. In that sense, without wanting to go into metaphysical analysis, it is a place 'beyond' this world.

The reasoning is interesting here. Taking Andrew's words as the basis for my ethical and religious practices seems to be a form of foundationalism. His words are the foundation of my life. But it is not the kind of foundationalism that analytical philosophy has spent so much time analysing, which is about beliefs I can be certain about, either through their being self-evident, or clearly demonstrated to be true, on the basis of other certain and self-evident beliefs. My belief in Andrew's words is different from, say, my conviction that the desk I sit at is really there. For my belief in Andrew depends on his self-testimony (and perhaps that of others too) that he has been to the place which I have not been to, and cannot even fully conceive. No doubt it depends on observations of Andrew too. But it cannot depend on my observations about the place I hope to go to, for I have not been there, and what is vital for me about Andrew is that he has, or at least he knows the way. My desk, by contrast, is clearly at a place I have been to and indeed am at. It has also remained silent and offered no self-testimony, neither about being in front of me nor having visited some other place that I *hope* to go to.

The kind of foundationalism here, then, is a strange one. It involves someone else, the 'Teacher' having gone on a journey, having done the observing, and on his or her reports of that place. Note these features: (1) the Teacher having been there, or experienced something of the 'world beyond'; (2) the self-testimony of the Teacher being accurate but also appropriately designed for the disciples so they can gain a measure of understanding (not having been there); (3) the disciple trusting the Teacher as well as the self-testimony; (4) the disciple having *hope* that he or she will reach the 'place' by following the example and teachings of the Teacher.

This 'foundationalism' is strange because it is not in any way dependent on the disciple having been to that place; indeed the disciple has to trust that the Teacher has been there (from now on I shall take this to include as an alternative that the Teacher has experienced that 'place' in some way, or has been well taught by those who have). The disciple is, so to speak, at level 1 or 2, but has to trust that the Teacher has been to level 7 (the maximum, say) and thus has in some sense been to that place. Because the disciple has not been to level 7, nor can fully grasp what it is like to be at level 7, it is difficult to see what kind of evidence that he or she can have to check that the Teacher has been there. A measure of trust seems necessary. But some form of remarkable powers being exercised by the Teacher, as well as remarkable character, may appeal as a form of evidence of contact or access to a place 'beyond' this world. Even this, though, may need further evaluation given that accounts of such powers and charisma seem to coalesce around teachers and prophets who teach rather different things about the 'place' and access to it.

We are faced with a pluralistic world. There are different 'Teachers' with a variety of claims about the final place, the place of ultimate fulfilment, moral perfection, or escape from suffering. It is as if we are faced with different guides all offering to take us on a difficult journey over a mountain range to a place that we hear is wonderful. They have different accounts of the journey, and even of the place we seek. How can we choose which is the best guide?

Now, however, look at it from the point of the guide, the one who is the best guide and knows the best and safest way. How can the guide persuade people that he or she is the best guide to a place that presently they cannot really know on a journey that they can know little of?

Imagine, just for a moment, that all the major religions have got it wrong. There is a God, the creator of all, but none of the guides, prophets and teachers that are followed in the major theistic religions spoke on God's behalf. In that sense they were mistaken. So too were atheists and non-theistic religious believers. It is just that God has not yet revealed himself. So we are imagining here that all the major religions have got significant parts of their teaching, particularly about divine special revelation, simply wrong. Now try to put ourselves into God's 'place', so to speak. Of course in one sense we cannot do this because God is 'the place' we cannot envisage without some form of special revelation. But in another sense it must be true that God has to operate within what we can understand if we are to understand anything about him. What then would we find convincing that *this* is God? (Some may say: 'Nothing, given the problem of evil' – I comment on this later.) What account is to be substituted for 'this' here? How can God persuade me to go on the journey towards ever-increasing understanding of his ways and what he is like? God is now in the position of one of the guides, or, if he sends a representative (assuming he has persuaded the representative and taught him or her) then the representative is in that position. What is necessary therefore is to understand what would win my trust, or your trust, and so on. And the very moment of me accepting that 'this' is God, or that this representative speaks on God's behalf or shows forth God aright, is the very moment when two things happen: (1) trust is exercised, and (2) belief in the existence of this God is formed. Trust in either God's self-testimony or the representative's testimony on behalf of God arises at the same time as belief in the existence of this God. Belief in this God cannot, it seems, arise without trust in divine self-testimony (either direct self-testimony, or indirect self-testimony through a representative who has been self-testified to, and so on if there is a chain of testimony via several representatives).

This account is only a sketch. But it suggests avenues for more rigorous enquiry. To win my trust there must be some form of divine self-testimony. God's options seem limited here, if for now we set aside direct cognition, or direct awareness of God, or truths about God. I look briefly at these later. For now, the divine options seems to be some form of divine 'speech' and various acts of power which might demonstrate God's power over nature. (A Christian will, of course, want to add incarnation and resurrection.) If we allow that God knows the future in advance then some form of prophecy might be particularly powerful as evidence, although even then there may be suspicions of some kind of arranging of events by a powerful being who was not God, or of human reinterpretation of 'history'. Assuming this 'God' has kindly intentions towards us perhaps acts of healing, or preventing disasters might count as evidence, but dramatic worldwide events may, of themselves, not count as decisive evidence of a trustworthy being, let alone God. Consider 'Gal', a being the size of a galaxy, trying to convince us of her kindly intentions and to win our trust. She has so much power she could instantly destroy our planet. Perhaps she knows all the details of our lives too. Many may find this rather frightening. How could we ever tell she was trustworthy given the enormous difference between her and us? If Gal 'faces a problem' it seems that God does. Indeed, God's actions could seemingly be duplicated by any Gal, or super-Gal that did not have kindly intentions towards us but was out to deceive us. How could we tell the difference between the actions of God and a possible Gal or super-Gal?

It seems then that self-testifying and acts of power are necessary (setting aside direct cognition), but may not be sufficient. They seem to be a part of the necessary part of the 'structure of revelation'. By 'structure of revelation' I mean the logically necessary structure of revelation in the sense that God cannot reveal himself to us without these forms of evidence. Note, though, that we will not see these as decisive evidence until we trust the divine self-testimony. Only some strategies will work to win trust: of necessity, if God wants to win that trust then these strategies form the range within which God must necessarily move: this range sets the boundaries of the necessary structure of revelation.

Not only are some things necessary, some things seem clearly better as potential evidence for God than others. Other things being equal, one act of power is not likely to be as good as many. Some types of acts of power may be better than other types. Healing an arm may be less impressive evidence than raising someone from the dead. In short, some strategies seem better than others at overcoming potential suspicion or doubts or confusion. Things to be overcome might be called 'obstacles to revelation'. For example, as Swinburne (1992: 78) points out, it is possible people may misunderstand God's intended message when it has to be translated into different cultural contexts. So there are epistemological obstacles to revelation, as well as providential ones in bringing about a situation where God can self-testify without epistemological obstacles. Studying why some strategies might be better than others at getting round such obstacles, so that our trust might be won, is a way of identifying things that are both necessary for revelation and things that might constitute good grounds, or 'evidence' for trust. (For further details see King 2004.)

From our point of view what might count as 'evidence' seems to coincide with a picture of the kind of things God, if there is a God, might do to persuade us to trust in him. There is an implicit notion of *divine plans*. Roughly: if there is a God, true belief in God would seem to arise when 'my' understanding of the divine plan and the related activities corresponds to God's plan and activities towards me and the human race, and I believe that the divine plan reflects the kind of character that God has self-testified about having, and that I think is worthy of my trust. Trust would be exercised not just because of the belief that God will carry out his intentions, but because his character (as self-testified to) would be seen as the source of all goodness and love, and in that sense worthy above all, or of supreme worth.

This seems to be potentially part of a universal discourse, not a tradition-specific one, in the same way as questions are that the whole human race might wrestle over, when confronted with Gal or super-Gal. God is, of course, not just a bigger version of Gal. But it is like a filter. God has to come down not just to Gal-size but in forms that could potentially win our trust.

Our concept of evidence for God, whether God with whatever attributes (G_1, G_2, G_3), involves a 'picture', or grasp of a plan, of the sort of actions we think such a God would or would not do. The point at which that picture, however inchoate, seems to match what we see as evidence, if we accept it as such, could be called conversion, or the moment of decision to trust. Whether or not it is a matter of probabilities that can be specified clearly, some notion of probability seems to be operative.

Perhaps many theologians would feel uncomfortable with this idea, but anyone who thinks there is a decisive problem of evil seems to be operating along these lines. The thinking, roughly speaking, is that it is overwhelmingly improbable that an omnipotent God of love (G_1, say) would plan to permit the evils that have occurred; therefore it is overwhelmingly improbable that such a God exists. Perhaps God has much less power, along the lines of the God of the process theology (G_3, say) so *that* kind of God may exist.

Of course, one may try to exit this kind of approach altogether and deny that notions of evidence for God are proper forms of religious discourse, and that theodicies using the notion of divine plans are morally deficient (e.g., Phillips 2004). I can only offer my reflections as offering a better fit of how people do reason religiously, but a fuller reflection on trust would have to deal with this type of approach indebted to Wittgenstein, as well as arguments, such as advanced by Surin (1986: 154-63), that any notion of divine plans allowing for evil leaves one with a coldly calculating theodicy.

If I am right, however, our concept of evidence for God is bound up with notions of divine plans. 'A God of love would not plan this kind of "place" or world for us but would provide us with a better one. Therefore such a God does not exist', an atheist might say. The concept of God here is based on the powers that God has and what are seen to be the likely divine plans. A notion of divine intention is operative in terms of a vision of a 'place' that is consonant with that God. Establishing whether God exists has some similarities to establishing if a certain intention exists or existed. (Plantinga [1967] was right to draw attention to the similarities between problems about the existence of God and the existence of other minds.) Roughly: I step into your shoes to figure out what intentions you might have and then the kind of plan you might adopt to reveal those intentions. I compare your actions to those ideas and then decide if they are adequate as evidence of your intentions; if the actions observed coincide with the expected actions associated with those plans then I exercise trust in you if I think you can carry out your plans, or at least that they are my best option.

This suggests that trust (and divine plans to win that trust) may be a missing link in discussions about evidence for God. The usual discussion seems to be as follows:

Version A
1) God (versions of: e.g. G_1, or G_2, G_3, etc.)
2) Putative evidence observed, E_O
3) Discussion about G_1, G_2, G_3, etc. compared to E_O

I think the underlying logic is different. I am referring to a process that may be generally implicit and unconscious here. The logic is:

Version B
1) God (versions of: e.g. G_1, G_2, G_3, etc.)
2) Estimate of divine plan for G_1 (etc.) towards this world including likely plans to win our trust
3) Estimate of divine actions relevant to those plans, i.e., estimate of expected type of evidence, E_1
4) Putative evidence observed, E_O
5) Comparison between E_1 and E_O

A fuller account, if one was referring to a God of love, would have to split analysis between the kinds of actions such a God would do anyway just by virtue of love, and then the actions that such a God might do to reveal his love for us by gaining our trust that he is a God of love.

Although only brief, this account indicates how trust is a missing link in discussions of revelation and evidence for God (in conjunction with divine plans to win that trust). Steps 2 and 3 in Version B must be included in accounts of evidence. Philosophy of religion has often focused on G_1 and E_O but the link between G_1 and E_1 is crucial, for it is that link that links divine plans with human *trust policies*. These trust policies are the underlying rationale in our decisions to trust, or that operate where we involuntarily place our trust in someone.

It is only the link between divine plans and human trust policies which makes E_O evidence, for if E_O is accepted by someone as adequate evidence to believe in God then both a trust policy and an implicit notion of a divine plan must be involved. E_O would *only* be adequate evidence because there is an implicit comparison with E_1. If philosophers of religion look from E_O to G_1 and argue whether E_O is, or is not, adequate evidence, this is as in Version A. But that is only one half of the story and it is a disconnected one at that. There is *no direct connection* from E_O to G_1. The only connection is via E_1 and the link between G_1 and E_1. The role of trust and divine plans in gaining that trust seems therefore to be crucial to our notions of evidence for special revelation. Without this our discussions about evidence for God are disconnected; we are trying to look at observed evidence E_O and a model of God and asking if the evidence is sufficient when we have no theory about how and why the evidence might be sufficient.

Version B needs exploring in future philosophy of religion. As noted, more sophisticated analysis would factor other divine plans not (directly anyway) oriented to us. These could include the kind of actions involved in creating and sustaining the world. Arguments from design, for example, rely on a notion of divine plan. These too can only be seen as evidence, rather than just putative evidence, by someone who has begun (at least) to trust in a divine plan.

Comparisons with science could also be made: the central difference is that evidence for a special revelation of God cannot be separated from God's plan to win our trust. Physical and chemical entities have no plans to wins our trust. However, analogies get closer with beings that can have plans, especially ones that we might not readily grasp.

Perhaps, though, God does not need to give us evidence as direct cognition would suffice? Can God be known directly, independently of any evidence? Can God's presence be known to us through 'direct perception'? Can truths about God also be known like this, as Plantinga (2000) has argued? Perhaps an overwhelming vision would suffice, along the lines of Alston's (1991) arguments that God can be perceived? Briefly, I doubt if any form of direct cognition can work independently of trust or notions of divine plans. One has to trust that it is God who has caused the conviction (of awareness of his presence, or of truth about God, etc.) to arise. But even that would seem to involve trust that the one perceived had not altered our faculties so that when we think we perceive the creator we do not. Descartes thought he had a decisive argument for God's existence; armed with this we could put our trust in God that he would not allow any such evil demon or other malevolent power to deceive us. But if we accept that none of the 'proofs' of God's existence are obviously decisive to most of us, then trust is still involved. Furthermore, one must consider that such action by God would be in line with the most likely divine plan, or at least a likely plan. Imagine, by contrast, Plantinga saying that he has a conviction that God has given direct cognition of a particular truth to him, but it is unlikely that God would do such a thing. This would be incoherent. Indeed, Plantinga (2000: 272–85) even argues that that it is *likely* that if God exists, he will use direct cognition to give knowledge of himself. Plantinga thus relies on a notion of divine plans to underpin his theory of direct cognition. I suggest there are implicit notions of divine plans and an underlying rationale of trust involved in all the core claims of 'Reformed epistemology'. The underlying logic of Version B must be present.

There are links here with debates about divine hiddenness. For example, Schellenberg (1993) has argued that God could give a kind of low-level continuous awareness of his presence, along Alstonian lines. But even this would seem to require trust that it was not just a very powerful being deceiving us. And since trust is, in part, a subjective matter it may not be quite so simple for God to bring this about as Schellenberg suggests. This is not to say it is impossible, but that more analysis would be needed to see if this could be done.

Hick, as is well known, has argued (e.g., Hick 1983: 56) for the concept of epistemic distance as a justification for divine hiddenness; that God wants us to choose him freely, so he does not force himself on us by so powerful a display of evidence that there would be no choice for us but to accept God's existence. But whilst I may accept that someone who bursts into my house with blazing fireworks is clearly a person, it is not so clear that I will think that person to be trustworthy. No doubt a powerful display will convince me that this is a mighty being, but what evidence is there that this is a God of love, the most trustworthy of all? Perhaps there are ways round this for God but – as already noted – things may be learnt about the necessary structure of revelation by studying the possibilities for winning trust.

There seem to be both objective and subjective elements in winning trust. Some divine plans are clearly better than others, just as some plans in chess are better than others. Those who reject belief in God may do so for many reasons but a common one is the problem of evil. *The problem of evil is really a dispute about divine plans.* A God of love would 'obviously' do far more in terms of removing evil; he could not have had the plan to leave the world pretty much as it is; therefore such a God does not exist. The claim here is that God, if he did exist, would do far more miracles, or other acts of power. In my view we have to bracket out the existence of evil and simply ask: what would be the best plan given the world as it is? Then the discussion about evil can be conducted separately. But anyone who thinks there is a problem of evil must believe *both* in divine plans and that these would include miracles. (So *pace* Hume – it is *virtually certain* in this context that some miracles will occur if there is such a God – and indeed *certain* if they are part of the necessary structure of revelation.) For the claim is in essence that there cannot be a God, because if there were he would have planned to have intervened (and done so) with more acts of power, relies on these two beliefs.

Although there clearly is disagreement here there seems to be agreement that a God of love would want to create a perfect world, or a perfect 'place', and restore that perfect world given that things had gone wrong. This is perhaps close to an 'objective' understanding of the longer-term goals of a God of love. The dispute seems more about whether the particular plan seemingly chosen is the best one. Suffice it to say that if the problem of evil does come down to different views over divine plans, including plans to gain human trust (and any other creatures capable of trust), then the nature of trust bears further examination.

I can only gesture at some key areas and aim to open up fresh questions. Perhaps it is helpful to return to the notion of the different guides over the mountain range. Who should I choose: Robin, Sheila or Thomas? None of them may strike me as trustworthy: they may all seem dubious characters. But it still can be rational to entrust myself to one of them if they are my only options and I am desperate to cross the mountains, perhaps because my life is in imminent danger from some pursuers. Sheila might even tell me that Ulay will meet us on the highest pass because she needs his help there. I could decide to put my trust in Ulay even though I have no evidence he exists. It might still be rational to do this with limited options. This is a form of practical rationality.

So it may be rational, given my goals, to entrust myself to one of the guides, but this does not mean I believe he or she is trustworthy. I am forced to make a choice, given my goals, and thus to entrust myself to one of the guides. I entrust myself to someone even though I may have little, or even no confidence, that they are trustworthy – they may just seem the best bet. This is a passional decision, in the language of William James (1970). My desires or goals are the relevant passion. There are limited options to achieve these goals. My belief is that it is rational to entrust myself to (say) Sheila. But this is quite different from believing that Sheila is trustworthy, either generally as a person or trustworthy in terms of having the intention and ability to lead me to my goal.

Much of the discussion about faith as a 'doxastic venture' (Bishop 2002), or replies that faith is 'sub-doxastic' (Buckareff 2005), or about it being sometimes practically rational to assume God's existence, seems to be about forms of goal-oriented trust. Buckareff, for example, suggests (2005: 440) that: 'Religious faith is a *sub-doxastic* venture that involves pragmatic assuming. One assumes that p as a means to achieve a religious goal. The assumption is an action guiding assumption.'

Golding (2003) has also argued that it may indeed be a matter of practical rationality to entrust oneself to God as understood in a particular tradition. It may even be that this kind of reasoning undergirded Kierkegaard's approach, if Emmanuel (1991) is correct. Such reasoning is indeed not about having grounds for belief that God exists. Grounds for entrusting oneself to X are quite different from grounds for belief that X is trustworthy or even (as with Ulay above) that X exists. It is not belief in the existence of God. It (like its ultimate ancestry in Pascal's wager) seems more akin to hope; rationally grounded hope, but no more. My suggestion here is that the notion of hope should be researched much more in philosophy of religion. This need not just be limited to theism, for all religions seem to offer hope as an incentive to discipleship.

There may be nothing wrong with hope; it may be a necessary component of any form of religious discipleship, but it seems distinct from grounds for belief in the existence of either God or the end point of any religious journey. Fundamental to the process of grounding religious belief seems to be an appropriate link between the self-testimony of the teacher or guide one is considering trusting and the existence of the 'place' that he or she is testifying about. I can rationally put my hope in someone (so hope seems to be a form of trust) – but not believe their self-testimony. By contrast, belief in the existence of a God who has revealed himself cannot, I suggest, be separated from belief in God's self-testimony. *This cannot be separated from trust in God that God has self-testified truthfully. So it is not possible to believe in God's existence without trusting him.*

My decision to become a disciple on the basis of that new-found belief would be a different trust: to *entrust* myself to God on the basis of that self-testimony, to put my hope in him. Discipleship thus seems to involve both beliefs based on trust and entrusting oneself. (This seemingly applies to a range of religions.)

The key point here is that if belief in God's existence cannot be separated from trust in God then *it is not possible to believe in God, or to believe that there is sufficient evidence for God, unless one trusts in God.* And since knowledge incorporates true belief, this also means that *it is impossible for God to give us knowledge of himself unless we trust in him.* So trust is pivotal for the concept of evidence for God. 'Evidence' is really 'evidence on which to base one's trust'.

When considering my potential guide, Sheila, let us grant that I have some evidence that she is a trustworthy person. This may beg the question, but I am interested here in the chain of testimony. If so, the evidence is only such that it is rational for me to decide to trust Sheila. By definition the evidence is not sufficient to show that claims about the final place are true. My evidence is not that 'y is the case' (where this is a truth-claim about the 'place' or end point), but only that it is rational to trust Sheila's claim that y is the case. So even where there is an appropriate chain from the end point to Sheila I still have to exercise trust. Clearly I do not need to exercise that kind of trust if I have seen sufficient evidence, but I cannot do that until I go on the journey. If this is so, then it seems that all religious claims must involve a trust component for those who have not started the journey. To ask for decisive evidence of the end-point seems to ask for something that it may not be possible to give. Perhaps the most one can have is confidence that it is rational to trust that y is the case (where y is a claim about the end point or final 'place').

The deeper question is then whether even God can give us such confidence that it is rational to trust that y, where y relates to God's existence and love and plans for us. Consider a chain of testimony: G has testified to F, F to E, and so on down to B to A. A is the person who testifies to me. But if God is the end of the journey, is not God in the situation of G? Everything hinges on the testimony of G and only God, so to speak, has seen himself, for God can never be fully perceived, to the extent of 'seeing' or being directly aware of, the fullness of his essence (to use theological language). It is not a question of finding enough evidence that A can be trusted that he or she has been there. It is now that even when any creature arrives 'there' there must be trust that *this* is God, that *this is that* of which the prophets have spoken, if one can put it that way. God, so to speak, finally can only 'say': 'this is who I AM; trust me or you can never know me'. As noted earlier, the principle seemingly applies in reverse: unless we place some trust in him God can never give us knowledge of himself. (Here I leave unexplored the possibility of a participatory ontology: if God could so unite us with himself that in some way we could know him as we know ourselves. If possible, this would seem to be God's 'best option', but perhaps this too cannot be achieved without trust.)

Even then, there are questions about knowledge and testimony: can testimony yield knowledge if (1) there is the right causal chain or chain of reporting from someone who has knowledge? Or: (2) should someone have independent evidence that would justify belief in the testimony? Coady (1992) has explored different approaches to this these questions. In general terms I think he would see what he calls the 'fundamentalist' view as in line with question 1 and the 'reductionist' view as in line with question 2 (Coady 1992: 22–23). Whether and how testimony can be a source of knowledge is a complex matter (see Lamont (2004), for a defence of the view that belief in testimony is an intellectual virtue that can produce knowledge); suffice it to note that if the reductionist view is true, it may be impossible for God to ever give us knowledge of himself if all potential knowledge of God from special revelation is rooted in divine self-testimony, for then no independent evidence is possible.

Is it just a matter of choice, of adopting a trust policy, of different attitudes to risk and different goals, purely a subjective matter? It seems more like an investment decision, where a measure of objectivity and rational strategising can still operate. Financial advisors want to know your attitude to risk. More generally, we might speak of trust policies which combine goals, emotions, desires, attitudes to potential costs and benefits, even attitudes to beauty, and so on. This echoes and expands the notion of 'belief policies' expounded by Paul Helm (1994). A belief policy is a strategy (which may be implicit, dispositional, or explicit) for 'accepting or rejecting or suspending judgement as to the truth of propositions in accordance with a set of evidential norms' (Helm 1994: 58). Helm argues that choosing between such policies must involve reliance on another principle (or principles) which cannot itself be evidentialist.

Human desires and attitudes form part of belief and trust policies. There may be a range of investments all of which are good, but some of which would not be good for people with the attitudes to risk that did not match the profile of those investments. With trust policies and God, however, God, we may assume, if he exists, knows our desires and attitudes. So a form of evidentialism is at least partially available: given that humans have a range of trust policies God *must* choose to become detectable through those very trust policies, if he wishes to win human trust. Thus progress can be made on understanding what would be good evidence, that is, actions appropriate to generating or winning human trust. Even raising the fact of there being 'obstacles' to God revealing himself suggests that there will be a good plan to overcome those obstacles. God's options are limited simply because we are limited. To study these limits is to study features of the necessary structure of revelation.

What though is needed is to bring me to the point where I can say it is rational to trust that I know that God exists? Further study is needed to see why some plans are better than others. But note that if I can come to a point where (1) I know that it is rational to trust that I know X has accurately testified to me (whether directly, or indirectly via an appropriate testimonial 'chain') that y is the case, and (2) X has in fact so testified, and did have knowledge that (3) y is the case, and (4) only X could ever directly know y, then it seems plausible to suggest that I have a form of knowledge. Of course I do not know that I have knowledge. But *I know that it is rational to trust that I know that* y *is the case*. I can be confident, perhaps in some circumstances even certain, of that. (I suggest this is the kind of certainty Descartes should have sought.) If I can be really confident that I know that it is rational to trust that I know God, is this not assurance that I know God? If so, then I suggest God could meet the requirements of 1 to 4 here and thus provide us with knowledge of himself after all.

In conclusion, the topic of trust and the notion of a journey-epistemology merit further research by philosophers across religious traditions.[1] Trust is clearly important for the process of discipleship in religion. Furthermore, finding the rationale for sufficient trust to start the journey at all seems deeply problematic. If there is a God then the 'most difficult' thing is getting us to start the journey. Perhaps in the case of theism some 'proofs' will work. But if there are none then not even God can furnish us with proofs of his existence.

The claim that we cannot rationally believe in the existence of a God (about whom claims of special revelation are made) unless we trust in that God, highlights the significance of both trust and the notion of a journey-epistemology. Such a God cannot give evidence of his existence without self-testifying, and the evidence *is* evidence sufficient on which to base trust. It cannot be seen to be evidence without trust being exercised in God. Such evidence cannot be separated from divine plans. This is distinct from evidential criteria for the entities of physics and chemistry which neither have plans nor self-testify in order to win our trust. Journey-epistemology requires self-testimony, and a judgement that there is sufficient evidence to trust the testifier. With God evidence can only be of divine plans being enacted. If there are such plans there is such a God. It is crucial to understand why some plans are better than others. Criteria for evidence for God can only be identified as we come to understand what the best plans might be. Here is another difference from normal science: those plans must factor in *our reactions*, our trust policies; thus *the notion of evidence for God cannot be separated from our self-understanding*; our image of God is always related to our image of ourselves.

I admit I have left much unclear. We face competing claims, competing guides, albeit mercifully with some overlap. In a world with sometimes daunting religious divisions, philosophy of religion would be important if it could help us to clarify some of the issues of religious epistemology, which may be one of the roots of much religious passion. My suggestion is that analysis of trust, divine plans and the notion of a journey-epistemology through the use of imagination and thought-experiments should be a part of the method and practice of philosophy of religion in a pluralistic world.[2]

Notes

1. Although I do not have space to explore the idea of a journey-epistemology further here, it has wider application than just in philosophy of religion. For example, earlier in this chapter one could substitute 'other' for 'place' at various points. Then notions of not just God as 'the Other', but people as 'other' come into play. In this link to the concept of 'alterity' the notion of a journey-epistemology provides a bridge between analytic and continental philosophy.
2. I am grateful to David Cheetham, Adam Hood and Mark Wynn for helpful comments on earlier drafts of this essay.

The Reasonableness of Philosophy of Religion

Philip Goodchild

Philosophy of religion is largely taught as an exercise in the application of critical reason to matters of religion. The object is usually to determine whether opinions can be justified. While religious revelations, insights, and faith commitments might be private and subjective matters, critical reasoning is not. Philosophy of religion is popular and accessible, because anyone can form a rational argument on religious opinions. Nevertheless, such arguments rarely achieve persuasive conclusions. If the debate between theists and atheists seems interminable, this is not necessarily because of faulty reasoning on one side or the other. If consensus is rarely achieved through argument, this seems to be because one's opponents are blinded by their prejudices. They fail to express in their premises a fully balanced and comprehensive vision of life. The question then arises: should critical reason be concerned exclusively with the quality of arguments? Or might there be a mode of critical reason that educates people to set aside their prejudices and teaches them the art of forming a balanced and comprehensive vision of life? Which of the following modes of reasoning should take priority: the construction of rigorous arguments, the interpretation of particular meanings within a cultural and social context, the elaboration of a fundamental metaphysical perspective, the cultivation of an ethical sensitivity within thought itself, or the discernment of the most rewarding objects of faith?

Recent philosophy of religion has concentrated on the construction of rigorous argument. Philosophy called 'Continental', primarily influenced by figures as diverse as Gottfried Hegel, Karl Marx, Friedrich Nietzsche, Martin Heidegger, and Franz Rosenzweig, has concentrated more on the role hermeneutics, metaphysics, and occasionally ethics play in the formation of thought. Similarly, those within religious or theological traditions are educated into strategies of interpretation, metaphysical perspectives, ethical sensitivities, and faith commitments as essential to the formation of opinion. The question arises of whether philosophy of religion is capable of making a critical engagement with such dimensions of thought itself. There is a widespread perception among some of those who are religious, as well as those who are educated in theology or Continental philosophy, that much critical argumentation is reductive, since the true formation of thought lies elsewhere. A hegemonic model of reasoning concerned primarily with propositions rather than thought itself has excluded a more attentive engagement with religion, leaving reason as an instrument of attack or defence in what is merely a clash of opinions.

It would be far too ambitious for this chapter to attempt to bring the full resources of other intellectual traditions to bear on the model of reason dominant in contemporary philosophy of religion. Instead, I hope to subject this model to critical scrutiny, and demonstrate that there are other practices of reason within the historical canon of philosophers of religion that should not be neglected. While Spinoza or Kierkegaard might be obvious choices here, I propose to explore some often overlooked implications of the mode of reasoning practised by Anselm in his *Proslogion*.

Anselm characterized his work as 'faith seeking understanding', a definition more commonly applied to theology than to philosophy of religion. Philosophy of religion is often distinguished from theology according to the difference between reason and revelation. A clear distinction between philosophy and theology was made by Spinoza (1951: 182–99): that which derives from reason is evident to the mind through comprehension of the very reasons why it is the case; that which derives from revelation is not self-evident, but must be signified by some extrinsic sign or special grace. One may therefore understand the work of theology as follows: it concerns the interpretation of signs that are given. When revelation concerns human life, whether in the prescription of laws and rituals, the sanctification of special places, occasions, objects or person, the inspiration of esoteric knowledge, or the evocation of powerful passions,[1] then the reason why the revelation can be deemed true or authoritative is extrinsic to the revelation itself. One cannot be certain that the revelation has actually happened, was given by God, was accurately reported, and concerns later ages.[2] Instead, the reason why the revealed content is true may be projected as a purpose, end or goal which cannot be fully disclosed, at least until the revelation is fulfilled by the faithful. In the meantime, any impulse towards faith in the revelation, any agreement between the nature of the recipients and the revealed content, is felt without being understood – it belongs within the affective domain of desire, or the domain of faith, hope and charity. The work of theology consists in interpreting projected purposes, so bringing that which begins beyond understanding within the realm of understanding. It proceeds on the basis of faith or desire rather than certainty. The style of theological reasoning is cooperative: it develops a tradition and community of interpretations.[3] If the task of philosophy of religion, as a quest for wisdom concerning religious matters, is to strengthen and confirm the understanding of reasons for judgements concerning matters of religion, then there is no sharp distinction between theology and philosophy for the likes of Anselm. For Anselm, according to his Augustinian heritage, understanding is grounded in the illuminated idea. By contrast, modern philosophy of religion[4] does not rely on purposes or final causes as its ultimate reasons since the truth of such causes lacks certainty. Instead, it proceeds by disclosing reasons or causes that are already implicit and understood within thought. It is a task that may be motivated by faith as much as by doubt; it is a task that may require the conversion of the understanding as much as justification of opinion; it is a task that may be initiated by revelation as much as by a desire to know what is the case.[5] If Anselm's thought must be distinguished from modern philosophy of religion, this is not simply because his work is 'faith seeking understanding', or because it is written in the form of a prayer, as though it is merely the outworking of a subjective presupposition or dogmatic commitment. Instead, his reasoning is different: where modern philosophy appeals to 'clear and distinct' ideas that can be made explicit, Anselm's understanding is illuminated by an idea 'that is greater than can be conceived'. It will be vital to explore what is at stake in this distinction.

The sharpest divisions in philosophy of religion are not over matters of opinion, as in the debate between theists and atheists, nor are they over presupposed concepts, such as the nature of God or eternity. They are divisions over the practice of reasoning itself. Philosophers have, over the centuries, adopted quite diverse practices of thinking, each of which they assumed was 'rational'. Perhaps we no longer have the same image and practice of thought as Plato, Aquinas, Descartes, Kant, or even each other. Many of the great philosophers have found a way of renewing the practice of thought: they have thought differently (Deleuze 1994b: 51). The sharpest contemporary division lies between a rationality that is based on an exclusive ideal and an institutional hegemony, whose primary mode of reasoning is to distinguish itself from any other thought that may be deemed 'irrational', and other forms of rationality that seek to disclose and develop the dimensions of reason that are actually present in thought.

1. The Hegemonic Model of Reason

The hegemonic model in contemporary philosophy of religion subjects religious beliefs to rational scrutiny in order to determine what is the case.

It seeks to determine whether opinions are justified, warranted or probable on the basis of evidence and argument. Since the model of reason is entirely separable from religious life and practice, it can be practised by almost anyone on the basis of a superficial acquaintance with religion. Indeed, one reason for its popularity may be this very accessibility, yielding an apparent mastery over the truth of religion that is superior to those who fail to think the matter through rationally.

Implicit within this model is a subjective presupposition about the nature of thought as such: the presupposition that everyone knows what it means to think, and that to reason is to follow a universal practice whose nature has been made explicit by key figures in the philosophical canon.[6] (One might appeal here to attempts by Aristotle, John Locke, Immanuel Kant, Gottlieb Frege and Bertrand Russell to make explicit what is involved in reasoning.) Such reasoning has the following characteristic presuppositions: (1) the aim of thought is to represent what is the case, (2) such representations are most clearly and distinctly expressed in the form of propositions, (3) reason aims primarily to distinguish truth from error by recognizing the implications of evidence and argument and (4) presuppositions of arguments may also be tested by first of all representing them explicitly in the form of propositions. Any questioning of the propriety of such a model for philosophy of religion may, at first sight, be charged with defending obscurantism and irrationality. For the style of this reasoning is adversarial: the goal is to become the most proficient master of public evidence and its rational implications. The goal is to marshal reasoning and evidence so successfully, avoiding all possible questionable presuppositions, logical fallacies, and objections, that even one's most intelligent opponents have to concede that one's opinions are justified, or at least plausible. There was a name for this rule of opinion in the era of Plato's academy: sophistry.[7] For is evidence and argument sufficient to distinguish reason from sophistry? Philosophy was born in an attempt to distinguish itself from the claims to wisdom embodied in the rule of opinion.

Nevertheless, the use of evidence and argument has served modern thought well in many other spheres. My question is not about the value of such reasoning in general, but about its applicability to questions of metaphysics and religion. Three fundamental presuppositions may be called into question here. First, there is the somewhat Epicurean assumption that the world consists in a set of individuated, atomic facts: the world is the totality of what is the case. Such facts have a unitary existence in respect of relation, quality, time and existence (Kant 1929: 366): that is, they are objective (independent of the thinker), simple (having the single quality of being factual), permanent (unchanging in time), and are either true or false. Such facts may be distinguished from other facts by specific differences, according to the laws of non-contradiction and the excluded middle. This is the form under which the contents of reality may be represented. The problem with such a presupposition is that religion and metaphysics concern the character of reality as a whole more than its specific contents, and 'being is not a genus'.[8] There is a large assumption involved in thinking that reality itself or God may be individuated according to specific differences. The fallacy, here, is a paralogism described by Kant:[9] the principles of a mode of representation in thought are taken as the metaphysical form of the represented content. There is a fallacy of equivocation when 'thinking the facts' in the sense of representing them is identified with 'thinking the facts' in the sense of considering evidence of the facts. Intuition is subsumed into representation. The 'fact' becomes the primary metaphysical form.

The consequence is that this form of representation is taken as universal in rational thought. Knowledge can be taken as such if it commands assent: it has to be based on evidence that is repeatable, public, and exchangeable. The content makes no difference: whatever one's opinion, a proposition can be written to express it. This mode of reasoning may therefore seem egalitarian, democratic and universal. Reasoning can be about anything; it does not matter what. Reason therefore seems to be entirely neutral in relation to value; it may be applied to the smallest as well as the greatest issues. If reason is independent of value, are we to follow the corollary that value is independent of reason? In other words, can we propose that reason does not matter? No philosopher could accede to such a claim without facing an existential crisis. If reason has value, then there are values intrinsic to reason, values which must be intuited. One such value is objectivity itself, or the indifference of reason to its content. There is a subtle logic at work here: on the one hand, what is the case is elevated above reason since it is independent of its rational demonstration; on the other hand, reason is liberated from subordination to what is the case since it may now choose to consider whatever it wishes. One seems to grant full autonomy to the object of thought; yet, in practice, it is thought itself that gains autonomy.[10]

One may question how valuable objectivity is in reason. A further assumption implicit here is the somewhat Cartesian hypothesis that thought is independent of being. If thought is considered as a representation, then the subject has complete mastery over what it may represent. The object is entirely passive. It can contribute nothing to the construction of knowledge. If reason is independent of its content, then a true proposition remains true independently of whether it is known or demonstrated. Yet what remains somewhat mysterious is that no objective reality can be known or demonstrated independently of reason. The objectivity of objective reality can never be encountered or demonstrated, for it remains beyond reason. As such, it can only ever be an object of faith. Indeed, far from there being a sharp distinction between subjective faith and objective reason, objective reason itself rests upon the metaphysical faith that truth is objective.[11] The pretension of the contemporary philosopher of religion to judge matters of truth in regard to religion rests entirely on pretension itself: it rests on the assumption that the truth of religion is objective, and accedes to objective reasoning; it rests on the assumption that the metaphysics of objectivity is superior to any metaphysics deriving from religions.

This metaphysics of objectivity is utopian. For while the work of thinking takes time, a proposition projects a time when thinking will be complete and the truth will be known. If the world is all that is the case, designated by the complete set of true propositions, then it has the constructed eternity of a perpetual present. True propositions belong to the secular order of an abstract present age. They project a world that is to come, when all may acknowledge all truths, and all sufficient reasons for what is the case will become evident. Every proposition, considered according to a model of objectivity, projects this utopia of complete knowledge, transparency, mastery and freedom as its unattainable ideal. While thinking takes time, such reasoning is timeless and instantaneous. It has no need of thought; it is thoughtless.

Now, in order to bring about such a secular utopia, it is necessary to treat propositions as hypotheses, as possibly true, in order to discover whether in fact they are, by means of their coherence with other true propositions. There is a somewhat Parmenidean assumption involved here that 'truth is true'. This is the basis for deductive logic, since valid conclusions can then be used as valid premises for subsequent argument. Constructing an argument is therefore a matter of making one's reasons explicit, expressing them also in the form of propositions. The apparent tautology, that 'truth is true', like all tautologies, contains a projection. In a tautology, a subject is identified with a predicate, yet a subject is not a predicate since they differ grammatically; if they are to be identified, it must be in respect of a projected third term to which both subject and predicate refer. The assumption is that the projected third term, the reason that is sought, can be made explicit in the form of a proposition. It is also the assumption that the truth of propositions is objective, independent of thought, since it remains unchanged when the proposition is taken from the context of one argument where it functions as a conclusion and placed in the context of another where it functions as a premise. It is something that can only ever be assumed; it cannot be shown. For context can, of course, change the meaning of concepts, and so also the truth value of propositions. So a specific privilege is given to propositions which do appear to function in this way. Far from such reasoning being neutral in relation to its content, then, it imposes its own metaphysics as the only valid one for rational argument. Of course, the objectivity of objective truth cannot be proven. Hypotheses remain forever hypothetical. Reason therefore remains under an unlimited obligation to demonstrate the objective truth of its propositions. Faith in the secular utopia of objective reality now entails the duty to treat all propositions solely in regard to their possible objective truth, in order to see if they will appear among the saved who appear in the secular utopia of true propositions. One has a duty to make one's thought plausible so that it may be accepted by others and have a chance of proving to be true. Moreover, this rational duty can never be discharged. It overrides all other metaphysics, all other models of reasoning. It supersedes all religious obligations, for one has no obligation to that which is not true.

David Hume and Immanuel Kant have taught us that there are illusions internal to reason itself.[12] When reason is taken beyond the limits of the analysis of experience, as in metaphysics or religion, then it exceeds its proper bounds. I wish to go further: there is a quasi-religion internal to the hegemonic model of reason, one characterized by faith and obligation in respect of the thinker, as well as a self-positing, all-encompassing and exclusive dynamic in respect of thought itself.[13] This internal dynamic is the reason for its hegemony, rather than the scraps of pleasure afforded to those who demonstrate through the force of their reasoning that their opinions are more objective than those of others. The decisive flaw in this model of reason is that, by means of its three fundamental presuppositions, it substitutes representation for intuition. Since the reason for the truth of any proposition must be expressed in a further proposition, the chain of deduction must regress until it reaches those propositions that are foundational, properly basic, or agreed by consensus with one's interlocutors. In short, the whole work of philosophy, which consists in conforming thought to truth, becomes displaced by a reasoning that must first conform truth to thought. Few philosophers deny that there is something like 'intuition', the recognition of truth or of the agreement of ideas. Yet since this model of reason must first make such ideas explicit in the form of propositions, then the vital task of discovering the truth is relegated to assumption, culturally agreed consensus, or theology.[14] Hence what is amiss in much contemporary philosophy of religion is that it is constitutionally incapable of fulfilling its primary function, the quest for wisdom. Since all basic judgements are represented in the form of propositions, then philosophy of religion is becomes merely a subtle means of representing the implications of an opinion under the guise of a quest for truth.

2. Faith Seeking Understanding

Saint Anselm of Canterbury is often taken as an initiator of deductive argument in philosophy of religion through his formulation of the 'ontological argument' in the *Proslogion*. In practice, however, his image of reason differs substantially from the contemporary hegemonic model. In the first place, his address is a prayer to God. He is engaged in the monastic practice of contemplation, as one can see from his opening admonition: 'Enter into the inner chamber of your soul, shut out everything save God and what can be of help in your quest for Him' (Anselm 1998: 84). This is a pious practice of disciplining attention. In the second place, God is not to be found through the capabilities of the thinker exercising the mastery of reason, but through the grace of illumination: 'Teach me to seek you, and reveal yourself to me as I seek, because I can neither seek You if You do not teach me how, nor find You unless You reveal Yourself' (Anselm 1998: 86). The object of thought is far from passive here; God gives understanding to faith. In the third place, this thought is 'faith seeking understanding': it is a temporal process of learning and transformation in which the goal never becomes a clear and distinct idea.[15] Moreover, it is not an understanding that is universally available, but one that presupposes faith: 'For I believe this also, that "unless I believe, I shall not understand"' (Anselm 1998: 87). Anselm has more or less explicitly stated that there is no deductive argument in his address that could demonstrate the existence of God to a fool.[16]

To explain the possibility of the fool, he distinguishes two senses of 'conceiving': 'For in one sense a thing is thought when the word signifying it is thought; in another sense when the very object which the thing is is understood' (Anselm 1998: 88–89). These correspond to differing kinds of reason, one consisting of the manipulation of signs and ideas by the mind, including the use of propositions that signify what is thought to be the case, the other when the very object discloses itself to the understanding through illumination. In the latter case, thought and existence are no longer independent, but thought depends upon existence. Here, existence is no mere predicate added to a representation; existence generates thought. This is hardly surprising, given that thought actually exists. The question is whether the reasons that generate a thought can be coextensive with the reasons for its truth; it is also a question of whether existence itself is thoughtful, or merely a passive object independent of thought. Even if Anselm phrases his approach to reasoning in theological terms, such reasoning is not theological if it does not depend upon any special revelation.

The argument of the *Proslogion*, therefore, is not a *reductio ad absurdum* designed to eliminate the error of belief in the existence of no God. As Kant was later to show in his discussion of the transcendental dialectic, *reductio ad absurdum* arguments can be used to demonstrate contradictory conclusions (Kant 1929: 393–421). In other words, they are not valid in the philosophy of religion where reason is carried beyond the limits of the analysis of experience. The contrary of reason, for Anselm, is not error (mistaking one individuated fact for another) but foolishness: a failure to understand, a failure to attend to the self-disclosure of the object to the mind. The disclosure of the existence of God, for Anselm, occurs through the contemplation of greatness by means of his concept of 'that than which nothing greater can be conceived'. Those who consider the existence of God as hypothetical before it is demonstrated, such as Kant, are being foolish, because they entertain the possibility of something lesser (a God who exists in the understanding alone) than they could conceive (a God who exists in reality also). God, when understood, can only be thought of as necessary, not possible. When searching for 'that than which nothing greater can be conceived', it is wise to start looking among the category of existing things, for one will never find it among the purely hypothetical. Anselm is constrained to think of God as existing. God's necessary existence is a constraint on thought rather than a property of the idea: Anselm concludes that 'there is absolutely no *doubt* that ...', that God 'cannot be *thought* not to exist', that he is unable 'not to *understand*' God's existence (Anselm 1998: 88–89; emphasis added). One may still affirm, of course, that 'there is no God', but such an affirmation is merely foolish it is foolish to consider that which is most significant as a mere object of the imagination.[17] The constraint upon Anselm's thought is not, therefore, one of strict logical necessity. Instead, the constraint is a disciplining of the understanding about how one is to consider God: God so truly exists that he cannot be conceived not to exist. This is where Anselm encounters what he takes to be God: in the very constraint placed upon his thought – in the directing of thought itself, rather than in the passive object of an active thought – in other words, within reason as its very force of necessity.

One may distinguish three vital characteristics of Anselm's alternative conception of reason. First, the object itself speaks in the understanding. Anselm does not believe that it is greater to exist in reality than in the understanding alone simply because he prefers existence (unlike Hamlet, who is undecided). Instead, he believes it because it is actually greater to exist in reality than in the understanding alone, and this fact makes itself evident to the understanding. For if God existed in the understanding alone, 'the creature would be above its Creator – and would judge its Creator and that is completely absurd' (Anselm 1998: 88). It is precisely such absurdity, hubris or foolishness that occurs whenever one seeks to determine whether

God exists by means of reason alone.[18] For a concept of God in the understanding is made possible by the mind, and the mind, in that sense, is greater than its ideas (especially if one is undecided as to whether such a God exists, since such a concept is inevitably a representation generated by the mind). The mind itself, for Anselm, is not that than which nothing greater can be conceived (as it would be for those who only consider possible facts), for the mind exists in time, and time exists in God (1998: 98). God, for Anselm, is greater than all other things in the sense that these things can in no way exist without God (1998: 99). So the mind can conceive of that which is greater than it – it can conceive of time, for example but the object is the basis upon which the idea is formed and judged, not vice versa. So the constraint upon the mind derives from the nature of the object which is considered – 'truth and light' belong to the object of understanding primarily in its effect upon the mind, and to the mind only secondarily (Anselm 1998: 95). The constraint upon the mind, 'light and truth' itself, derives from the nature of the object which is considered. Then the contrary to such a reason is not error, but inattentiveness and misunderstanding.

Secondly, Anselm's reasoning, like those of Socrates and Descartes, also involves the discipline of turning inwards for the purpose of self-examination. To be rational is to be self-critical. Anselm learns that he is constrained to think of God as existing. Yet this, we can say following Kant, is a necessity that belongs to pure reason alone, and not necessarily to the properties of an object corresponding to an idea. When Anselm considers that than which nothing greater can be conceived, he establishes the rules for the formation of a concept of a metaphysical absolute. It makes little difference whether the absolute is considered as nature, as the world, as being, as time, or as God: the same rules should apply. The difference between the naturalist and the theist, then, concerns less the existence of an object called 'the absolute' or 'that than which nothing greater can be conceived', than it does the nature of metaphysical conditioning, and whether this is conceived according to a model of physical causality, logical entailment, emanation, or creation. Anselm's Augustinian model of metaphysics (which is not strictly Kantian), based on a doctrine of creation through the Logos (which is Christian rather than Neoplatonic), does not separate the realm of objective existence (reality) from the realm of thought (understanding) at the level of the metaphysical absolute. The distinction between understanding and reality, so applicable to objects of the imagination (such as perfect islands) or representation (such as a painting), no longer applies to God. For thought is not independent of reality: it exists in reality, and is conditioned by it.[19] To reason carefully is to understand or observe how thought is actually conditioned by existence; it is not a celebration of the freedom and mastery of thought in the imagination.[20] Anselm's rule is a way of engaging with the actual by means of the intellect instead of solely by means of the senses.

Thirdly, Anselm's reasoning involves an ongoing transformation. It is not exactly the same thing that exists in thought and in reality. If Anselm begins with faith, it is because he has a dim awareness or vague apprehension of God under the concept of that than which nothing greater can be conceived. Contemplation of this concept yields a transformation of the understanding whereby the concept is filled out and enriched. Anselm explains that although his soul 'saw both the truth and the light ... yet it did not see You because it saw You only partially but did not see You as You are' (1998: 95). God is 'light inaccessible' (96) because understanding occurs through this light, but it does not perceive the source itself. Since God alone is what he is and who he is (99), the understanding, which is not God even when it attempts to contemplate God, falls short of what it understands. The distance is no longer that between imagination and reality, the possible and the actual, but between effect and cause, conditioned and condition, understanding and reason. Anselm prays to progress until his understanding comes to fullness. Just as joy does not enter into those who rejoice, but those who rejoice enter wholly into joy (103), so it is the same with understanding: truth does not enter into understanding, but understanding enters into truth, for God permeates and embraces all things (99). God is no longer a transcendent projection of the imagination but is encountered as an immanent mode of understanding. God is at once the inaccessible object of the understanding, yet also within and around the understanding, as well as the source of illumination of the understanding – such is the significance of a Trinitarian reason.

My aim, here, is not to claim that Anselm is correct in his reasoning (after all, he only claims to understand partially).[21] My aim is to show that Anselm practises a form of reasoning that regards some of the fundamental presuppositions that structure the hegemonic model of reason as foolish. For to consider the existence of God solely in respect of its possibility, in order to attempt to establish either its truth or its necessity, as nearly all philosophical commentaries on the 'ontological argument' have done, is perhaps a little foolish.

3. A Reasonable Philosophy of Religion

How, then, are we to pursue philosophy of religion a little more wisely, once it has left the monastery for the university? In the first place, following Plato, we may pay more attention to the elaboration of the definition of concepts. For while the hegemonic model of reason attempts to eliminate all objective presuppositions apart from those grounded in consensus or evidence, including the presuppositions deriving from faith, it allows arbitrary subjective presuppositions to be smuggled in under the meaning of concepts, such as 'person', 'infinite', 'power', 'knowledge', 'free will', 'time', 'eternity', 'good', 'evil', 'nature', 'life', 'death', 'reason' and 'truth'. All too often, arguments are decided on the basis of everyday notions of such concepts which may have little relevance to the absolute. Even many of the problems pursued in philosophy of religion arise in this way, such as: 'Can God create a stone too heavy for him to lift?', 'Is God's foreknowledge compatible with free will?', 'Does God command what he does because it is good or is it good because he commands it?', 'Is God's goodness compatible with the existence of evil?' and 'Why is there something rather than nothing?' The pursuit of such problems has little merit. At best, consideration of them can disclose how everyday notions are inapplicable to metaphysical matters. The elaboration of concepts is not a matter of determining their 'true' meaning – for if there is such a true meaning, it is known to God alone. It is a matter of determining a wise understanding of such concepts, one that is compatible with the complex reality of experience. The fundamental issues that decide positions in philosophy of religion are often coextensive with other branches of philosophy, while also addressing the fundamental limits of experience embraced by religion: what is meant by life, death, enlightenment, time, love, desire, law, grace, signification, goodness, or divinity, for example? Concepts are the proper objects of philosophical thought. Judgements and opinions always follow on from concepts.

In the second place we may pay attention to the elaboration of problems. The fundamental distinction to make is between those problems that derive from judging existence by ideas (purely abstract or academic problems) and those that derive from judging ideas by existence (existential problems). Thus, 'Why is there something rather than nothing?', is a purely abstract problem because it attempts to judge existence (something) by a mere concept (nothing). Similarly, 'How is the existence of a good God compatible with the existence of evil in the world?', is an abstract problem because it attempts to judge reality by a superficial concept of 'good'. By contrast, the thought experiment of considering whether the world would be better without some apparent evil such as death (see Swinburne 1998: 212–15) is a valid work of imagination because it enables us to revise our notions of 'good' on the basis of what is actually the case. The nature of what is may be disclosed by imagining what life would be like without it.

The true philosophical problem is always that of making our thought conform to the lineaments of reality: it is to make thought enter truth, not truth enter thought. The normal operation of reason is to explore reality in an atomized and piecemeal fashion: it is to determine what is the case. By means of such individuation, truth is subordinated to freedom of thought, and sought on extrinsic grounds. The grounding of truth, by contrast, is not individuated: it cannot be effectively considered as 'what is the case' or represented in the form of a proposition. The lineaments of reality are what ground truth; they are dimensions of reality as a whole, dimensions that belong to thought as well. Such dimensions are encountered intrinsically within thought in the form of existential problems. Hence, for example, there is a true philosophical problem in determining whether space and time are dimensions of reality as such, or merely transcendental dimensions that thought uses to arrange experience (as according to Kant). On this issue, Spinoza perceived that the fundamental lineaments of reality (attributes of substance) are thought and extension. He did so by treating reality (substance) as that which is in itself and is conceived through itself, and then by finding how the intellect conceives of reality (this is his definition of attributes). The method is more important than the conclusions here. For there is no need to take Newtonian physics, which conceives of reality in terms of space and time, as the most adequate expression of reality. Religions teach variously that law, desire, unity, nature, grace, enlightenment, awareness, suchness, morality, life, goodness, truth, eternity or God characterize reality as such. The problem for philosophy of religion is not one of determining which, if any, of these religious teachings are true, nor is it a matter of reconciling competing truth-claims. It is a matter of determining how such concepts can be conceived so that reality itself is conceived in itself through them. One must endeavour to raise them to the level of the absolute. Thought rejoins existence when the character of existence is encountered as a character of thought. The difference between theology and philosophy, here, is that where theology takes such concepts as either symbols expressive of reality or analogies referring to reality, holding them on the grounds of desire, faith or revelation, philosophy seeks to discover the reasons why such concepts may disclose reality. The touchstone of philosophy is pure immanence: reality is conceived in itself and through itself.

In the third place, we may pay attention to the cultivation of insights or intuitions. In this respect, philosophy remains a spiritual exercise (Hadot 1995), even when it is conducted by atheists. In some cases, such insights vivify received doctrines and concepts. In this case, the difficulty lies in communicating such insights, since the doctrines and concepts may be well known to those who lack insight. In other cases, such insights may require the elaboration of new concepts, or even an entirely new philosophical approach or system. The effort required to comprehend the new concepts or new orientation in thought may result in the repetition of such insights in others. Yet more significant than whether philosophy is traditional, conforming to an established doctrine, or modern, creating a new thought, is the issue of how much the insight promises to enrich life. For insights always arrive as a dim awareness – one does not quite know what one knows. Thinking and being are not the same.[22] Truth is not yet true. Pure immanence is an impossible ideal. What one perceives only becomes clearer when it is reflected through another aspect of reality. Just as evolutionary advance makes possible the emergence of a host of new species to fill new environmental niches, and just as technological advance makes possible the production of a host of further new technologies, so also insights are cultivated through each other when one aspect of reality sheds light upon another. Cross-disciplinary fertilization is part of the philosophical method.

Such a philosopher of religion may enjoy a greater degree of freedom and creativity than a religious thinker or theologian. Herein lies a greater promise; as well, perhaps, as a greater danger. For the religious way of life involves a disciplined practice of directing attention. Insights must be expressed through existing concepts, opinions must conform to established doctrine, and passions must be directed in accordance with established laws and values. If religious life occasionally evokes powerful passions and energies, that energy is largely channelled into constructive social activities, although it may sometimes give rise to a dangerous enthusiasm. Similarly, as Anselm, Kierkegaard and Spinoza have taught, the philosophical path of the cultivation of insight also evokes the most powerful of emotions. If the philosopher is free to question everything, and so lacks the constraints of religious life, then there may be no constraint over the direction of such emotions or new possibilities of life other than a working body of concepts, problems and insights, and these often fall short of providing a pattern for a whole way of life, or new circumstances. This is not merely a personal problem. If the influence on the modern world of philosophers such as Descartes, Locke, Adam Smith, Kant, Marx, and Nietzsche has been immense, the consequences have not always been beneficial. This is why a philosophy (like a religion) cannot simply be evaluated according to its intrinsic rationality, but also according to its influence, outworking, and even the ways in which it is betrayed. It is not that one should hold Locke, Smith or Marx responsible for what has been done in their name, or through their reasoning. It is simply that the task of conforming thought to reality remains to be undertaken afresh in each generation. A philosophy that attends to what matters in reality, that attends to its own process of thinking, and that attends to its insights or dim awareness of reality itself at an absolute level, is the direction that should be taken by future philosophy of religion.

Notes

1. See the list of superstitions that Kant seeks to eliminate from religion within the limits of reason alone (1960: 47–48).
2. It was such an argument, formulated by Lord Herbert of Cherbury, that was essential in setting aside revelation for the sake of modern reason. Versions of such arguments were used by the philosophical founders of the modern secular state, such as Thomas Hobbes, John Locke and Thomas Paine (see Gay 1968: 43).
3. The situation is a little different, however, when revelation concerns divine life and so discloses the purpose of human life. Such a revelation is self-authenticating for it discloses its own reasons. There remains a role for theological interpretation, however, in that the meaning of all human concepts is generated and maintained in the everyday process of making sense of experience, rather than in the divine contemplation of perfect ends. In this respect, such a revelation still exceeds the limits of human reason. Where revelation may give insight to the individual, the work of theology is still necessary to give shape to a community of interpretation.
4. I take modern philosophy of religion as emerging with the work of Lord Herbert of Cherbury (see Goodchild 2002b: 3).
5. See my brief summary of some of the explicit motives of the early modern philosophers of religion in Goodchild (2002b: 5–7).
6. Such subjective presuppositions are interrogated by Gilles Deleuze (1994a: 129–67).
7. The relevant characteristic of sophistry here is not indifference to truth, nor the payment for teaching, but making the production of knowledge into an objective technique rather than requiring the moral conversion of a soul. See Plato, *Hippias Major* (Plato 1982: 281–82); see also the discussion of the sophists in Hénaff 2002: 44.
8. Aristotle's *Metaphysics*, III, 3 (998b), cited in Aquinas (1975: 127).
9. See Kant (1929: 328–67). Where Kant explores this in terms of a 'paralogism of pure, rational psychology', I have generalized this to epistemology (see Goodchild 2002a: 45).
10. There are precise analogies here with the relation of thought to God explored by Feuerbach (1989). See also the metaphysical revolution proposed by Duns Scotus, who, in order to maintain the liberty of God over human systems of reason, effectively proposes the full liberty of creatures.
11. Søren Kierkegaard's pseudonymous author, Johannes Climacus, speaks of a 'parting of the ways' between subjective and objective thought. Yet the full implication of his consideration of the subjective dimension of thought in Socrates is that 'the

truth is objectively a paradox', that is, a leap is required in objective reason (see Kierkegaard 1968: 183; 1983: 42).
12. See, in particular, the commentaries of Gilles Deleuze (1984; 1991).
13. The nearest analogy for such a human-made yet autonomous, self-propagating system, is economic value as described by Marx.
14. For example, in Alvin Plantinga's Reformed epistemology the discernment of properly basic truths is relegated to theology or revelation in the form of his Aquinas/Calvin model (see Plantinga 2000).
15. Anselm argues that God is 'something greater than can be thought' (Anselm 1998: 96).
16. He responds to Gaunilo as a Catholic, and not as a fool (Anselm 1998: 111).
17. Unless such objects of the imagination come to take on a life of their own and determine human life, as may indeed by true in the case of concepts of God, sovereignty, truth, and money.
18. See the argument of Johannes Climacus in Kierkegaard 1983: 39–41.
19. This is why Kant's critique of the ontological argument fails to apply to Anselm, for Kant presupposes that thought is a representation, entirely independent of existence (see Kant 1929: 501–07).
20. Hence Kant may wish to reject the existence or givenness of Descartes' triangle with its logically necessary three angles, but he would be foolish to reject the existence of something greater than he has previously conceived should it actually be given to him. To do so is to prefer the lesser to the greater, the hypothetical over the actual.
21. For my critical revision of Anselm's argument, see Goodchild 2005.
22. Here I part company with Spinoza, for the most that can be known is the effect of reality upon thought.

Bibliography

Abraham, W. J. (2006) *Crossing the Threshold of Divine Revelation* (Grand Rapids: Eerdmans).
Adams, M. M. (2000) *Horrendous Evils and the Goodness of God* (Ithaca, NY: Cornell University Press).
Akhtar, S. (1991) 'An Islamic Model of Revelation', *Islam and Christian-Muslim Relations* 2: 95–105.
—— (2007) *The Quran and the Secular Mind: A Philosophy of Islam* (London and New York: Routledge).
Al-Ghazali, A. H. M. (1953) *The Faith and Practice of Al-Ghazali* (trans. W. Montgomery Watt; London: Allen & Unwin).
—— (2000a) *The Incoherence of the Philosophers* (trans. M. Marmura; Provo, UT: Brigham Young University Press).
—— (2000b) *Deliverance from Error* (trans. R. McCarthy; Louisville, KY: Fons Vitae, 2nd edn).
Alston, W. (1991) *Perceiving God: the Epistemology of Religious Experience* (Ithaca, NY: Cornell University Press).
Anselm (1998) *The Major Works* (Oxford: Oxford University Press).
Aquinas (1975) *Summa Contra Gentiles Book One: God* (trans. A. C. Pegis; Notre Dame: University of Notre Dame Press).
—— (1981) *Summa Theologica* (New York, NY: Benziger Bros).
—— (1989) *Summa Theologiae: A Concise Translation* (ed. T. McDermott; London: Methuen).
Augustine (1952) *De Mendacio*, in *Treatises on Various Subjects* (ed. R.J. Deferrari; trans. M.S. Muldowney *et al.*; Washington: Catholic University Press of America).
—— (1991) *Confessions* (trans. Henry Chadwick; Oxford: Oxford University Press).
Baillie, J. (1939) *Our Knowledge of God* (New York: Charles Scribner's Sons).
Banner, M. (1999) *Christian Ethics and Contemporary Moral Problems* (Cambridge: Cambridge University Press).
Bartky, S. L. (2002) 'Suffering to be Beautiful', in C. L. Mui and J. S. Murphy (eds) *Gender Struggles: Practical Approaches to Contemporary Feminism* (Lanham, MD: Rowman and Littlefield Publishers).
Bavinck, H. (2003) *Reformed Dogmatics* (vol. 1; ed. J. Bolt; trans. J. Vriend; Grand Rapids: Baker Academic).

Bergson, H. (1965) *An Introduction to Metaphysics: The Creative Mind* (trans. M. L. Andison; Totowa, NJ: Littlefield, Adams & Co.).

Bhikkhu, T. (1993) *The Mind Like Fire Unbound* (Massachusetts: Dhamma Dana Publications).

Bhikkhu, T.N.-T. (2006) 'Kusala and Akusala as Criteria of Buddhist Ethics', *Buddhism Today*: ⟨http://quangduc.com/English/kusala.htm⟩. (accessed 4 June 2006).

Bishop, J. (2002) 'Faith as Doxastic Venture', *Religious Studies* 38: 471–87.

Bodhi, B. (1995) *The Middle Length Discourses of the Buddha* (trans. B. Ñāṇ amoli; Massachusetts: Wisdom Publications).

Bok, S. (1982) *Secrets: On the Ethics of Concealment and Revelation* (New York: Pantheon Books).

Broglie, G. de (1953) 'La Vraie notion thomiste des "praembula fidei"', *Gregorianum* 34: 341–89.

Brown, D. (2004) *God and Enchantment of Place: Reclaiming Christian Experience* (Oxford: Oxford University Press).

Buckareff, A. A. (2005) 'Can Faith be a Doxastic Venture?', *Religious Studies* 41: 435–45.

Bull, M. (1992) 'Who was the First to make a Pact with the Devil?', *London Review of Books* (May 14): 22–24.

Butler, Joseph 1736 *Analogy of Religion* (Dublin: J. Jones for George Ewing).

Byrne, P. (2003) *God and Realism* (Aldershot: Ashgate).

Caldecott, A. (1901) *The Philosophy of Religion in England and America* (London: Methuen and Co.).

Casey, E. S. (1996) 'How to get from Space to Place in a Fairly Short Stretch of Time: Phenomenological Prolegomena', in S. Feld and K. Basso (eds) *Senses of Place* (Santa Fe, NM: School of American Research Press).

Cavarero, A. (1995) *In Spite of Plato: A Feminist Rewriting of Ancient Philosophy*. (New York: Routledge).

Cheetham, D. (2005) 'The University and Interfaith Education', *Studies in Interreligious Dialogue*, 15/1: 16–35.

—— (2006) 'Some Preliminary Reflections on the Role of Theology and Religion in Public Discourse', in V. Mortensen (ed.) *Religion and Society: Crossdisciplinary European Perspectives* (Højbjerg: Forlaget Univers).

Chung, S. (2007) 'Existence of God and Worldview: MacIntyrean Account of "The Five Ways"' (unpublished seminar paper).

Cixous, H. and C. Clément (1986) *The Newly Born Woman* (trans. B. Wing; Minneapolis: University of Minnesota Press).

Clark, K. J. (1990) *Return to Reason: A Critique of Enlightenment Evidentialism and a Defense of Reason and Belief in God* (Grand Rapids: Eerdmans).

—— (2000) 'Reformed Epistemology Apologetics', in S. Cowan (ed.) *Five Views on Apologetics* (Grand Rapids: Zondervan Publishing House).

Clark, K. J. (ed.) (1992) *Our Knowledge of God: Essays on Natural and Philosophical Theology*. (The Hague: Kluwer).

Clayton, J. (2006) *Religions, Reasons and Gods: Essays in Cross-Cultural Philosophy of Religion* (prepared by A. M. Blackburn and T. D. Carroll; Cambridge: Cambridge University Press).

Clooney, F. (2001) *Hindu God, Christian God* (Oxford: Oxford University Press).

Clouser, R. (2005) *The Myth of Religious Neutrality: An Essay on the Hidden Role of Religious Belief in Theory* (South Bend, IN: University of Notre Dame Press, rev. edn).

Coady, C. A. J. (1992) *Testimony: A Philosophical Study* (Oxford: Clarendon Press).

Coakley, S. (ed.) (2003) *Religion and the Body* (Cambridge: Cambridge University Press).

Connolly, W. (1999) *Why I am Not a Secularist* (Minneapolis: University of Minnesota Press).

Daneau, L. (1583) *Christianae isogoges* (Geneva: E. Vignon).

Dann, G. E. (2006) *After Rorty: The Possibilities for Ethics and Religious Belief* (London: Continuum).

Davidson, H. A. (1974) 'The Study of Philosophy as a Religious Obligation', in S. D. Grotein (ed.) *Religion in a Religious Age* (Cambridge: Association for Jewish Studies).

Davis, S. T. (2006) *Christian Philosophical Theology* (Oxford: Oxford University Press).

Dawkins, R. (1998) *Unweaving the Rainbow: Science, Delusion and the Appetite for Wonder* (Boston and New York: Houghton Mifflin).

Deleuze, G. (1984) *Kant's Critical Philosophy* (trans. H. Tomlinson and B. Habberjam; London: Athlone Press).

—— (1991) *Empiricism and Subjectivity* (trans. C. V. Boundas; New York: Columbia University Press).

—— (1994a) *Difference and Repetition* (trans. P. Patton; London: Athlone Press).

—— (1994b) *What is Philosophy?* (trans. G. Burchill and H. Tomlinson; London: Verso).

Deol, J. (2001) 'The Eighteenth Century Khalsa Identity: Discourse, Praxis and Narrative', in C. Shackle, G. Singh and A. Mandair (eds) *Sikh Religion, Culture and Ethnicity* (Surrey: Curzon).

Dooyeweerd, H. (1999) *In the Twilight of Western Thought: Studies in the Pretended Autonomy of Philosophical Thought* (Collected Works, B/4; ed. J. K. A. Smith; Lewiston, NY: Edwin Mellen Press).

Eliade, M. (1965) *The Two and the One* (New York: Harper Torchbooks).

Emmanuel, S. (1991) 'Kierkegaard's Pragmatist Faith', *Philosophy and Phenomenological Research*, 51: 279–302.

English, A. C. (2006) *The Possibility of Christian Philosophy: Maurice Blondel at the Intersection of Theology and Philosophy* (Radical Orthodoxy Series; London: Routledge).

Faber, B. (2006) 'Ethical Hermeneutics in the Theatre: Shakespeare's Merchant of Venice', in K. Vanhoozer, J. K. A. Smith, and B. E. Benson (eds) *Hermeneutics at the Crossroads* (Bloomington: Indiana University Press).

Feuerbach, L. (1989) *The Essence of Christianity* (trans. G. Eliot; Amherst: Prometheus Books).

Feyerabend, P. (1970) 'Consolations for the Specialist', in I. Lakatos and A. Musgrave (eds) *Criticism and the Growth of Knowledge* (Cambridge: Cambridge University Press) pp. 197–230.

Fiddes, R. (1718–20) *Theologia Speculativa* (Dublin: John Hyde, George Grierson and Richard Gunne).

Flew, A. (1961) *Hume's Philosophy of Belief* (London: Routledge).
—— (1966) *God and Philosophy* (New York: Dell).
Flew, A. and MacIntyre, A. (eds) (1955) *New Essays in Philosophical Theology* (London: SCM).
Flint, R. (1893) *Theism: Being the Bard Lecture for 1876* (New York: Charles Scribner's Sons, 7th edn).
Foucault, M. (1988) *The History of Sexuality*, vol. 3: *The Care of the Self* (trans. R. Hurley; New York: Vintage).
Freud, S. (1974) *The Standard Edition of the Works of Sigmund Freud* (ed. James Strachey; London: Hogarth).
Fuller, P. (2005) *The Notion of Ditthi in Theravada Buddhism: The Point of View* (London: Routledge).
Gadamer, H.-G. (1989) *Truth and Method* (New York: Crossroad).
—— (1993) *Truth and Method* (trans. J. Weinsheimer and D. G. Marshall; New York: Continuum, rev. edn).
Gallagher, S. (2005) *How the Body Shapes the Mind* (Oxford: Clarendon Press).
Ganeri, J. (2002) 'Why Truth? The Snake Sūtra', *Contemporary Buddhism* 3/2: 127–39.
Gay, P. (1968) *Deism: An Anthology* (Princeton: D. Van Nostrand).
Gethin, R. (1997) 'Wrong View (micchā-dit t hi) and Right View (sammā-diṭṭhi) in the Theravāda Abhidhamma', in Dhammajoti *et. al.* (eds) *Recent Researches in Buddhist Studies* (Hong Kong: Y. Karunadasa Felicitation Committee, Colombo & Chi Ying Foundation) pp. 211–21.
Gilson, E. (1993) *The Spirit of Medieval Philosophy* (trans. A. H. C. Downes [1933]; Toronto: PIMS).
Goldenberg, N. (1995) 'The Return of the Goddess: Psychoanalytic Reflections on the Shift from Theology to Thealogy', in U. King (ed.) *Religion and Gender* (Oxford, UK and Cambridge, USA: Blackwell).
Golding, J. (1992) 'Faith and Doubt Reconsidered', *Tradition* 26: 33–48.
—— (1997) 'Maharal's Conception of the Human Being', *Faith and Philosophy* 14:444–57.
—— (2003) *Rationality and Religious Theism* (Aldershot: Ashgate).
Gombrich, R. F. (1996) *How Buddhism Began: The Conditioned Genesis of the Early Teachings* (London: Athlone Press).
Goodchild, P. (2002a) *Capitalism and Religion: The Price of Piety* (London: Routledge).
—— (2002b) *Rethinking Philosophy of Religion: Approaches from Continental Philosophy* (New York: Fordham University Press).
—— (2005) 'Proslogion', in B. E. Benson and N. Wirzba (eds) *The Phenomenology of Prayer* (New York: Fordham University Press).
Griffith-Dickson, G. (2005) *The Philosophy of Religion* (London: SCM Press).
Griffiths, P. J. 1997 'Comparative Philosophy of Religion', in P. L. Quinn and C. Taliaferro (eds) *A Companion to Philosophy of Religion* (Oxford: Blackwell) pp. 615–20.
Hadot, P. (1995) *Philosophy as a Way of Life: Spiritual Exercises from Socrates to Foucault* (ed. A. I. Davidson; trans. M. Chase; Oxford: Blackwell).
Harrison, V. S. (2006) 'The Pragmatics of Defining Religion in a Multi-Cultural World', *International Journal for Philosophy of Religion* 59: 133–52.

—— (forthcoming) 'Feminist Philosophy of Religion and the Problem of Epistemic Privilege', *Heythrop Journal*.

Hartshorne, C. (1968) 'The God of Religion and the God of Philosophy', in *Talk of God: Royal Institute of Philosophy Lectures, 1967–68* (vol. 2; London: Macmillan) pp. 152–67.

Harvey, P. (1990) *An Introduction to Buddhism* (Cambridge: Cambridge University Press).

Hauerwas, S. (2001) *With the Grain of the Universe: The Church's Witness and Natural Theology* (Grand Rapids, MI: Brazos Press).

Hebblethwaite, B. (2005) *Philosophical Theology and Christian Doctrine* (Oxford: Blackwell).

Hegel, G. W. F. (1988) *Lectures on the Philosophy of Religion. One-Volume Edition. The Lectures of 1827* (trans. P. C. Hodgson; Berkeley: University of California Press).

Heidegger, M. (1962) *Being and Time* (trans. J. Macquarrie and E. Robinson; London: SCM).

—— (1969) 'The Onto-Theo-logical Constitution of Metaphysics', in M. Heidegger, *M. Identity and Difference* (trans. J. Stambaugh; San Francisco: Harper & Row).

—— (1992) 'Phenomenological Interpretations with Respect to Aristotle: Indications of the Hermeneutic Situation' (trans. M. Baur [1922]) in *Man and World* 25: 355–93.

—— (2002) *The Essence of Truth* (London: Continuum).

Helm, P. (1994) *Belief Policies* (Cambridge: Cambridge University Press).

Hénaff, M. (2002) *Le Prix de la Verité* (Paris: Éditions de Seuil).

Hick, J. (1983) *The Second Christianity* (London: SCM Press).

—— (1989) *An Interpretation of Religion* (New Haven: Yale University Press).

Hodge, A. A. (1878) *Outlines of Theology* (Chicago: Robert Carter and Brothers, rev. edn).

Hoitenga, D. J. (1991) *From Plato to Plantinga: An Introduction to Reformed Epistemology* (Albany: State University of the New York Press).

Holbach, P.-H. T. Baron d' 1770 *Système de la nature* (2 vols; London); ET: *System of Nature* (trans. H. D. Robinson; New York: Burt Franklin, 1970).

Holder, J. J. (2006) 'The Purpose and Perils of Comparative Philosophy', in E. S. Nelson (ed.) *The SACP Forum for Asian and Comparative Philosophy*, 23/46: 35–51. (Published online www.sacpweb.org)

Horner, I. B. (trans.) (1963–64) *Milinda's Questions Vol.1* (London: Pali Text Society).

Hyperius, A. (1568) *Methodus theologiae* (Basel: Ioannem Oporinum).

Irigaray, L. (1993) *Sexes and Genealogies* (trans. G. C. Gill; New York: Columbia University Press).

Jakobsh, D. (2003) *Relocating Gender in Sikh History* (New Delhi: Oxford University Press).

James, W. (1902) *Varieties of Religious Experience* (New York: Longmans, Green and Co.).

—— (1970) 'The Will to Believe' [1896], in G. Mavrodes (ed.) *The Rationality of Belief in God* (Eaglewood Cliffs, NJ: Prentice-Hall) pp. 161–83.

Jantzen, G. M. (1999) *Becoming Divine: Toward a Feminist Philosophy of Religion* (Bloomington: Indiana University Press).

John Paul II (1998) *Fides et Ratio* (Sydney, NSW: St Paul's Publications).

Johnson, K. D. (2007) *Theology, Political Theory, and Liberalism: Beyond Tolerance and Difference* (Cambridge: Cambridge University Press).

Joyce, G. H. (1924) *Principles of Natural Theology* (London: Longmans, Green and Co.).
Kalupahana, D. (1976) *Buddhist Philosophy: A Historical Analysis* (Hawaii: University Press of Hawaii).
Kant, I. (1929) *A Critique of Pure Reason* (trans. N. K. Smith; Basingstoke: Macmillan).
—— (1960) *Religion within the Limits of Reason Alone* (trans. T. H. Greene and H. H. Hudson; New York: Harper Brothers).
—— (1996) 'An Answer to the Question: What is Enlightenment?', in *Practical Philosophy* (trans. and ed. M. J. Gregory; Cambridge: Cambridge University Press) pp. 11–22.
Kellner, M. (2006) *Must a Jew Believe Anything?* (Oxford: Littman Library of Jewish Civilization).
Keown, D. (1992) *The Nature of Buddhist Ethics* (London: Macmillan).
Kierkegaard, S. (1968) *Concluding Unscientific Postscript to the Philosophical Fragments* (trans. D. F. Swenson; Princeton: Princeton University Press).
—— (1983) *Philosophical Fragments* (trans. H. V. Hong and E. H. Hong; Princeton: Princeton University Press).
King, R. H. (2004) 'Obstacles to Revelation' (unpublished PhD thesis: University of Birmingham).
Klauber, M. I. (1994) *Between Reformed Scholasticism and Pan-Protestantism: Jean-Alphonse Turretin (1671–1737) and the Enlightened Orthodoxy at the Academy of Geneva* (Selinsgrove: Susquehanna University Press).
Klein-Franke, F. (1995) 'Al-Kindi', in S. H. Nasr and O. Leaman (eds) *History of Islamic Philosophy* (London: Routledge) pp. 165–77.
Kripke, S. (1980) *Naming and Necessity* (Oxford: Blackwell).
Kuhn, T. (1970) *The Structure of Scientific Revolutions* (Chicago: University of Chicago Press, 2nd edn).
Kuyper, A. (1943) *Calvinism: Six Stone Foundation Lectures* (Grand Rapids: Eerdmans).
Lakatos, I. (1970) 'Falsification and the Methodology of Scientific Research Programs', in I. Lakatos and A. Musgrave (eds) *Criticism and the Growth of Knowledge* (Cambridge: Cambridge University Press) pp. 91–196.
Lamm, N. (1972) 'Faith and Doubt', in N. Lamm (ed.) *Faith and Doubt: Studies in Jewish Thought.* (New York: Ktav).
Lamont, J. R. T. (2004) *Divine Faith* (Aldershot: Ashgate).
Leaman, O. (ed.) (1998) *The Future of Philosophy: Towards the Twenty-First Century*, (London: Routledge).
Leigh, E. E. (1654) *Body of Divinity* (London: A.M. for William Lee).
Levinas, E. (1969) *Totality and Infinity* (trans. A. Lingis; Pittsburgh: Duquesne University Press).
Lindbeck, G. (1984) *The Nature of Doctrine: Religion and Theology in a Postliberal Age* (Louisville, KY: Westminster/John Knox Press).
Lindberg, D. and Numbers, R. (eds) (1986) *God and Nature: Historical Essays on the Encounter between Christianity and Science* (Berkeley, Los Angeles, and London: University of California Press).
Livingston, D. (1984) *Hume's Philosophy of Common Life* (Chicago: University of Chicago Press).

Long, D. S. (2006) 'The Way of Aquinas: Its Importance for Moral Theology', *Studies in Christian Ethics* 19: 339–56.

McCormick, J. F. 1943 *Scholastic Metaphysics: Part II, Natural Theology* (Chicago: Loyola University Press).

MacIntyre, A. (1977) 'Epistemological Crises, Dramatic Narrative, and the Philosophy of Science', *Monist* 60: 453–72.

—— (1984) *After Virtue* (Notre Dame: University of Notre Dame Press, 2nd edn).

—— (1988) *Whose Justice? Which Rationality?* (Notre Dame: University of Notre Dame Press).

—— (1989) 'Epistemological Crises, Dramatic Narrative, and the Philosophy of Science', in S. Hauerwas and L. G. Jones (eds) *Why Narrative? Readings in Narrative Theology* (Grand Rapids, MI: Eerdmans) pp. 138–57 (reprint of MacIntyre 1977).

—— (1990) *Three Rival Versions of Moral Enquiry: Encyclopaedia, Genealogy, and Tradition* (Notre Dame: University of Notre Dame Press).

Magee, B. (1997) *Confessions of the Philosopher* (London: Phoenix).

Mandoki, K. (1998) 'Sites of Symbolic Density: A Relativistic Approach to Experienced Place', in A. Light and J. Smith (eds) *Philosophy and Geography III: Philosophies of Place* (New York: Rowman & Littlefield Publishers) pp. 73–95.

Maritain, J. (1954) *Approaches to God* (New York: Harper and Brothers Publishers).

Masek, L. (2000) 'Petitionary Prayer to an Omnipotent and Omnibenevolent God', in *Philosophical Theology: Reason and Theological Doctrine* (Proceedings of the American Catholic Philosophical Association, 74) pp. 273–83.

Mehta, J. L. (1990) *Philosophy and Religion: Essays in Interpretation* (Delhi: ICPR).

Melanchthon, P. (1532) *Commentary on Romans* (Wittenberg: Joseph Clug).

—— (1535) *Loci Communes* (Wittenberg).

—— (1540) *Commentary on Romans* (Strasburg: apud Cratonem Mylium).

—— (1543–44) *Loci Communes* (Basel).

Midgley, M. (1992) *Science as Salvation: A Modern Myth and its Meaning* (London and New York: Routledge).

Milbank, J. (1990) *Theology and Social Theory: Beyond Secular Reason* (Oxford: Blackwell).

Milligan, G. (1922) *Here and There Among the Papyri* (London: Hodder and Stoughton).

Muller, R. (2003a) *Post-Reformation Reformed Dogmatics* (vol. 1; Grand Rapids: Baker Academic).

—— (2003b) *Post-Reformation Reformed Dogmatics* (vol. 3; Grand Rapids: Baker Academic).

Murphy, F. A. (2004) 'Gilson and Chenu: The Structure of the *Summa* and the Shape of Dominican Life', *New Blackfriars*, 85: 290–303.

Murphy, N. (1990) *Theology in the Age of Scientific Reasoning* (Ithaca, NY and London: Cornell University Press).

—— (1996) *Beyond Liberalism and Fundamentalism: How Modern and Postmodern Philosophy Set the Theological Agenda* (Valley Forge, PA: Trinity Press International).

—— (1998) *Anglo-American Postmodernity: Philosophical Perspectives on Science, Religion, and Ethics* (Boulder, CO: Westview Press).

Murphy, N. and Ellis, G. F. R. (1996) *On the Moral Nature of the Universe: Theology, Cosmology, and Ethics* (Minneapolis: Fortress Press).

Musculus, W. (1560) *Loci communes* (Basel: Johann Herwagen).

Nauriyal, D. K., Drummond, M. and and Lal, Y. B. (eds) (2006) *Buddhist Thought and Applied Psychological Research: Transcending the Boundaries* (London: Routledge).

Ni, P. (2006) 'Traversing the Territory of Comparative Philosophy', in E. S. Nelson (ed.) *The SACP Forum for Asian and Comparative Philosophy*, 23/46: 17–34. (Published online www.sacpweb.org)

Niebuhr, R. (1949) *The Nature and Destiny of Man* (vol. 1; New York: Charles Scribner's Sons).

Nietzsche, F. (1967) *Ecce Homo* [1888] (trans. W. Kaufmann; New York: Vintage).

—— (1979) 'Truth and Lies in the Non-moral Moral Sense', in *Philosophy and Truth: Selections from Nietzsche's Notebooks of the Early 1870s* (trans. and ed. D. Breazeale; Amherst, NY: Humanity Books) pp. 79–91.

—— (1995) *Human, All Too Human* (trans. G. Handwerk; Stanford: Stanford University Press).

—— (2001) *The Gay Science* (trans. J. Nauckhoff; Cambridge: Cambridge University Press).

Nussbaum, M. (1997) *Cultivating Humanity: A Classical Defense of Reform in Liberal Education* (Cambridge, MA: Harvard University Press).

Ochs, P. (2006a) 'Morning Prayer as Redemptive Thinking', in C. C. Pecknold and R. Rashkover (eds) *Liturgy, Time, and the Politics of Redemption* (Grand Rapids: Eerdmans) pp. 50–90.

—— (2006b) 'Philosophic Warrants for Scriptural Reasoning', *Modern Theology* 22: 465–82.

Olivelle, P. (1998) *The Early Upanishads: An Annotated Text and Translation* (New York: Oxford University Press).

Pascal, B. (1958) *Pensees* (New York: E. P. Dutton).

Pattison, G. (2001) *A Short Course in the Philosophy of Religion* (London: SCM).

Pecknold, C. C. and Rashkover, R. (eds) (2006) *Liturgy, Time, and the Politics of Redemption* (Grand Rapids: Eerdmans).

Phillips, D. Z. (1999) *Recovering Religious Concepts: Closing Epistemic Divides* (London: Palgrave).

—— (2004) *The Problem of Evil and The Problem of God* (London: SCM).

Pickstock, C. (1998) *After Writing: On the Liturgical Consummation of Philosophy* (Oxford: Blackwell).

Plantinga, A. (1967) *God and Other Minds: a Study of the Rational Justification of Belief in God* (Ithaca, NY: Cornell University Press).

—— (1980) 'The Reformed Objection to Natural Theology', *Proceedings of the American Catholic Philosophical Association* 15: 49–63.

—— (1981) 'Is Belief in God Properly Basic?', *Nous* 15/1, reproduced in W. Rowe and W. Wainwright (eds) (1998) *Philosophy of Religion: Selected Readings* (Fort Worth, TX: Harcourt, Brace and Jovanovich, 3rd edn, 1998) pp. 472–81.

—— (1992a) 'Augustinian Christian Philosophy', *Monist* 75: 291–320.

—— (1992b) 'Belief in God', in R. Boylan (ed) *Introduction to Philosophy* (New York: Hartcourt, Brace, and Jovanovich) pp. 390–96.

—— (1993) 'A Christian Life Partly Lived', in K. J. Clark, *Philosophers Who Believe* (Downers Grove, IL: InterVarsity Press) pp. 45–82.

—— (1998) 'Christian Philosophy at the End of the Twentieth Century', in J. Sennett (ed.) *The Analytic Theist: An Alvin Plantinga Reader* (Grand Rapids, MI: Eerdmans Publishing Company) pp. 339–40.

—— (2000) *Warranted Christian Belief* (New York: Oxford University Press).

Plantinga A. and N. Wolterstorff (eds) (1983) *Faith and Rationality* (Notre Dame: University of Notre Dame Press).

Plato (1982) *Hippias Major* (trans. P. Woodruff; Oxford: Basil Blackwell).

Platt, J. (1982) *Reformed Thought and Scholasticism: The Arguments for the Existence of God in Dutch Theology, 1575–1650* (Leiden: E. J. Brill).

Polansdorf, A. P. von (1617) *Syntagma theologiae christianae* (Geneva: Iacobi Stoer).

Quine, W. V. O. (1951) 'Two Dogmas of Empiricism', *Philosophical Review* 60: 20–43.

Quinn, P. L. (2005) 'Religious Diversity: Familiar Problems, Novel Opportunities', in William J. Wainwright (ed.) *The Oxford Handbook of Philosophy of Religion* (Oxford: Oxford University Press) pp. 392–417.

Robbins, J. (1991) *Prodigal Son/Elder Brother: Interpretation and Alterity in Augustine, Petrarch, Kafka, Levinas* (Chicago: University of Chicago Press).

Ronkin, N. (2005) *Early Buddhist Metaphysics: The Making of a Philosophical Tradition.* (London: Routledge).

Rorty, R. (1979) *Philosophy and the Mirror of Nature* (Princeton: Princeton University Press).

—— (2003) 'Analytic and Conversational Philosophy', in C. G. Prado (ed.) *A House Divided: Comparing Analytic and Continental Philosophy* (Amherst, NY: Humanity Books) pp. 17–32.

Ross, T. (1985) 'The Implicit Theology of Carl Sagan', *Pacific Theological Review* 18(2): 24–32.

Ryle, G. (1990) *The Concept of Mind* [1949] (London: Penguin).

Saddhatissa, H. (trans.) (1994) *The Sutta-Nipāta* (Surrey: Curzon Press).

Schellenberg J. (1993) *Divine Hiddenness and Human Reason* (Ithaca, NY: Cornell University Press).

—— (2005) *Prolegomena to a Philosophy of Religion* (Ithaca, NY: Cornell University Press).

—— (2007) *The Wisdom to Doubt: A Justification of Religious Skepticism* (Ithaca: Cornell University Press).

—— (forthcoming) *The Will to Imagine: A Justification of Skeptical Religion* (Ithaca: Cornell University Press).

Scruton, R. (1992) 'Imagination', in D. Cooper (ed.) *A Companion to Aesthetics* (Oxford: Blackwell).

Seamon, D. (1980) 'Body-Subject, Time-Space Routines, and Place-Ballets', in A. Buttimer and D. Seamon (eds) *The Human Experience of Space and Place* (London: Croom Helm) pp. 148–65.

Shapiro, M. B. (2003) *The Limits of Orthodox Theology: Maimonides' Thirteen Principles Reappraised* (Oxford: Littman Library of Jewish Civilization).

Sharma, A. (1997) *The Philosophy of Religion: A Buddhist Perspective* (Delhi; New York: Oxford University Press).
Singh, Guru G. 1973 '*Bacitra Natak*', in *Sabdarath Dasam Granth* (vol. 1; Patiala: Punjabi University).
Singh, H. (1983) *The Heritage of the Sikhs* (New Delhi: Manohar Publications).
—— (1992) *Encyclopaedia of Sikhism*. (Patiala: Punjabi University).
Singh, N. K. (1993) *Feminine Principle in the Sikh Vision of the Transcendent* (Cambridge: Cambridge University Press).
—— (2004) 'The Body of the Gurus: Sikh Scripture from a Contemporary Feminist Perspective', *Religious Studies and Theology* 23: 27–52.
—— (2005) *The Birth of the Khalsa: A Feminist Re-Memory of Sikh Identity* (Albany: State University of New York Press).
Singh, S. (1944) *Philosophy of Sikhism* (Lahore: Sikh University Press).
Smith, J. K. A. (1997) 'The Art of Christian Atheism: Faith and Philosophy in Early Heidegger', *Faith and Philosophy*, 14: 71–81.
—— (1999) 'Dooyeweerd's Critique of "Pure" Reason', introduction to H. Dooyeweerd, *In the Twilight of Western Thought: Studies in the Pretended Autonomy of Philosophical Thought* (Collected Works B/4; ed. J. K. A. Smith; Lewiston, NY: Edwin Mellen Press).
—— (2000) *The Fall of Interpretation: Philosophical Foundations for a Creational Hermeneutic* (Downers Grove, IL: InterVarsity Press).
—— (2002) *Speech and Theology: Language and the Logic of Incarnation* (London: Routledge).
—— (2004) *Introducing Radical Orthodoxy: Mapping a Post-Secular Theology* (Grand Rapids: Baker Academic; Carlisle: Paternoster).
Spinoza, B. (1951) *A Theologico-Political Treatise* (trans. R. H. M. Elwes); New York: Dover Publications).
Sprengnether, M. (1990) *The Spectral Mother: Freud, Feminism, and Psychoanalysis* (Ithaca, NY: Cornell University Press).
Stapfer, J. F. (1756–57) *Institutiones theologiae polemicae universae, ordine scientifico dispositae* (5 vols; Heideggerum & Socios).
Stout, J. (1981) *The Flight from Authority: Religion, Morality, and the Quest for Autonomy* (Notre Dame: University of Notre Dame Press).
Stump, E. (1979) 'Petitionary Prayer', *American Philosophical Quarterly* 16: 81–91.
Stump, E. (ed.) (1993) *Reasoned Faith: Essays in Philosophical Theology in Honor of Norman Kretzmann* (Ithaca, NY: Cornell University Press).
Sudduth, M. (1999a) 'The Internalist Character and Evidential Implications of Plantingian Defeaters', *The International Journal for Philosophy of Religion* 45: 167–87.
—— (1999b) 'Proper Basicality and the Evidential Significance of Internalist Defeat: A Proposal for Revising Classical Evidentialism', in G. Bruentrup and R. K. Tacelli (eds) *The Rationality of Theism* (Dordrecht: Kluwer Academic Press).
—— (forthcoming) *The Reformed Objection to Natural Theology* (Aldershot: Ashgate).
Surin, K. (1986) *Theology and the Problem of Evil* (Oxford: Blackwell).
Swinburne, R. (1981) *Faith and Reason*. (Oxford: Clarendon Press, 1981).
—— (1992) *Revelation: From Metaphor to Analogy* (Oxford: Clarendon Press).

—— (1998) *Providence and the Problem of Evil* (Oxford, Clarendon Press).
—— (2004) *The Existence of God* (2nd edn) (Oxford: Clarendon Press, 2nd edn).
Taylor, C. (2004) *Modern Social Imaginaries* (Durham: Duke University Press).
Til, S. van (1704) *Theologiae utriusque compendium* (Lugduni Batavorum: apud Jordanum Luchtmans).
—— (1719) *Theologiae utriusque compendium* (Leiden).
Turner, J. (1985) *Without God, Without Creed: The Origins of Unbelief in America*. (Baltimore, MD: Johns Hopkins University Press).
Turretin, F. (1679–85) *Institutio theologiae elencticae* (Geneva: apud Samuelem de Tournes).
Vandervelde, G. (2005) ' "This is My Body": The Eucharist as Privileged Theological Site', in J. K. A. Smith and J. H. Olthuis (eds) *Radical Orthodoxy and the Reformed Tradition* (Grand Rapids: Baker Academic) pp. 263–76.
Vasu, R. B. S. C. (trans.) (1912) *The Vedāntasūtras of Bādarāyan a with the Commentary of Baladeva* (Allahabad: The Pān in i Office).
Vos, A. (1985) *Aquinas, Calvin, and Contemporary Protestant Thought: A Critique of Protestant Views on the Thought of Thomas Aquinas* (Grand Rapids: Eerdmans).
Ward, G. (2001) *Cities of God* (London: Routledge).
—— (2006) 'The Future of Religion', *Journal of the American Academy of Religion* 74/1: 179.
Walshe, M. (trans.) (1995) *The Long Discourses of the Buddha* (Boston: Wisdom).
Webster, D. (2005) *The Philosophy of Desire in the Buddhist Pali Canon* (London: Routledge).
Welch, C. (1972) *Protestant Thought in the Nineteenth Century: Volume 1, 1799–1870* (New Haven: Yale University Press).
Wesselius, J. (1997) 'Points of Convergence Between Dooyeweerdian and Feminist Views of the Philosophic Self', in J. H. Olthuis (ed) *Knowing Other-Wise: Philosophy at the Threshold of Spirituality* (Bronx, NY: Fordham University Press) pp. 54–68.
Westphal, M. (1993) *Suspicion and Faith: The Religious Uses of Modern Atheism* (Grand Rapids, MI: Eerdmans).
—— (1999) 'Overcoming Onto-Theology', in J. D. Caputo and M. Scanlon (eds) *God, the Gift, and Postmodernism* (Bloomington: Indiana University Press).
White, H. (1978) *Tropics of Discourse: Essays in Cultural Criticism* (Baltimore and London: Johns Hopkins University Press).
Williams, B. (2002) *Truth and Truthfulness* (Princeton: Princeton University Press).
Williams, R. (1984) ' "Religious Realism": On not quite Agreeing with Don Cupitt', *Modern Theology*, 1: 3–24.
Wilson, T. D. (2002) *Strangers to Ourselves: Discovering the Adaptive Unconscious* (Cambridge, MA: Harvard University Press).
Wolterstorff, N. (1976) *Reason Within the Bounds of Religion* (Grand Rapids: Eerdmans).
—— (1983) 'Can Belief in God be Rational if it has no Foundations?', in A. Plantinga and N. Wolterstorff (eds) *Faith and Rationality* (Notre Dame: University of Notre Dame Press) pp. 135–86.
Wright, A. (2004) *Religion, Education and Post-modernity* (London: Routledge).

Wright, N. T. (2000) 'Paul's Gospel and Caesar's Empire', in R. A. Horsley (ed.) *Paul and Politics: Ekklesia, Israel, Imperium, Interpretation* (Harrisburg, PA: Trinity Press International) pp. 161–62.

Wykstra, S. J. (1989) 'Toward a Sensible Evidentialism: On the Notion of "Needing Evidence"', in W. L. Rowe and W. J. Wainwright (eds) *Philosophy of Religion: Selected Readings* (New York: Hartcourt, Brace and Jovanovich, 2nd edn) pp. 426–37.

Wynn, M. (forthcoming) 'God, Pilgrimage and Acknowledgement of Place', *Religious Studies*.

Yearley, L. H. (1990) *Mencius and Aquinas: Theories of Virtue and Conceptions of Courage* (Albany: State University of New York Press).

Index

Abbasids 65
Abraham 47, 62
Abraham, W. 144
Abrahamic tradition 5, 6
Adams, M. 133, 145n. 2
Advaita Vedanta 76, 81, 83
  advaitic 76
  vedantic 117
Aesthetic(s) 28, 42, 48, 71, 106, 107, 114, 118, 119.
  art 21, 46, 48, 49, 50, 107, 114
Agnosticism 15, 22, 29, 69, 96
  agnostic 15, 161
Akhtar, S. 5, 72n. 1, 72n. 3
akusala 95
Alston, W. 10, 149, 160, 163, 181
Anabaptist 32
  Anabaptist-Christian tradition 44
Analogical 60, 62, 143
Analytic philosophy of religion 89, 148, 157, 174
Ananda 82
Anderson, B. 142
Anglo-American philosophy of religion 3, 4, 11, 32, 146, 160
anicca 95
Anselm 13, 14, 37, 165, 189–90, 195–98, 201, 203, 203n. 15, n. 16, n. 19, n. 21
  Proslogion 189, 195
Anthropology 10, 70, 135, 137, 138, 141
Anti-realist(s) 8, 113–14
Apologetics 21, 39, 42, 52, 89, 91, 93, 162
Aquinas 37, 40, 47, 50, 86, 111, 145n. 3, 148, 150–53, 163, 165, 173n. 10, 190, 202n. 8, 203n. 14.
  Thomism 71
  Aristotelian-Thomist tradition 35, 40

Aristotle 40, 47, 56, 86, 146n.17
  Aristotelian tradition(s) 37, 47
Atheism 4, 29, 40, 41, 72n. 3
  atheists 41, 167, 176, 188, 190, 200
  atheistic claims 2
Augustine 36, 50, 78, 109, 154
  and Anselm 197
  Augustinian tradition(s) 13, 36, 37, 40, 109
  Augustinian heritage 190

Baillie, J. 163
Baisakhi 127
Baladeva 81
Banner, M. 159n. 4
Bartky, S.L. 130
Bavinck, H. 173n. 8, n. 14
Bergson, H. 114
Bhai Rupa 132n. 3
Bhikkhu, Thich Nhat-Tu, 99n. 11
Bibi Bhani 126
Bishop, J. 183
Blondel, M. 145n. 3
Body, the 9, 11, 18, 118–20, 122–27, 129–31, 144, 158
Bok, Sissela 80, 81
Bonaventure 165
Brown, D. 156
Buber, M. 72n. 2
Buckareff, A.A. 183
Buddhism 7, 76, 87–99
  enlightenment 24, 92, 94, 99n. 7, 103
  Madhyamaka Buddhism 83, 85
  Therevada Buddhism 88
  'Undetermined Questions' 92
Bull, M. 20, 146n. 20
Byrne, P. 113, 159n. 9

Caitanya 81
Caldecott, A. 164
Calvinism 138, 173n. 14
Candrakīrti 77, 86
Casey, E. 151
Cavarero, A. 120–21
Cheetham. D. 7, 8, 115n. 2, 116n. 6, 187n. 2
  Christianity 4, 16, 22, 23, 32, 40, 43, 53, 89, 91, 140, 165, 168
  Christendom 41
  Christian philosophy 89, 90, 143, 145n. 3
  Christian theism 3
  Christian tradition 3, 37–40, 42–44, 150, 165
  non-Christian tradition 4
Chung, S. 37
Cixous, H. 121
Clark, K.J. 145n. 2, n. 5, 162, 173n. 13
Clayton, J. 8, 109, 111, 114
Clément, C. 121
Clooney, F. 8, 104, 111
Clouser, R. 140, 146n. 21
Coady, C.A.J. 185
Coakley, S. 146n. 19, 147n. 31
Cognitive stories 6, 84–86
Common sense 61
Connolly, W. 146n. 25
Conservative conformism 2, 30
Constantine 43
  Constantianism 43
Contemplation 13, 120, 195, 196, 198, 202n. 3 (see Meditation)
Continental philosophy 2, 13, 134, 139, 146n.13, 187n. 1, 188, 189
Corrosive cynicism 30
Croce, B. 118
Crusades 43
Cuneo, T. 147n.31
Curiosity (intellectual) 17, 20–22, 103

Daly, M. 129
Dann, G.E. 145
Davidson, H. A. 47
Davis, S. 134, 145n. 2
Dawkins, R. 42, 91

Deleuze, G. 190, 202n. 6, 203n. 12
Dennett, D. 91
Derrida, J. 145n. 8
Descartes, R.
Desire 6, 8, 10, 13, 18, 98, 138, 175, 189–90, 199, 200
desires 6, 12, 36, 81, 183, 185, 186.
Dhamma 82, 91, 92
Dialogue (critical) 103, 105, 107–09, 114.
Discipleship 12, 175, 183, 184, 186
diṭṭhi 95–97
  micchā-diṭṭhi 95–96
  sammā-diṭṭhi 95–97
Dogmatic theology 161 (see Natural Theology)
Dooyeweerd, H. 21, 139, 146n. 21
Drummond, M. 99
dukkha 88, 95

Eliade, M. 128
Emmanuel, S. 183
Empiricism
  empirical observation 20
  empirical discoveries/findings 34
  empirical evidence 38, 39, 90
English, A.C. 145n. 3
Enlightenment, 103, 199, 200
  Enlightenment tradition 3, 35, 37, 40, 43, 105–07, 138, 139, 141
  post-Enlightenment 168, 171, 172
Epistemology/ies 3, 5, 6, 11, 32–36, 38, 41, 42, 60, 67, 72, 74, 78, 79, 84, 85, 89, 90, 108, 113, 115, 133–36, 139–41, 145, 146, 148, 150, 155, 157, 158, 160–73, 178, 181
  epistemic distance 182
  epistemological obstacles 178
  epistemic point of view 149
  epistemic spaciousness 114
  journey-epistemology 175, 186, 187, 187n. 1, 12
Ethics 4, 10, 11, 12, 33, 36, 41, 48, 50, 72n. 2, 75, 76, 87, 94, 118, 127, 130, 139, 146n. 17, 175, 188
  ethics of self-deception 80–84
  theological ethics 153

Evidence 5, 11, 13, 36, 38, 39, 41, 63, 64, 67, 95, 96, 174, 177–87
  evidentialism(t) 161–63, 168–71, 172, 172n. 4, 185, 186
  evidential(ist) approach 11, 13, 14, 160, 161
  evidential atheism 40
  non-evidential 11, 25, 160–63
  self-evident 12, 63, 175, 176
Evil 41, 43, 60, 111, 133, 171, 176, 179, 181, 182, 199
Evolution(ary) 41, 57, 201
  of natural theology 167
Experience 9, 21, 22, 34, 42, 61, 66, 69, 90, 95, 98, 102–06, 119, 121, 124, 128, 129, 134, 136, 137, 146n. 14, n. 17, 165, 170, 175
  embodied 137
  experiential epistemology 90
  experiencing God 67
  experience of self/lessness 81, 83
  mystical 51, 108
  perceptual 149
  religious 39, 50, 51, 137, 149, 160–63, 170, 171

Faber, B. 146n. 15
Faith 1, 4, 5, 7, 11, 13, 14, 25, 29, 36, 49, 51–54, 61–66, 68–71, 89, 90, 124, 134, 137, 140–2, 160, 161, 165, 168, 171, 172
  and reason 4, 69, 71, 72, 172
  Christian 161, 165, 167, 169
  faith-based belief 91
  'faith seeking understanding' 13, 189, 190, 195
  Jewish 5
Fanaticism 14, 52, 64
Feminism(t) 8, 9, 20, 22, 28, 57, 117–32, 146n. 22
Feyerabend, P. 34, 39
Fichte, J.G. 103
Fiddes, R. 168
Fideism 53
  fideist 5, 53
Fisher, G. 163
Five k-s 9, 118, 127, 128, 130, 131
Flew, A. 145n. 1

Flint, R. 172n. 2
Form(s) of life 9, 10, 21, 22, 24, 134, 136–38, 141, 146n. 19
Foundation(s) 36, 37, 39, 41, 61, 72, 167–71, 175
  foundational(ism) 5, 32, 37, 134, 138, 139, 169, 175, 194
  foundationalist 134
  non-foundationalist 134, 139, 145n. 8
  post-foundationalist 141
Free will 17, 18, 199
Frege, G. 191
Freud, S. 41, 120, 122
Fuller, P. 100n.13

Gabbai, M. 47
Gadamer, H.-G. 130, 134, 139
Galileo 34
Gallagher, S. 146n.19
Game(s) 7, 75, 88, 110
Ganeri, J. 6, 99n. 8
Gay, P. 202n. 2
Genealogy 84, 103, 119, 120
  genealogical tradition 40
Gethin, R. 96, 97
al-Ghazali 5, 65, 66, 70, 73n. 7
Gifford, Lord 168
Gilson, E. 140, 145n. 3, 146n. 26
Globalization 4, 50, 105, 106
  global perspective 105
  global project 108, 110
  global scepticism 26
Goldenberg, N. 122
Golding, J. 4, 5, 47, 51, 115n. 1, 183
Gombrich, R. 97
Goodchild, P. 13, 202n. 4, n. 5, n.9, 203n. 21
Greek Philosophy 56, 59, 64–66.
Griffith-Dickson, G. 111
Griffiths, P.J. 111, 116n. 5
Guru Arjan 123
Guru Gobind Singh 9, 123, 125–28, 130–32
Guru Nanak 119, 123

Hadith 72n. 4
Hadot, P. 102, 138, 200

Halbfass, W.   114
Hanifah, A.   66
Harrison, V.   116n. 4, 146n. 22
Hartshorne, C.   153
Harvey, P.   99
Hauerwas, S.   140, 173n. 10
Hebblethwaite, B.   133, 145n. 2
Hegel, G.W.F.   103, 105, 106, 110, 118, 188
Hegemonic model (of reasoning)   189, 190–95, 198, 199
Heidegger, M.   84, 134, 137–39, 145n. 8, n. 10, 146n. 14, n. 17, 147n. 28
Helm, P.   185
Hénaff, M.   202n. 7
Herbert of Cherbury   202n. 2
Heresy   57
  heretic(s)   43, 55, 68
Hermeneutics   60, 66, 112–15, 118, 134, 188
  hermeneutics of suspicion   41, 118
  hermeneutical philosophy   104
  hermeneutical strategies/styles   13, 104, 111
Hick, J.   22, 31n. 3, 93, 94, 110, 116n. 5, 145n. 9, 182
Hinduism   165
Hindu(s)   1, 6, 24, 28, 93, 104, 111, 123, 126, 127, 130, 140
  philosophy   75
  texts   6, 76
History/Historical
  account   36
  accidents/events   33, 39
  argument   35
  comparison   109
  contexts   111, 112
  evidence   36, 41, 44, 165, 171
  reason   35
  historically conditioned   33
Hobbes, T.   202n. 2
Hodge, C.   163, 164, 172n. 2
Hoitenga, D.J.   164
Holbach, P.-H. T. Baron d'   40
Holder, J.   109, 110
Hood, A.   187n. 2
Horner, I.B.   86n. 8
Hume, D.   27, 40, 42, 50, 114, 182, 194

Husserl, E.   137, 139
Hyperius, A.   167

'Ibn Rushd   65
Imagination   8, 10, 20, 30, 35, 102, 105, 112, 114, 115, 118, 119, 129, 143, 144, 174, 186, 196–99, 203n.17,
  imaginary   114, 118, 119, 121
Incarnation(s)   125, 126, 150, 165, 177
Incommensurability   108, 109, 112, 114, 115
Indian philosophy   6, 85
  brahman   24, 81
  brahmanical   99n. 5
  guhya   76
  māyā   85
Intellect, the   16, 20, 36, 55, 61, 62, 64, 198, 200 (*see* Mind, the)
Irigaray, L.   120, 130
Islam   5, 53, 59, 60, 62, 65–67, 70, 71, 72n. 3, 165
Islamic philosophy   5, 60, 61, 67, 72n. 2
  ʿ*aql*   61
  ʿ*aqliyy*   61
  ʿ*ilm al-riyal*   72n. 4
  ʿ*ulama*   70
  al-ʿalimun   70
  al-ʿaqida   69
  al-falsafa   59
  faqih   70
  fiqh   66
  kalam   69
  naqliyy   61

Jakobsh, D.   118
James, W.   163, 183
Jantzen. G.   22, 31n. 2, 117, 121
John Paul II   150–52
Johnson, K.D.   146n.25
Joyce, G.H.   172
Judaism   45, 52–59.
  Jews   5, 24
  Jewish   2, 4, 60, 72n. 2, 123, 140, 145n. 9
    morning prayer   144
    philosophy   45, 54–58.

Kalapuhana, D. 90
Kant, I. 31n. 3, 36, 86n. 4, 103, 105, 114, 190–92, 194–97, 200, 201, 202n. 1, n. 9, 203n.19
   Kantian 139, 168, 197
Kellner, M. 57
Keown, D. 99n.11
Kierkegaard, S. 67, 183, 189, 201, 202n. 11, 203n. 18
'al-Kindi 61, 65, 66, 73n. 5
King, R. 11, 116n. 7
Klauber, M.I. 167
Klein, M. 122
Klein-Franke, F. 73n. 5
Kripke, S. 159n. 6
Kṛṣṇa 85
Kuhn, T. 33, 34, 39
kusala 98
Kuyper, A. 138, 139, 146n. 20, 173n. 14

Lakatos, I. 34, 39
Lal, Y.B. 99
Lamm, N. 51
Lamont, J.R.T. 185
Leaman, O. 102
Leftow, B. 133
Leigh, E.E. 167
Levinas, E. 135, 140, 146n. 26
Liberal(s) 28, 39
   democracy 50
   post-liberal 141, 146n. 16, 147n. 30
Lindbeck, G. 146n.16
Lindberg, D. 43
Liturgy/ical 8, 9, 10, 134–47
   prayers 123
Livingstone, D. 42
Locke, J. 130, 191, 201, 202n. 2
Locus de Deo 166, 167
Loew, J. 47
Logos 154, 197, 124
Long, D.S. 145

MacIntyre, A 3, 10, 32, 33–36, 37, 40, 42–44, 134, 139, 141, 144, 145
Madrasah 70
Magee, B 102

Mahābhārata 76
Maimonides, M. 5, 55
Malik ibn Anas 66
Maṇḍanamira 78
Mandoki 153
Maritain, J. 172n. 2
Marx, K. 41, 188, 201
Marxism 43
   Marxist 43
Masek, L. 146n. 12
McCormick J.F. 173n. 11
Meditation 7, 51, 90, 92, 99
   (*see* Contemplation)
   Meditative 98
Mehta, J.L. 86n. 10
Melanchthon, P. 166, 172n. 6
Menander 82
Mencius 111
Meta-discourse 45, 54
Metaphysics 8, 13, 32, 65, 74, 85, 188, 191–92, 194, 197
   as matricide 120
   and objective truth 193
   metaphysical 9, 13, 23, 25, 33, 61, 94, 120, 128, 158, 175, 188, 192, 197, 199
   metaphysical absolute 197
   Sikh metaphysics 117, 118, 120, 128, 130, 131
Method 79, 87, 115, 175
   and conceptions of God 149
   and liturgy 135
   literary 104
   methodology 1, 71
   and Buddhism 88
   and comparative philosophy of religion 105–06, 111–12, 115
   and philosophy 56, 105–6, 201
   and practice (of philosophy of religion) 1, 4, 7, 14, 105–06, 111–12, 115, 150, 155, 157, 158, 187
   and prejudice 68
   and rationalism 137
   scientific 72
   Spinoza's 200
   and texts 85
   and truth 64

Midgley, M. 42, 43
Milbank, J. 10, 109, 134, 139, 141, 146n. 24
Milligan, G. 58n. 1
Mind, the
  and body 18, 120, 122
  believer's 67
  and contemplation 196
  deception of 83
  human 67, 85
  philosophy of – *see* Philosophy of mind
  rational 66
  re-orientation of 80, 90
  of God 36
Modernity 38, 139
Muller. R. 166, 172n. 7, 173n. 8, 173n. 9
Murphy, F.A. 145n. 3
Murphy, N. 1, 3, 10, 32, 39
Musculus, W. 167
Mutakallim 70
Mysticism 51, 59
  mystical 57, 108
  mystic 112

Nāgārjuna 86
Nāgasena 82
Ñāṇamoli 99n. 12
Narrative 33, 34, 35, 75–78
  narratives 6, 11, 34, 77, 108, 113
Natural sciences 3, 32, 148
Natural theology 11, 89, 114, 160–72
  dogmatic 11, 166, 170–72
  pre-dogmatic 167–72
Naturalism 3, 27, 29, 40, 42–44
  naturalist 27, 40–44, 197
  naturalist tradition 33, 40, 42, 44
Nauriyal, D.K. 99n. 1
Neoplatonic 197
Neutrality 109, 133, 134, 171
  myth of 140–41
Ni, P. 101, 105
Nibbana/nirvana 24, 92, 93, 94, 95
Niebuhr, R. 63, 64
Nietzsche, F. 40, 41, 50, 75, 79, 80, 113, 117, 188, 201
Numbers, R. 43
Nussbaum, M. 108, 112
Nyāya 77

Objective genitive 102, 116n. 5, 133
Ochs, P. 114, 146n. 12
Olivelle 86n. 9
Ontological argument 14, 148, 195, 198, 203n. 19
Opinio 38
Otto, R. 142
Oxford philosophy 102

Pagan 59, 62, 63
Paine, T. 202n. 2
Paley, W. 37,
Pali Canon 88, 94, 95, 96
Paradigm 33, 74, 120–21, 130, 142, 147n. 27
Participation 10, 134–35, 142, 144
Pascal, B. 47, 53, 54
Patriarchy,
  patriarchal 8, 117, 118, 119, 120, 122, 124, 131
  androcentric 8, 118, 120, 131
Pattison, G. 102, 113
Pecknold, C.C. 147n. 30
Perception 114, 115, 120, 155, 161, 181, 189
  perceptual beliefs 10, 149, 150, 152, 155, 156
Persuasion 13, 104, 115
Phenomenology 70, 81, 83, 137, 142, 159
Phillips, D. Z. 22, 31n. 2, 179
Philo 50, 56
Philosophical theology 3, 7, 37, 39, 60, 71, 101, 133, 136, 142, 147, 150, 171
Philosophy of mind 18, 74, 107
Philosophy of science 33, 34, 39
Pickstock, C. 143
Pilgrimage 11, 156, 158
Place, concept of 10, 150
  genius loci 10, 151–53
  genius mundi 154, 155
  knowledge of 150, 155
Plantinga, A. 22, 133–34, 139, 140, 159n. 1, 160, 163, 172n. 3, 179, 181, 203n. 14
Plato 36, 56, 75, 79, 80, 120, 190, 191, 198
  Platonic 34, 36, 56, 61

Pluralism 44n. 1, 50, 57, 93–94, 145n. 9, 146n. 25
  pluralist 91, 93, 139, 140, 176, 187
  pluralistic hypothesis 110
Polansdorf, A.P. von 167
Polanyi, M. 139
Politics 4, 46, 48, 49, 50
  political 20, 50, 59, 64, 65, 67, 68, 72, 108, 109, 112, 118, 123, 124, 142
Postmodern 3, 32, 108, 134, 146n. 20
  Postmodernism 134, 145n. 8
  Postmodernist 20, 22, 28, 30
  Postmodernity 106
Practice
  liturgical 134–47
  and method *see* Method
  social practice 10, 33, 41, 130–31
  of philosophy of religion 1, 4, 14, 19, 63, 88, 93–94, 102, 105, 107–08, 110–12 115, 142–44, 150, 155, 157–59, 174, 187, 190, 191
  praxis 8
Pre-theoretic 8
  pre-discursive 8, 11, 158
Probable 38, 39
  probability 38, 178
  probable reasoning 38–39
Process theology 179
Proper basicality 149, 163, 164
Protestant 39, 63, 166–68, 172
  Protestant Scholasticism 163, 164, 166–8
Protreptic narratives 6, 77
Ptolemy/Ptolemaic 34

Quine, W. V. O. 33
Quinn, P.L. 116n. 3

Radhakrishnan 86n. 1
Radical Orthodox/y 28, 143, 145n. 7
Ramanuja 114
Rashkover, R. 147n. 30
Reason
  age of 60
  and revelation 5, 72, 189
  Cartesian rationalism 10, 61, 137, 138
  practical rationality 183

Reductionism 32, 136, 141
Referentialism 32
Reformation, the 38
  Radical Reformation 32
Reformed epistemology 11, 133–34, 139, 140, 141
Relativism/t 33–4
Revelation 2, 5, 12, 39, 50, 61, 61–62, 64, 65, 68, 69, 71–72, 79, 137, 140, 144, 146n. 26, 161, 165–68, 169, 171, 173n. 11, 180, 189, 190, 200
  and reason *see* Reason and revelation
  'obstacles to revelation' 178
  special 176, 180–81, 185, 186, 195
  structure of 177–78, 182
Richard of St. Victor 165
Robbins J. 146n. 26
Ronkin, N. 99n. 2
Rorty, R. 36–37, 104, 145n. 8
Rosenzweig, F. 188
Ross, T. 42
Russell, B. 191
Ryle, G 104

Sagan, C. 41
Salvation 41–42, 94
Sāṃkhya 77
Santayana, G. 52
Scepticism 2, 15–16, 19, 22, 24, 26–30, 108, 149
Schellenberg, J.L. 1–3, 4, 7, 22, 25, 27, 31n. 3, n. 4, n. 6, 115n. 1, 174, 181
Schleiermacher, F. 39
Scholasticism 71
  Buddhist 89, 92
  Islamic 71
  Protestant *see* Protestant Scholasticism
Science 3, 4, 17, 26, 34, 36, 46, 48–50
  analogies with God 149–50, 153
  and Christianity 32, 43
  cognitive 146n. 19
  historicization 33
  late mediaeval 34
  and morality 43
  naturalist world view 41–44
  philosophy of *see* Philosophy of science

Science (*continued*)
  and religion 4, 21, 32, 36, 48, 50
  and rationality 39, 43
  scientific evidence and evidence for God 181, 187
  scientific method *see* Method
Scientia 38
Scruton, R. 114
Seamon, D. 159n. 7
Second-order discourse 110, 156
Secular
  secular age 68, 72
  secular reason 5, 10, 69, 71, 134, 138, 139–41
Self, the 6, 74–86
  no-self *(anatta)* 75, 95
Shapiro, M. B. 57
Sharma, A 99n. 9
Shedd, W. 163, 164
Sikhism 9, 117, 118, 126, 129
  Mother (as Ultimate reality) 119, 122, 131
  Sikh philosophy 9
Singh Sabha writers 117
Singh, Bhai Chet 132n. 3
Singh, Harbans 132n. 3
Singh, Nikky-Guninder K., 8–9, 127, 132n. 1
Singh, Sher 117
Sirah 72
Smith, Adam 201
Smith, James K. A. 9–10
Social imaginary 10, 142–3
Socrates 56, 197, 202n. 11
Spinoza, B. 189, 200, 201, 203n. 22
Sprengnether, M. 120
Stapfer, Johann F. 167
Stout, J. 38
Strong, Augustus 163, 164
Stump, E. 133, 145n. 2, 146n. 11
Subjective 9, 12, 129, 141
subjective genitive 133
Sudduth, M. 11
Sunni 65, 66
Surin, K. 171
Swinburne, R. 10, 22, 149, 159n. 2, 174, 178
Symbolism 8, 9

Talmud, the 55–56
Tathāgata 82
Taylor, C. 10, 142–43
Testimony 12, 38, 162, 170, 177, 184, 185
  self-testimony 12, 175, 177, 184, 185, 187
Theism 2, 3, 16, 22–24, 29–30 , 38, 42, 89, 91, 95, 144, 164, 165–67, 183, 186
  'canonical theism' 144
Theodicy (*see also* Evil) 60, 93, 179
Theology
  Christian 3, 33, 69, 93
  Natural *see* Natural theology
  Philosophical *see* Philosophical theology
  Systematic 89
  Thealogian 119, 122
Therevada *see* Therevada Buddhism
Til, Salomon van 167, 173n. 14
tilakkhana 95
Tillich, P. 145n. 9
Tolerance 50
Torah 55, 57, 140
Tradition(s)
  competing traditions 3, 34–35, 42–44
  Enlightenment *see* Enlightenment tradition
  tradition-constituted reason 35
  tradition-dependent rationality 1, 3, 32
  tradition-ladenness 4
  traditionless reason 35
Trinity/Trinitarian 49, 142, 165, 166
Trust 11–13, 36, 91, 174–87
  trust policy 12, 180, 185–86, 187
  trustworthy 81
Truth(s)
  Eternal 105
  Revealed 64,
  truth-claims 63, 93–95
  universal 33
Turner, J. 40
Turrentin, F. 167
Turrentin, J-A. 167

Ultimate reality 2, 9, 23, 33, 41, 91, 93
  'Real', the 31n. 3, 93
  Ultimism 2–3, 23–25, 27–30

Umayyads 65
Universal discourse 45, 156, 178
Unskilful (See also *akusala*) 94–95, 98
Upanisads 6, 76, 81–82, 84
   Upanisadic 76, 77, 81–82, 83, 85

Vaiśeṣika 77
Vajrāyana 76
Van der Leeuw, G. 142
Vandervelde, G. 147n. 9
Vasubandhu 77
Vos, A. 173n. 11

Walshe, M. 86n. 6, 86 n.7
Ward, G. 106–07, 143
Webster, D. 7, 99n. 11, n. 13
Wesselius, J. 146n. 22
Westphal, M. 40–41, 145n. 10
White, H. 117
Will, the 36, 80
Williams, B. 83

Williams, R. 150, 151, 152
Wilson, T.D. 146n. 19
Winnicott, D. W 122
Wisdom 5, 13–14, 46, 55, 57, 60, 65, 71, 90, 125, 129, 130, 140, 190, 191, 194
   of God 165, 171
Wittgenstein, L. 50, 52, 67, 138, 159n. 3, 179
   Wittgensteinian thought 22
Witvliet, J. 147n. 31
Wolff, Christian 167
Wolterstorff, N. 133–34, 139, 145n. 5, 146n. 22, 146n. 31
Wright, A. 113
Wright, N.T. 142
Wykstra, S. 162
Wynn, M. 10–11, 156, 159n. 8, 187n. 2
Wyttenbach, D. 167

Yearley, L. 111
Yogācāra 77
Yudhiṣṭhira 76